The Nonpartisan League 1915–22

The Nonpartisan League 1915–22

An Annotated Bibliography

Compiled by
Patrick K. Coleman and Charles R. Lamb

MINNESOTA HISTORICAL SOCIETY PRESS
St. Paul • 1985

Minnesota Historical Society Press, St. Paul 55101

Copyright © 1985 by the Minnesota Historical Society

All rights reserved

The photographs used in this book are from the collections
of the Minnesota Historical Society

International Standard Book Number 0-87351-189-1

Manufactured in the United States of America

10 9 8 7 6 5 4 3 2 1

Library of Congress Cataloging-in-Publication Data
Coleman, Patrick K., 1952-
   The Nonpartisan League, 1915-22.

   Includes index.
   1. National Nonpartisan League--Bibliography.
I. Lamb, Charles R., 1953-   . II. Title.
Z5075.U5C6 1985   016.3224   85-21480
[HD1485.N4]

Contents

INTRODUCTION	vii
ABBREVIATIONS and REPOSITORIES	x
BOOKS	1
ARTICLES	13
PAMPHLETS AND EPHEMERA	32
PERIODICALS	52
GOVERNMENT PUBLICATIONS	54
COURT CASES	58
ARCHIVAL AND MANUSCRIPT COLLECTIONS	61
UNPUBLISHED PAPERS	70
INDEX	77

Introduction

The Nonpartisan League started organizing farmers in western North Dakota in 1915. What began with a handful of enthusiastic planners eventually became one of the most successful movements in the history of agrarian protest. North Dakota farmers, motivated by intolerable marketing conditions and inspired by the fiery rhetoric of the League's president, Arthur C. Townley, took political power into their own hands. By 1919 politicians and farmers backed by the Nonpartisan League (or NPL) controlled the North Dakota governor's office, both houses of the state legislature, and most of the other constitutional offices. After many difficult battles, these officials established the League's program of state-owned industries. During this time, the North Dakota NPL became a national organization, allying with farmers in other midwestern and western states who also built state Nonpartisan Leagues, although none was as successful as the North Dakota League. By 1922, when Townley resigned the national presidency, even the North Dakota organization had lost most of its momentum. With the demise of the first NPL, the sun had set on the "New Day in North Dakota"; the state-owned industries would remain as the League's legacy.

The history of the League is a compelling chapter in the struggle for economic justice that has been waged by farmers throughout our country's history. The dramatic story of the NPL's rapid rise to power and equally rapid decline has long been of interest to historians and other scholars—as the number of their dissertations, theses, and articles on the League shows. The League appeals to nonacademic readers as an exciting story of political and social confrontation played out by seemingly larger-than-life characters. The intensity and bitterness of the League's struggle underscore the challenge that the movement presented to the existing economic and political structure.

Despite this long-standing interest, the most complete guide to sources for NPL history —the bibliography in Robert L. Morlan's _Political Prairie Fire: The Nonpartisan League, 1915-1922_—is thirty years old (see entry No. 78). _The Nonpartisan League, 1915-22: An Annotated Bibliography_ is our effort to expand on Morlan's base and add the works that have become available since his book was published. We have attempted to compile a listing of works by and about the NPL that is exhaustive within well-defined limits of time and content. Only works relating to the original NPL, which existed from 1915 to about 1922, have been included. Historians recognize the unique character of the League during those years in its methods and accomplishments and in the intensity of the debate it engendered. The League had other incarnations in North Dakota: in the middle 1920s the organization, weakened by factionalism, nevertheless elected legislative majorities and a governor. The North Dakota NPL was known as the "Langer League" in the 1930s, when William Langer, who had avidly supported the first NPL, then staunchly opposed it, once again became a leader of the organization. In 1956 the League merged with the North Dakota Democratic party to form the Democratic-NPL party, which exists today. Many sources, however, do not focus so neatly on specific periods, so we have included some that are helpful to the study of the original NPL, even if they are primarily concerned with the post-1922 period.

The bibliography is also limited to works with significant, direct reference to the NPL, and we have excluded those that deal with subjects tangentially important to the NPL, such as the history of other agrarian groups and labor organizations of the period. Works with a brief reference to the League have been included if they pertain to an aspect of NPL history (such as the League in Canada) that has been difficult to research due to a scarcity of sources. The annotations indicate the extent and nature of these sources.

The works in this bibliography have been divided into eight categories according to type: books (full-length monographs); articles; pamphlets and ephemera; periodicals; records from court cases; government publications; archival and manuscript collections; and doctoral dissertations, master's theses, and other unpublished papers.

Although the criteria for inclusion were applied to all categories, some sections presented special problems. We have listed all known pamphlets and fliers concerning the NPL, including pieces produced both by the NPL and by anti-NPL organizations (such as the Independent Voters' Association) and individuals. Because these items are often difficult to locate, we have indicated a repository in which each can be found; researchers should note that institutions other than the one named may hold copies of a pamphlet. A large number of the pamphlets held by the Minnesota Historical Society were part of the National Nonpartisan League records (see entry No. 864) and the Henry G. Tiegan papers (see No. 901); while the original copies are now available in the Society's Reference Library, the pamphlets also appear in the microfilm edition of the National Nonpartisan League papers.

The periodical section includes only those newspapers and magazines that were directly owned and operated by the NPL or groups organized specifically to oppose the League. The NPL, working through the Publishers' National Service Bureau, had indirect control over many local newspapers, but it is nearly impossible to establish clearly the importance of this influence for each local paper.

Government publications presented a special problem. Virtually all public documents published by North Dakota's NPL-controlled state government are potentially relevant. Fortunately, the major state documents from the NPL years have been bound into volumes for each legislative session. Besides listing these volumes (see No. 751), we have included public documents relating to departments that were most affected by League rule in North Dakota. We also cite government publications that were widely distributed as part of the "pamphlet war." It should be noted that collections in the North Dakota State Archives, which are listed with other archival and manuscript collections, often contain public documents. Public documents from other states are listed if they make specific reference to the League.

The bibliography includes legal citations for court cases that involved the League, its leaders, or its members. The citations that are listed refer to the final hearing of each case before its highest court of litigation; researchers can trace proceedings in lower courts through the records of the final hearing. Most of the citations refer to published reports in Northwestern Reporter (abbreviated as NW), Federal Reporter (F), and United States Reports (US). The entries follow standard style for legal citations, listing plaintiff and defendant, volume number, reporter title, and page number. Some cases are listed without legal citations because cases from certain jurisdictions are not reported in the legal literature.

Researchers who have worked with manuscript and archival sources can appreciate the difficulty of searching a large collection for a few relevant documents. But the importance of these primary sources has led us to include collections that contain only a small amount of material related to the NPL. Because it was impossible to travel to every repository to check every possible collection, we have relied, in many cases, on the knowledge of reference archivists and the information available in the finding aids of institutions holding the materials.

With the exception of some of the archival and manuscripts collections, the compilers have seen all but a few of the works listed. We have annotated most of the entries and provided locations of items or collections when appropriate. An extensive index, prepared by Susan Tertell, provides access to the authors, subjects, and people mentioned in each entry.

Our efforts in compiling this bibliography have shown us many areas of NPL scholarship in which much work remains to be done. Few works on the NPL reflect the revolution in the study of political history that has taken place over the past twenty years. The "new" political history, which revitalized the discipline in the 1960s and 1970s, has shifted the focus of study from individual political leaders and episodic, dramatic events to a concern for understanding political history in its larger social context.[1] Using a variety of new techniques, historians have expanded their explanation of politics to include economic, social, and cultural factors. In the process many long-held assumptions concerning American political life have been revised.

Too often historians have concentrated on the personalities of League history, largely ignoring the thousands of men and women whose collective actions determined the movement's course. There are many questions concerning the NPL rank-and-file members that have not been fully answered. Was ethnicity a factor in the movement's history? Were NPL members primarily farm owners, tenant farmers, or agricultural laborers? What was the role of farm women in the League? Almost nothing has been written of NPL organizers and legislators. Who were these people? What course did their careers take before and after the NPL interlude? Although it is difficult to find sources that will shed light on the people who were a vital

---

[1] See Allen G. Bogue, "The New Political History in the 1970s," in Michael Kammen, ed., The Past Before Us: Contemporary Historical Writing in the United States (Ithaca, N.Y.: Cornell University Press, 1980).

part of League history but were not prominent leaders, the gap can be partially filled by lists of NPL members and legislative candidates, personal papers of League organizers and elected officials, and NPL-owned newspapers. We have tried to indicate these sources as they appear in the bibliography. For these and other questions concerning the League, we hope that this bibliography will help researchers to discover the answers. We also encourage users to notify us of items they find that have not been included.

This bibliography would never have been completed without the help of the archivists and librarians who answered our many questions and pointed us toward useful sources. Their patience and guidance made our work possible. Especially helpful were John Bye of the North Dakota Institute of Regional Studies, North Dakota State University; Delores Vyzralek and David Gray of the State Historical Society of North Dakota; and Daniel E. Rylance of the Department of Special Collections, Chester Fritz Library, University of North Dakota. We also offer our special thanks to Larry Remele of the State Historical Society of North Dakota for his advice and suggestions throughout the course of this project. We began to feel that all work on the NPL would grind to a halt without his generous help to the many researchers who consult him.

Jean A. Brookins, director of the Publications and Research Division of the Minnesota Historical Society, and the late June D. Holmquist, her predecessor, encouraged us to proceed with our idea for this bibliography and offered initial suggestions. We are grateful to Kay Spangler, who was both tolerant and cheerful while typing the entries, and June Sonju, who entered the manuscript on a word processor. Ann Regan, the editor who guided this project from nearly illegible handwritten notecards to finished book, deserves our warmest thanks. Her tough questions, insightful critique, and unending prodding made this a much more useful reference work than it otherwise would have been.

The research and publication of this bibliography were made possible through a grant from the Minnesota Historical Society's Public Affairs Center, which is funded by the Northwest Area Foundation.

Patrick K. Coleman
Charles R. Lamb

ABBREVIATIONS

IVA	Independent Voters' Association
MHS	Minnesota Historical Society, St. Paul
NPL	Nonpartisan League
NDSU	North Dakota Institute for Regional Studies, North Dakota State University, Fargo
SHSND	State Historical Society of North Dakota, Bismarck
UND	Department of Special Collections, Chester Fritz Library, University of North Dakota, Grand Forks

REPOSITORIES

Idaho State Historical Society, Boise
Kansas State Historical Society, Topeka
Library of Congress, Washington, D.C.
Provincial Archives of Alberta, Edmonton
Minneapolis Public Library, Minneapolis
Minnesota Historical Society, St. Paul
Nebraska State Historical Society, Lincoln
North Dakota State University, Fargo
Saskatchewan Archives Board, University of Saskatechewan, Saskatoon, and University of Regina, Regina
State Historical Society of North Dakota, Bismarck
State Historical Society of Wisconsin, Madison
University of Colorado, Boulder
University of Iowa, Iowa City
University of Montana, Missoula
University of North Dakota, Grand Forks
University of Oregon, Eugene
University of Washington, Seattle

Books

1. Adamson, Madeleine, and Seth Borgos. <u>This Mighty Dream: Social Protest Movements in the United States.</u> Boston: Routledge & Kegan Paul, 1984. 143 p.
   Brief chapter on NPL, heavily illustrated with cartoons and photographs. Published to accompany an exhibit of the same name; authors are members of ACORN (Assn. of Community Organizers for Reform Now).

2. Andre, Pearl, ed. <u>Women on the Move.</u> Bismarck: North Dakota Democratic-NPL Women, 1976. 274 p.
   Primarily concerned with women in Democratic-NPL party post-1954, but contains histories of early NPL womens' clubs and biographical sketches of women in NPL, including Lydia Cady Langer, Rhea Hagen, Viola Liessman, Emma Stenehjen, Berta E. Baker, and Minnie D. Craig, the first woman to serve as speaker of a legislative body in the U.S.

3. Beecher, John. <u>Tomorrow Is a Day: A Story of the People in Politics.</u> Chicago: Vanguard Books, 1980. 386 p.
   Three chapters give a popular account of movement from people's party to "prairie Tammany" and charge that NPL had fascist tendencies.

4. Bizzell, W. B. <u>The Green Rising: An Historical Survey of Agrarianism, with Special Reference to the Organized Efforts of the Farmers of the United States to Improve Their Economic and Social Status.</u> New York: Macmillan Co., 1926. 264 p.
   Chapter on NPL (p. 177-91) places it in context of other agrarian crusades and summarizes its birth, programs, and expansion.

5. Blackorby, Edward C. <u>Prairie Rebel: The Public Life of William Lemke.</u> Lincoln: University of Nebraska Press, 1963. 339 p.
   Definitive and sympathetic biography of one of NPL's and N.Dak.'s most important figures.

6. Borner, Florence. <u>Modern Poems for Modern People.</u> Bismarck: Bismarck Tribune, [1919]. 158 p.

Nonpartisan League meeting, ca. 1918

Poems on NPL, including "The Flivver Campaign," "Where the League Begins," and "A Modern Hiawatha" (dedicated to A. C. Townley).

7. Brinton, J[ob] W[ells]. Wheat and Politics. Minneapolis: Privately published, 1931. 270 p.
   The author, an important NPL official who broke with League in 1919, attempts to show the "dirty hands of pillage covered by the white glove of 'Farm Relief'" in actions of groups ranging from NPL to Federal Farm Board.

8. Bruce, Andrew Alexander. Non-Partisan League. New York: Macmillan Co., 1921. 284 p.
   An unfavorable history designed to show NPL excesses and Bolshevik nature. Carries half-title: "The Citizen's Library of Economics, Politics and Sociology--New Series." Author was former N.Dak. Supreme Court justice.

9. Burdick, Usher L. History of the Farmers' Political Action in North Dakota. Baltimore: Wirth Brothers, 1944. 140 p.
   Includes one chapter on NPL with rest of text on its third-party predecessors, the Farm Bureau Federation, and the Farmers Union. Contains photographs and bibliography.

10. _____. The Life of George Sperry Loftus: Militant Farm Leader of the Northwest. Baltimore: Wirth Brothers, 1939. 92 p.
    Biography of head of Equity Cooperative Exchange and prominent farm leader. Describes his 1913 speech, said to have begun NPL idea, which demanded that farmers receive pledges from politicians to support certain legislation.

11. Burgess, Eugene Willard. La "Nonpartisan League" Une Expérience Américaine de Socialisme d'état Agraire. Paris: Marcel Giard, 1928. 244 p.
    Preface describes this as a more objective and "serene" history of NPL than could be written in U.S. Indexed. French not read by compilers.

12. Buttree, J. Edmund. The Despoilers: Stories of the North Dakota Grain Fields. Boston: Christopher Publishing House, [1920]. 314 p.
    Emphasizes NPL's anti-business and anti-city nature. Author notes that first two chapters, which describe farmers' attitudes, were published in 1918 under the title "The Psychology of Suspicion."

13. Chafee, Zechariah, Jr. Free Speech in the United States. Cambridge, Mass.: Harvard University Press, 1942. 634 p.
    Includes passing references to prosecutions of NPL leaders during WWI and a section on trial of Joseph Gilbert at Jackson, Minn., for sedition (p. 285-98).

14. Cheney, Charles B. The Story of Minnesota Politics: High Lights of Half a Century of Political Reporting. [Minneapolis], 1947. 78 p.
    Reminiscences of a reporter for the Minneapolis Tribune; covers NPL years (p. 45-49).

15. Chrislock, Carl H. Ethnicity Challenged: The Upper Midwest Norwegian-American Experience in World War I. Norwegian-American Topical Studies, vol. 3. Northfield: Norwegian-American Historical Association, 1981. 174 p.
    Contains chapter on NPL and loyalty issue as well as material on Sigvard Rodvik, who maintained the liaison between NPL and Norwegian-Danish press.

16. _____. The Progressive Era in Minnesota, 1899-1918. St. Paul: Minnesota Historical Society, 1971. 242 p.
    Good chronological account of NPL in Minn.; covers well the campaigns of 1916 and 1918, Charles A. Lindbergh, Sr., the loyalty issue, and the Commission of Public Safety. Ties NPL to a "breakdown of the Progressive consensus" (p. 183).

17. Cole, Wayne S. Senator Gerald P. Nye and American Foreign Relations. Minneapolis: University of Minnesota Press, 1962. 293 p.
    Biography of man who, with help of Publishers' National Service Bureau, managed and edited Griggs County Sentinel-Courier (Cooperstown, N.Dak.), a leading NPL newspaper, after editing Fryburg (N.Dak.) Pioneer (later Billings County Pioneer) which supported NPL. Describes influence of NPL on his foreign policy views.

18. Conrad, Charles, and Joyce Conrad. 50 Years: North Dakota Farmers Union. N.p.: [North Dakota Farmers Union, 1976]. 269 p.
    Contains references to NPL and its relationship to Farmers Union, 1915-25 and later; describes Farmers Union tie to A. C. Townley's National Producers' Alliance.

19. Crawford, Harriet Ann. The Washington State Grange, 1889-1924: A Romance of Democracy. Portland: Binfords and Mort, 1940. 334 p.
    Contains discussion of cooperation between Grange and NPL, 1916-20; support of William Bouck, Grange master; NPL newspaper The Commonwealth (Seattle); activities of J. L. Freeman and A. W. Swigart, NPL organizers at Yakima convention, 1920.

20. Crawford, Lewis F. History of North Da-

kota. 3 vols. Chicago: American Historical Society Inc., 1931.
General state history with discussion of NPL years (vol. 1, p. 410-55).

21. Doan, Edward N. The La Follettes and the Wisconsin Idea. New York: Rinehart, 1947. 311 p.
Contains discussion of Robert M. La Follette's speech to NPL convention, 1917, and petitions filed to expell La Follette from U.S. Senate as the result of its misquotation.

22. Douthit, Davis. Nobody Owns Us: The Story of Joe Gilbert, Midwestern Rebel. Chicago: Cooperative League of the U.S.A., 1948. 240 p.
Biography of the socialist organizer who edited Nonpartisan Leader; includes detailed accounts of Gilbert's trials in Jackson and Martin counties, Minn., and his conviction for sedition. Author was editor of Midland Cooperator; he worked under Gilbert.

23. Dyson, Lowell K. Red Harvest: The Communist Party and American Farmers. Lincoln: University of Nebraska Press, 1982. 259 p.
States that rise of NPL killed western socialism and made farmer proud to be branded "as a red." Deals mainly with American Communist party after first League's decline.

24. Fine, Nathan. Labor and Farmer Parties in the United States, 1828-1928. New York: Rand School, 1928. 445 p.
Good background material with one chapter (p. 363-97) on NPL.

25. Fite, Gilbert C. Peter Norbeck: Prairie Statesman. Columbia: University of Missouri Press, 1948. 217 p.
Discusses NPL in S.Dak. 1918 gubernatorial election between Norbeck and Mark P. Bates, the NPL-endorsed candidate; charges of disloyalty aimed at L. J. Duncan and other S.Dak. NPL leaders; support of NPL by Daily Republican and South Dakota Leader, both published in Mitchell.

26. Folwell, William Watts. A History of Minnesota. 2d ed. 4 vols. St. Paul: Minnesota Historical Society, 1956-69.
Vol. 3 contains appendixes on NPL (p. 538-55) and Minn. Commission of Public Safety (p. 556-78).

27. Fossum, Paul R. The Agrarian Movement in North Dakota. Baltimore: Johns Hopkins Press, 1925. 183 p.
Contains good background information and a chapter (p. 94-129) on NPL. Argues that NPL failed because it was political, appealed to class prejudices, and sought to make government a business machine; author favors cooperatives.

28. Friesen, Gerald. The Canadian Prairies: A History. Toronto: University of Toronto Press, 1984. 524 p.
Not seen by compilers.

29. Gaston, Herbert E. The Nonpartisan League. New York: Harcourt, Brace & Howe, 1920; Westport, Conn.: Horizon Press, 1975. 325 p.
Written in response to anti-NPL books. Author served as officer of Northwest Publishing Co. and editor of Minnesota Daily Star.

30. Geelan, Agnes Kjorlie. The Dakota Maverick: The Political Life of William Langer, Also Known as "Wild Bill" Langer. Fargo: Kaye's Printing Co., 1975. 166 p.
Sympathetic treatment, including information on Langer's career as NPL attorney general, break with Townley, and IVA campaign. Uses many interviews.

31. _____. North Dakota's Workmen's Compensation Bureau: Fifty Years of Progress, 1919-1969. Bismarck: Conrad Publishing Co., 1969. 162 p.
Early history of bureau, explaining origins in NPL legislature. Also contains some staff biographies from 1919-22 period. Illustrated.

32. Geiger, Louis G. University of the Northern Plains: A History of the University of North Dakota, 1883-1958. Grand Forks: University of North Dakota Press, 1958. 490 p.
Includes a brief analysis of relationship between NPL administration and UND, 1916-ca. 1921, and discusses actions of UND presidents Frank McVey and Thomas Kane. Also mentions activities of Neil C. Macdonald, N.Dak. superintendent of public instruction under NPL.

33. Gieske, Millard L. Minnesota Farmer-Laborism: The Third Party Alternative. Minneapolis: University of Minnesota Press, 1979. 389 p.
Briefly deals with transition from NPL to Farmer-Labor party in Minn.

34. Gilbert, A. B. Making the Farm Pay: A Study in Better Social Organization Affecting Farming. St. Paul: Riverside Press, [1920]. 183 p.
NPL program and its benefits to farmers, emphasizing importance of political activity over technological changes. Appendix of Minn. NPL program and index. Author was associate editor of Nonpartisan Leader.

35. Goldberg, Ray. *The Nonpartisan League in North Dakota: A Case Study of Political Action in America.* Fargo: Midwest Printing and Lithographing Co., 1955. 95 p.
   Emphasizes farm movements prior to 1916; discusses structure of NPL organization and status of League in 1940s. Originally written as undergraduate honors thesis at Harvard University (1948).

36. Green, James R. *Grass-Roots Socialism: Radical Movements in the Southwest, 1845-1945.* Baton Rouge: Louisiana State University Press, 1978. 450 p.
   Discusses NPL in Tex. and Okla., including 1922 Tex. race for governor in which NPL supported Fred S. Rodgers. Mentions that Covington Hall and E. R. Meitzen left Tex. during WWI repression to work for NPL in N.Dak.; Socialists merged with NPL in order to gain respectability because NPL was not "tainted with disloyalty" in Tex.

37. Groves, Donald B., and Kenneth Thatcher. *The First Fifty: History of Farm Bureau in Iowa.* Lake Mills, Iowa: Graphic Publishing Co., 1968. 288 p.
   Includes references (p. 7-9) to NPL-endorsed Governor William Harding; explains that Farm Bureau kept NPL influence to a minimum by organizing first; identifies northern Iowa as area most strongly influenced by NPL.

38. Gutfeld, Arnon. *Montana's Agony: Years of War and Hysteria, 1917-1921.* Gainesville: University Presses of Florida, 1979. 174 p.
   NPL move into Mont. and attacks on it by Council of Defense and by individuals. Includes material on E. B. Craighead and his newspaper *New Northwest* (Missoula).

39. Haines, Lynn, and Dora B. Haines. *The Lindberghs.* New York: Vanguard Press, 1931. 307 p.
   Biography of Charles A. Lindbergh, Sr., with one chapter on his 1918 race for governor of Minn. as NPL candidate and effect of war hysteria on the League. Lynn Haines was Lindbergh's friend and political adviser; Dora Haines finished the book after her husband's death.

40. Hargreaves, Mary Wilma M. *Dry Farming in the Northern Great Plains, 1900-1925.* Cambridge, Mass.: Harvard University Press, 1957. 587 p.
   Mentions NPL's encouragement of farm diversification, Bank of N.Dak. programs, and promotional appeals.

41. Haynes, Frederick Emory. *Social Politics in the United States.* New York: Houghton, Mifflin Co., 1924. 414 p.
   Legislative history and rise and fall of NPL (p. 299-331).

42. Haynes, John Earl. *Dubious Alliance: The Making of Minnesota's DFL Party.* Minneapolis: University of Minnesota Press, 1984. 264 p.
   Passing mention of NPL and how Governor J. A. A. Burnquist's policies forced the unions and farmers to unite and form the Farmer-Labor party. Gives much information on William Mahoney, president of Working People's Nonpartisan Political League and chief founder of Farmer-Labor party.

43. Holbrook, Franklin F., and Livia Appel. *Minnesota in the War with Germany.* 2 vols. St. Paul: Minnesota Historical Society, 1932.
   Unsympathetic view of NPL's "helping to foster discontent" in WWI and an uncritical view of attempt by Minn. Commission of Public Safety and local authorities to quiet the League (vol. 2, p. 44-51).

44. Holzworth, John Michael. *The Fighting Governor: The Story of William Langer and the State of North Dakota.* Chicago: Pointer Press, 1939. 140 p.
   Uncritical biography of former NPL leader who broke with NPL in 1919 and was endorsed by IVA for governor in 1920. Author was Langer's close friend; book was published during Langer's second campaign for U.S. Senate.

45. Howard, Joseph Kinsey. *Montana: High, Wide and Handsome.* New Haven: Yale University Press, 1943. 347 p.
   Good general history, stressing powers against which NPL struggled; passing mention of NPL.

46. Howard, Thomas W., ed. *The North Dakota Political Tradition.* North Dakota Centennial Heritage Series. Ames: Iowa State University Press, 1981. 220 p.
   Includes essays relating to NPL by Robert P. Wilkins ("Alexander McKenzie and the Politics of Bossism"); Charles N. Glaab ("John Burke and the Progressive Revolt"); Larry Remele ("Power to the People: The Nonpartisan League"); D. Jerome Tweton ("The Anti-League Movement: The IVA," an especially important summation); and Glenn H. Smith ("William Langer and the Art of Personal Politics").

47. Howe, Frederic Clemson. *The High Cost of Living.* New York: Charles Scribner's Sons, 1917. 275 p.
   Mentions NPL's program as one of state socialism and modified single tax; applauds NPL's exemption of farm improvements from taxation. Endorsed by NPL (see No. 593).

48. Irvine, W[illiam]. *The Farmer in Poli-

tics. Toronto: McClelland and Stewart, 1920, J. Lorimer, 1979. 253 p.
    Discusses background and aims of United Farmers of Alba.; argues for cooperation and political action. Author had been organizer for NPL. Reprint edition includes introduction by Reginald Whitaker.

49. Janes, George Milton. Who Should Have Wealth and Other Papers. Milwaukee, Wis.: Morhouse Publishing Co., 1925. 170 p.
    Author, a professor of economics, argues that N.Dak. farmers would have made the same gains without a political party (p. 69-88) as they did with NPL.

50. Jenkinson, Clay. A Humanities Guide to Northern Lights. Mandan, N.Dak.: North Dakota Humanities Council, 1981. [184] p.
    Chapters include "A Thumbnail History of the Nonpartisan League," "Northern Lights and Feminism," and a biographical sketch and chronology of A. C. Townley, all by the editor; "The Power of Northern Lights" by Robert W. Lewis; "Who Were Your Grandmothers, John Hanson?" by Ann Markusen (see No. 269); a list of reviews of Northern Lights by Robert Behling; and others.

51. Johnson, Claudius O. Borah of Idaho. New York: Longmans, Green and Co., 1936; Seattle: University of Washington Press, 1967. 511 p.
    Briefly discusses (p. 305-8) NPL endorsement of Borah; loyalty issue; NPL strength in Idaho; Ray McKaig's work for Borah; Governor Frank R. Gooding's attacks on NPL. Reprint edition includes new introduction by author.

52. Karlin, Jules A. Joseph M. Dixon of Montana, Part 2: The Governor versus the Anaconda, 1917-1934. Missoula: University of Montana, 1974. 269 p.
    Discusses Dixon's sympathy for NPL. Includes material on NPL-endorsed candidates Jeanette Rankin and Burton K. Wheeler; NPL petition drives to save voting reforms; Mont. Labor League; campaign of 1920; NPL-endorsed State Senator Peter Rorvik; and organizer A. J. (Mickey) McGlynn.

53. Kile, Orville Merton. The Farm Bureau Movement. New York: Macmillan Co., 1921. 282 p.
    Contrasts NPL with Farm Bureau (p. 233-43), praising NPL but adding that Farm Bureau's less political course was "safer and more in accord with our American ideals."

54. _____. The Farm Bureau through Three Decades. Baltimore: The Waverly Press, [1948]. 416 p.
    One-page discussion of how NPL was beaten by Farm Bureau in organizing Iowa.

55. Knight, Harold V. Grass Roots: The Story of the North Dakota Farmers Union. Jamestown: North Dakota Farmers Union, 1947. 183 p.
    Very brief mention of NPL, arguing that political action was not the answer to farmers' problems and that it "brought no millennium."

56. Kramer, Dale. The Wild Jackasses: The American Farmer in Revolt. New York: Hastings House, 1956. 260 p.
    A sympathetic and readable account of NPL in four chapters, putting NPL in context of other agrarian movements. Author had been associated with NPL and other farm protests.

57. La Follette, Bell C., and Foca La Follette. Robert M. La Follette. 2 vols. New York: Macmillan, 1953. 1,305 p.
    Comprehensive biography of La Follette by his wife and daughter. Includes detailed account of his 1917 speech before NPL conference in St. Paul.

58. Langer, William. The Nonpartisan League: Its Birth, Activities and Leaders . . . Published under Penalty of the Anti-liars Law of North Dakota Providing for One Year in the Penitentiary. . . . Mandan, N.Dak.: Morton County Farmers Press, [1920]. 240 p.
    Written while author was attorney general and candidate for N.Dak. governor in June 1920 primary. Claims to support original intentions of NPL but charges "corrupt leaders" with espousing socialism, free love, and other radical ideas. Promises to take state industries out of politics by appointing governing boards.

59. Larson, Bruce L. Lindbergh of Minnesota: A Political Biography. New York: Harcourt Brace Jovanovich, 1973. 363 p.
    Definitive biography, with much information on Charles A. Lindbergh, Sr., as NPL candidate for Minn. governor in 1918 and transition from NPL to Farmer-Labor party. Also contains detailed description of Lindbergh's economic ideas and of Working People's Nonpartisan Political League.

60. Le Sueur, Meridel. Crusaders. New York: Blue Heron Press, 1955; St. Paul: Minnesota Historical Society Press, Borealis Books, 1984. 94 p., 104 p.
    Highly personal biography of the author's mother and stepfather, with references to NPL. Borealis edition carries subtitle The Radical Legacy of Marian and Arthur Le Sueur and includes new introduction by author (p. xi-xxix), index, and photographs.

61. Limvere, Karl. Economic Democracy for the Northern Plains: Cooperatives and North Dakota. N.p.: North Dakota Farmers Union, 1980. 80 p.

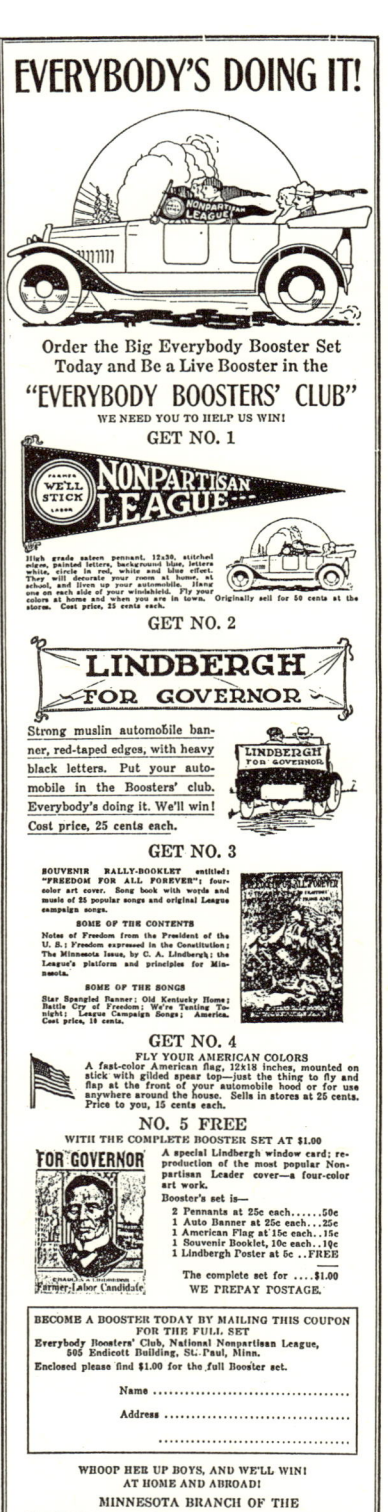

Advertisement from Minnesota Leader, May 11, 1918

Includes history of agrarian discontent, a chapter on NPL, and a photo of NPL members in front of U.S. Capitol in 1933.

62. Lindbergh, Charles A., Sr. Why Is Your Country at War and What Happens to You after the War and Related Subjects. Washington, D.C.: National Capital Press, Inc., 1917. 220 p.
  An anti-war treatise that was often quoted out of context to accuse Lindbergh and NPL of being unpatriotic. Used against Lindbergh in 1918 Minn. gubernatorial campaign; A. C. Townley was questioned about it by a U.S. Senate committee. Contains a chapter by Mrs. Lillian Lindbergh Roberts entitled "Your Vote for Suffrage." Printing plates were destroyed in 1918 in WWI hysteria.

63. _____. Your Country at War and What Happens to You after a War. Philadelphia: Dorrance and Co., 1934. 215 p.
  Reprint of 1917 edition. The reprint was to be published in 1924 for use in Lindbergh's campaign for governor, but he died in May of that year. Introduction by Walter E. Quigley tells a few NPL annecdotes and explains relevance of Lindbergh's arguments to New Deal.

64. Lindstrom, David E. American Farmers' and Rural Organizations. Champaign, Ill.: Garrard Press, 1948. 457 p.
  Short synopsis (p. 128-31) of NPL leaders, purpose, program, and decline. Based on Bruce's unfavorable book (see No. 8).

65. Lipset, S[eymour] M. Agrarian Socialism: The Cooperative Commonwealth Federation in Saskatchewan, A Study in Political Sociology. Berkeley: University of California Press, 1950. 315 p.
  Short history of NPL and its role as a model for the socialist Cooperative Commonwealth Federation. Also mentions revived NPL.

66. McConnell, Grant. The Decline of Agrarian Democracy. Berkeley: University of California Press, 1953. 226 p.
  Two short paragraphs stating that NPL amounted to nothing more than bitter class rhetoric.

67. McCurry, Dan C., ed. The Farmer-Labor Party: History, Platform, and Programs. American Farmers and the Rise of Agribusiness: Seeds of Struggle. New York: Arno, 1975. Various paging.
  Includes a reprint from the Congressional Record (74th Cong., 2d sess., 1936, 80, pt. 10:9694-9725) of a speech by Ernest Lundeen, Minn. Farmer-Labor congressman, that describes tie of Farmer-Labor party to NPL.

68. MacKay, Kenneth Campbell. *The Progressive Movement of 1924*. New York: Columbia University Press, 1947. 298 p.
   Considers role of NPL in setting groundwork for La Follette's 1924 presidential bid. States that "progressives were encouraged by the remarkable readiness of farmers to join a political organization devoted to liberal principles" (p. 53).

69. McKenna, Marian C. *Borah*. Ann Arbor: University of Michigan Press, 1961. 450 p.
   Biography of Idaho governor endorsed by NPL in 1918 primary. Argues that NPL "invasion" of Democratic party discredited state's direct primary law, bringing repeal of the legislation. Summaries of NPL program and background are mediocre; the book seems to rely heavily on Johnson's biography (see No. 51).

70. MacPherson, C. B. *Democracy in Alberta: The Theory and Practice of a Quasi-Party System*. Toronto: University of Toronto Press, 1953. 258 p.
   Mentions that United Farmers of Alba. was forced to take over NPL when the latter's "business government" ideas became so widespread.

71. Malone, Michael P. *C. Ben Ross and the New Deal in Idaho*. Seattle: University of Washington Press, 1970. 191 p.
   Brief discussion (p. 16-18) of Ray McKaig, Idaho Federation of Agriculture, and NPL success in 1918 Idaho Democratic primary election.

72. Malone, Michael P., and Richard B. Roeder. *Montana: A History of Two Centuries*. Seattle: University of Washington Press, 1976. 352 p.
   Passing mention of NPL, including its effort to get Anaconda Copper Mining Co. to pay its share of taxes; support of labor leader William F. Dunne for NPL; Burton K. Wheeler's NPL-backed campaign for governor, 1922.

73. Manahan, James M. *Trials of a Lawyer*. [Minneapolis: Privately published, 1933]. 248 p.
   Entertaining autobiography. Describes author's recruitment into Progressive movement by George Loftus; pleading of cases for the American Society of Equity; offer of NPL support to union members on strike against Twin City Rapid Transit Co. (1917); and defense of Joseph Gilbert at Jackson, Minn. (see No. 849), where author was threatened with lynching.

74. Mardiros, Anthony. *William Irvine: The Life of a Prairie Radical*. Toronto: James Lorimer & Co., 1979. 298 p.
   Biography of important speaker and organizer for NPL in Alba. Describes work of other Canadian organizers, including S. E. Haight, Harry Johnson, Alex Ross; program of NPL in Alba.; growth of other organizations, including Labor Representative League and United Farmers of Alba.; and Irvine's newspaper (see No. 716).

75. Martin, Boyd A. *The Direct Primary in Idaho*. Palo Alto, Calif.: Stanford University Press, 1947. 149 p.
   Discusses NPL's 1918 Idaho primary victory (p. 61-69).

76. Martinson, Henry R. *History of North Dakota Labor*. N.p., [1970?]. 69 p.
   Contains two-page section on relationship between NPL and N.Dak. labor groups such as IWW and N.Dak. State Federation of Labor. Martinson was an NPL organizer from 1916 to 1920.

77. Mayer, George H. *The Political Career of Floyd B. Olson*. Minneapolis: University of Minnesota Press, 1951. 329 p.
   Brief history of NPL, dealing with the "marriage of convenience" between farmers and laborers in 1918 campaign. Argues that A. C. Townley never understood labor and resented power of Working People's Nonpartisan Political League and that Olson filled the leadership gap left by Townley.

78. Morlan, Robert L. *Political Prairie Fire: The Nonpartisan League, 1915-1922*. Minneapolis: University of Minnesota Press, 1955; Westport, Conn.: Greenwood Press, 1974; St. Paul: Minnesota Historical Society Press, Borealis Books, 1985. 408 p.
   The best history of NPL to date. Sympathetic treatment with good chronology; much new research has been done since its publication. Based on Ph.D. dissertation (see No. 970). Borealis edition includes new introduction by Larry Remele and new index.

79. Morton, W. L. *The Progressive Party in Canada*. Toronto: University of Toronto Press, 1950. 331 p.
   Discusses NPL in Man., Alba., and Sask. and its ties to N.Dak. NPL. Mentions Man. Grain Growers' Assn., Free Trade League, and United Farmers of Alba.; various progressive politicians and organizers, including George Chipman, Roderick McKenzie, D. J. Sykes, H. W. Johnson, William Irvine, J. S. Woodsworth, James Weir, Louise McKinney, H. W. Wood, and O. L. MacPherson.

80. Murphy, Paul L. *World War I and the Origin of Civil Liberties in the United States*. New York: W. W. Norton & Co., 1979. 285 p.
   Discusses support of Woodrow Wilson and George Creel for NPL and their reluctance to

interfere with Minn. Commission of Public Safety. Describes interpretations and enforcement of laws affecting NPL.

81. National Conference on Marketing and Farm Credits. *Marketing and Farm Credits: A Collection of Papers Read at the Fourth Annual Session . . . .* Madison, Wis.: The Conference, 1917. 546 p.
   Includes paper by Lynn J. Frazier, "Marketing Problems of Northwestern Grain Growers" (p. 309-21), read at conference in Chicago, 1916. Discusses farming methods, marketing of farm produce, and NPL activities during 1915 and 1916. Author was NPL governor of N.Dak. (1917-21). Includes account of his nomination and analysis of relationship between NPL and small-town businesses.

82. The *National Nonpartisan League Debate*. American *Farmers and the Rise of American Agribusiness: The Seeds of Struggle*. New York: Arno Press, 1975. Various paging.
   Reprints of three pamphlets: Jerry Dempster Bacon, *A Warning to the Farmer . . .* (see No. 446); NPL, *Facts for the Farmers . . .* (see No. 576); and NPL, *Facts Kept from the Farmer . . .* (see No. 577).

83. Nelson, Bruce Opie. *Land of the Dakotas*. Minneapolis: University of Minnesota Press, 1946. 354 p.
   Chapter on "The Revolt of the Farmers" has biographical information on Townley and NPL organizational methods; it is a good, sympathetic, but occasionally unreliable introduction to NPL.

84. Nelson, Theodore Gilbert. *Scrapbook Memories*. Salem, Oreg.: Your Town Press, 1957. 160 p.
   Autobiography of organizer of farm cooperatives and secretary of IVA. Book's organization as a scrapbook makes use difficult. Includes written instructions for recall election.

85. Neubeck, Deborah Kahn. *Guide to a Microfilm Edition of the National Nonpartisan League Papers*. St. Paul: Minnesota Historical Society, 1970. 22 p.
   A short history of NPL and description of NPL papers held at MHS (see No. 864).

86. North Dakota. University. Bureau of Governmental Affairs. *A Compilation of North Dakota Political Party Platforms*. Bismarck, 1979. 388 p.
   All NPL platforms (sometimes in summary) and those of their opposition.

87. Nye, Russell B. *Midwestern Progressive Politics: A Historical Study of Its Origins and Developments, 1870-1950*. East Lansing: Michigan State College Press, 1951. 422 p.
   General summary of NPL history. Mentions NPL organizers Oliver S. Evans in Nebr. and O. A. Stolin in Wis.; Business Men's Protective Assn., an anti-NPL organization in Omaha, Nebr. Author calls NPL "nothing more or less than the renaissance of Grangerism."

88. O'Hare, Kate Richards. *In Prison*. New York: Alfred A. Knopf, 1923; Seattle: University of Washington Press, 1977. 211 p.
   Prison memoirs of woman convicted of sedition for a 1917 speech given in Bowman, N.Dak.; her conviction was used to discredit NPL. Introduction to reprint edition by Jack M. Holl gives a short biography of O'Hare. Author's foreword includes a brief account of trial.

89. Omdahl, Lloyd B. *Insurgents*. Dakota Territory Centennial Edition. Brainerd: Lakeland Color Press, 1961. 252 p.
   Short history of NPL, with description of the "shift of the Nonpartisan League to the Democratic column" in 1954-56. In 1960 author was NPL chairman of Burleigh County, N.Dak., and Democratic-NPL candidate for secretary of state.

90. Penniman, Howard R. *Sait's American Parties and Elections*. 5th ed. New York: Appleton-Century-Crofts, Inc., 1952. 574 p.
   Includes NPL (p. 137-43).

91. Peterson, H[orace] C., and Gilbert C. Fite. *Opponents of War, 1917-1918*. Madison: University of Wisconsin Press, 1957. 399 p.
   Succinct description of harassment of NPL in S.Dak. and Minn. during WWI. Discusses activities of S.Dak. Governor Peter Norbeck; events surrounding Robert M. La Follette's 1917 speech; loyalty issue; trial of Joseph Gilbert and A. C. Townley at Jackson, Minn.; Minn. Commission of Public Safety; and campaign of Charles A. Lindbergh, Sr.

92. *The Red Flame: A Chronicle of the Fierce Controversy Surrounding the Early Days of North Dakota's Non-Partisan League*. Minot, N.Dak.: Lowe & Larson Printing, Inc., 1975. 446 p.
   Reprint of complete run (Nov. 1919-Oct. 1920) of rabidly anti-NPL monthly publication. Includes introduction by Robert L. Morlan. Indexed.

93. Rice, Stuart A. *Farmers and Workers in American Politics*. New York: Columbia University, 1924. 233 p.
   Compares and contrasts farmers' and laborers' backgrounds and interests. Discusses political alliances to support candidates in Wash. (Robert Bridges), Wis. (John J. Blaine), Minn. (Henrik Shipstead, Magnus Johnson), S.Dak. (Mark P. Bates), and Nebr.

(R. B. Howell, Charles W. Bryan). Argues that farmers' friendliness to labor was proven by N.Dak. legislation in 1919 session.

94. Robinson, Elwyn B. History of North Dakota. Lincoln: University of Nebraska Press, 1966. 599 p.
   The best history of N.Dak. in print. Chapter 15 (p. 327-51), "The Great Socialist Experiment," and Chapter 16 (p. 352-70), "A Socialist State in the First World War," are brief histories of NPL's rise to power and legislative activity. Contains a general bibliography, as well as bibliographic essays for each chapter.

95. Robinson, James Eugene. Wrongs and Remedies: Economic Live Wire Essays. New York: The Knickerbocker Press, 1923. 301 p.
   Contains short chapter describing the author's view of NPL. Robinson, an NPL-endorsed justice of the N.Dak. Supreme Court, strongly disagreed with NPL tax program.

96. Rogin, Michael Paul. The Intellectuals and McCarthy: The Radical Specter. Cambridge, Mass.: MIT Press, 1967. 366 p.
   Quantitative history; shows NPL to be strongest among poorer farmers. Argues that many NPL leaders became reactionary because foreign policy questions became more important than economic ones. Discusses impact of German-Russian immigrants.

97. Ross, Martin. Shipstead of Minnesota. Chicago: Pacard and Co., 1940. 140 p.
   Admiring biography of dentist from Glenwood, Minn., who was an NPL candidate for Congress in 1918, governor in 1920, and--successfully--for U.S. Senate in 1922. Published for his 1940 election campaign.

98. Russell, Charles Edward. Bare Hands and Stone Walls: Some Recollections of a Side-Reformer. New York: Charles Scribner's Sons, 1933. 441 p.
   Decline of NPL explained (p. 343-44) by well-known Socialist brought to Fargo to help publish Nonpartisan Leader.

99. ____. The Story of the Nonpartisan League: A Chapter in American Evolution. New York: Harper & Bros., 1920; Arno Press, 1975. 332 p.
   Insider's history of NPL at its height.

100. Saloutos, Theodore, and John D. Hicks. Agricultural Discontent in the Middle West, 1900-1939. Madison: University of Wisconsin Press, 1951. 581 p.
   Includes an excellent study of NPL in N.Dak., S.Dak., Minn., Nebr., Kans., Mont., and Wis. Discusses Arthur Le Sueur's opposition to political nature of NPL program for state industries; W. C. Zumach and relationship of Wis. Socialists with NPL; role of N.Dak. Farm Bureau and Farmers Union in decline of NPL.

101. Schneider, Richard. West of the Red: The Role of Transportation in the Development of North Dakota. (Fargo: Upper Great Plains Transportation Institute, North Dakota State University, 1977). 250 p.
   Chapter 11 summarizes NPL history, 1915-22, largely following Morlan's account (see No. 78). Does not mention transportation in the context of NPL history.

102. Schutz, Mary Neal. Plowing Up a Storm: The History of Midwestern Farm Activism. Lincoln: Nebraska Educational Television Network, 1985. 27 p.
   Published to accompany 90-minute public television special of the same name. Covers farm movements from Grange to farm protests of the 1980s. Includes synthesis of NPL history in a chapter by Larry Remele entitled "The Nonpartisan League: The Courage to Stand Up for Farmers."

103. Sharp, Paul F. The Agrarian Revolt in Western Canada: A Survey Showing American Parallels. Minneapolis: University of Minnesota Press, 1948. 204 p.
   A general history of Canadian farm protest groups, including two chapters on NPL that describe its relationships with other organizations, including United Farmers of Alba., Sask. Grain Growers' Assn., and Grain Growers' Grain Co. Mentions influence of American immigrants and their experience with agrarian movement in U.S.

104. Socialist Party of the United States. A Political Guide for the Workers: Socialist Party Campaign Book 1920. Chicago: Department of Labor Research, Rand School of Social Science, 1920. 183 p.
   Rejects any attempt by Socialists to affiliate with the NPL (p. 82-83).

105. Stedman, Murray Salisbury, Jr., and Susan W. Stedman. Discontent at the Polls: A Study of Farmer and Labor Parties 1827-1948. New York: Columbia University Press, 1950. 190 p.
   Passing mention of NPL. Claims farmer-labor parties of 1950s did well in areas that had been dominated by NPL.

106. Stuhler, Barbara. Ten Men of Minnesota and American Foreign Policy, 1898-1968. St. Paul: Minnesota Historical Society, 1973. 263 p.
   Short biographies of Charles A. Lindbergh, Sr., NPL-endorsed candidate for governor of Minn. in 1918, and of Henrik Shipstead, endorsed by NPL and Working People's Nonpartisan Political League for U.S. House in

1918, governor in 1920, and U.S. Senate in 1922.

107. _____, and Gretchen Kreuter, eds. Women of Minnesota: Selected Biographical Essays. St. Paul: Minnesota Historical Society Press, 1977. 402 p.
Includes brief biographies of two women elected in 1922 to Minn. State House of Representatives: Myrtle Cain, backed by Working People's Nonpartisan Political League, and Hannah Kempfer, an Independent who refused NPL endorsement.

108. Thomas, L. G. The Liberal Party in Alberta: A History of Politics in the Province of Alberta 1905-1921. Toronto: University of Toronto Press, 1959. 230 p.
Brief mention of Alba. NPL and support it received from large number of Americans living in southern Alba.

109. Thomason, O. M. The Beginning and the End of the Nonpartisan League. St. Paul: Ramaley Printing Co., 1920. 225 p.
First half of book is fictionalized biography of A. C. Townley ("Arthur D. Parker") and founding of NPL; argues "end" of NPL will come when its program is enacted. Author was NPL speaker and writer who urged Townley to accept more democratic methods; he had edited the Iconoclast (Minot, N.Dak.), a Socialist paper, and he wrote a satirical column for the Nonpartisan Leader.

110. Tideman, Philip L., ed. Fourscore and Twelve: The Letters of Oscar F. Hawkins. Lincoln, Nebr.: Union College Press, 1965. 161 p.
Excerpts of letters (p. 103-6) concerning NPL. Hawkins was an educator and Socialist activist.

111. Tittemore, J[ames] N., and Vissers, A. A. The Non-Partisan League vs. the Home. Milwaukee: Burdick-Allen Co., 1922. 184 p.
Anti-League history of NPL written by leaders of Wis. State Union of the American Society of Equity. Attacks NPL as socialist; urges formation of cooperatives. Contains valuable list, with brief identifications, of 72 paid NPL leaders and organizers.

112. Tofsrud, Ole T. Fifty Years in Pierce County. Rugby, N.Dak.: n.p., 1943. 87 p.
A short discussion of NPL, its programs, and A. C. Townley.

113. Toole, K. Ross. Twentieth-Century Montana: A State of Extremes. Norman: University of Oklahoma Press, 1972. 307 p.
Mentions beating of NPL organizer A. J. (Mickey) McGlynn in Miles City, Mont., and WWI hysteria. Deals with NPL's involvement in Burton K. Wheeler's 1920 campaign for governor and League's support for Jeannette Rankin, first woman elected to U.S. Congress (1916).

114. Tostlebe, Alvin S. The Bank of North Dakota: An Experiment in Agrarian Banking. Studies in History, Economics, and Public law, vol. 114. New York: Columbia University Press, 1924. 210 p.
Good background of economic and political conditions, NPL legislative achievements, bank operations. Critical of state bank legislation. Author concludes bank must be freed from political control of Industrial Commission; bank's principal function should be to guarantee credit.

115. Tweton, D. Jerome. In Union There Is Strength: The North Dakota Labor Movement and the United Brotherhood of Carpenters and Joiners. Grand Forks: North Dakota Carpenter/Craftsman Heritage Society, 1982.
Includes discussion of relationship between NPL and organized labor, with description of clash between Jerry Dempster Bacon and leaders of State Federation of Labor. Argues that downfall of NPL hurt labor.

116. _____, and Theodore B. Jelliff. North Dakota: The Heritage of a People. Fargo: North Dakota Institute for Regional Studies, University of North Dakota, 1976. 242 p.
Includes a chapter (p. 135-46) on the League and various other references to NPL. Index.

117. Veblen, Thorstein. Vested Interest and the Common Man. New York: B. W. Huebsch, Inc., 1920. 183 p.
Brief and unflattering mention of NPL at end of author's treatise on the discrepancy between business and industry.

118. Weinsten, James. The Decline of Socialism in America, 1912-1925. New York: Vintage Books, 1967. 367 p.
Mentions NPL and Working People's Nonpartisan Political League in relation to other socialist and left-wing groups. Much material on William Mahoney and 1924 campaign of Minn. Farmer-Labor party.

119. Weist, Edward. Agricultural Organization in the United States. Lexington: University of Kentucky, 1923. 618 p.
Very brief mention of NPL, N.Dak. Industrial Commission, and expansion of government's role in managing public utilities for the benefit of farmers.

120. Wheeler, Burton K., with Paul F. Healy. Yankee from the West: The Candid, Turbulent Life Story of the Yankee-born U.S. Senator

Cartoon from The Red Flame, Jan., 1920

from Montana. New York: Doubleday & Co., 1962. 436 p.
  Discusses NPL in Mont., including candidates Charles Cooper, Roland C. Arnold, and Louis S. Irvin; petition drive to postpone referendum on primary law; violence against NPL and Wheeler in 1920 gubernatorial campaign; opposition from Anaconda Copper Mining Co. and Montana Development Assn.; charges of "free love."

121. Whitman, Alden, comp. Great American Reformers. New York: H. W. Wilson Co., forthcoming.
  Includes biographical articles on A. C. Townley, William Langer, Gerald P. Nye, and William Lemke (by Larry Remele) and on George Loftus (by Scott Ellsworth).

122. Wilkins, Robert P., and Wynona H. Wilkins. North Dakota: A Bicentennial History. The States and the Nation Series. New York: W. W. Norton & Co., 1977. 218 p.
  Chapter on NPL (p. 137-52) concludes the "great socialist experiment was a failure."

123. Witham, James W. Fifty Years on the Firing Line: My Part in the Farmers' Movement by "The Cornfield Philosopher." Chicago: Privately published, 1924. 214 p.
  A folksy account of the agrarian movement.

Author was sympathetic to NPL but not a member; he had covered legislative sessions in three states for various papers and settled in Minn. Gives brief biographies of Progressives he knew, including O. M. Thomason, Ole J. Kvale, and many other NPL members and editors of farm newspapers. Lists Minn. newspapers supporting reform.

124. Wood, Louis Aubrey. A History of the Farmers' Movement in Canada. Toronto: Ryerson Press, 1924; University of Toronto Press, 1975. 372 p.
  General history of Canadian agrarian protest groups that includes brief mentions of NPL, its Sask. organizer S. E. Haight, and Nonpartisan Leader (Swift Current). Author says NPL and Sask. Grain Growers' Assn. never established "harmonious relations" (p. 294).

125. Youmans, Grant S. Legalized Bank Robbery. 4th ed. Minot, N.Dak.: Grant S. Youmans, June, 1919. 112 p.
  First edition, Aug. 1914. A pre-NPL plea for state-owned banks.

126. Young, Walter D. The Anatomy of a Party: The National CCF 1932-61. Toronto: University of Toronto Press, 1969. 328 p.
  History of Canada's Cooperative Commonwealth Federation. Mentions J. S. Woodsworth, Salem

Bland, William Irvine, and Fred Dixon as NPL organizers. Argues that opposition to conscription hurt League but NPL had impact on reform movement.

127. _____. Democracy and Discontent: Progressivism, Socialism and Social Credit in the Canadian West. Toronto: Ryerson Press, 1969. 122 p.
Passing mention of NPL influences on farm movements in Sask. and Alba.

128. Youngdale, James M. Populism: A Psychohistorical Perspective. Port Washington, N.Y.: Kennikat Press, 1975. 220 p.
Much material on Working People's Nonpartisan Political League and its ties to farmers' NPL. Discusses leaders and organizers William Mahoney, W. W. Royster, Thomas Van Lear, Henry Martinson. Stresses the importance of socialist influence in Minn. populism.

129. _____, ed. Third Party Footprints: An Anthology from Writings and Speeches of Midwest Radicals. Minneapolis: Ross and Haines, 1966. 357 p.
Introductory essay by author places NPL in setting of historical protest movements. Biographical information, speeches, and writings of Charles A. Lindbergh, Sr., James Manahan, Edwin F. Ladd, A. C. Townley, William Mahoney, and Joseph Gilbert, and NPL supporters Marian Le Sueur, Susie Stageberg, Knud Wefald, and Ole J. Kvale.

130. Zimmerman, Carle C. Farmers' Marketing Attitudes. [St. Paul, 1927]. 55 p.
Published Ph.D. dissertation, 1925, studying farmers in eight Minn. communities in 1924; NPL had 1,586 members in those postal areas before that date. Shows a slight negative relationship between membership in Farm Bureau and membership in cooperatives and a positive relationship between membership in NPL and in cooperatives. Calls the League "economic and political" (p. 49). Same as Nos. 130 and 1010.

131. _____, and John D. Black. The Marketing Attitudes of Minnesota Farmers. Agricultural Experiment Station Technical Bulletin 45. St. Paul: University of Minnesota, 1926. 54 p.
Same as Nos. 130 and 1010.

Articles

132. "Address of President Townley." *Report of the Proceedings of the American Federation of Labor,* 1917, p. 237-40.
    Speech delivered to an American Federation of Labor convention. Explains farmers' economic grievances and urges cooperation between farm groups and organized labor.

133. Anderson, D. "Revolt of a State, North Dakota." *LaFollette's Magazine* 9 (Aug. 1917): 6-7.
    Description of NPL history and program. Includes cartoons by John M. Baer.

134. "Arthur C. Townley, the Radical Autocrat of North Dakota." *Literary Digest* 61 (Apr. 19, 1919): 62-64.
    Summary of national press reaction to Townley's position in NPL.

135. Asher, Robert. "Radicalism and Reform: State Insurance of Workmen's Compensation in Minnesota." *Labor History* 14 (Winter 1973): 19-41.
    Account of struggle spearheaded by Minn. State Federation of Labor in alliance with NPL.

136. "Attorney Holds Newspaper Law Inoperative." *North Dakota Press Association Bulletin* 3 (June 1920): 1, 3.
    Discussion of case before N.Dak. Supreme Court challenging NPL-backed newspaper legislation passed by 1919 legislature.

137. Babcock, C. D. "Report on the Activities of the Non-Partisan Political League. Particularly in the States of North Dakota and Minnesota." *Oregon Voter* 11 (Oct. 27, 1917): 108-11, 128-30, 132.
    Brief history of NPL stressing its socialist connections. Author was secretary of the Insurance Federation of Oreg.

138. Bakken, Douglas. "NPL in Nebraska--1917-1920." *North Dakota History* 39 (Spring 1972): 26-31.
    Includes reasons for NPL's lack of success in Nebr.

139. "Bank of North Dakota." *New Republic* 19 (May 10, 1919): 40-41.
    Organization of bank and its benefits to N.Dak.

140. "Bar and the Nonpartisan League." *Public* 22 (Sept. 13, 1919): 974.
    Defends NPL against denunciation by American Bar Assn.

141. Baum, Dale. "The New Day in North Dakota: The Nonpartisan League and the Politics of Negative Revolution." *North Dakota History* 40 (Spring 1973): 4-19.
    Applies Richard Hofstadter's re-interpretation of Populism (*Age of Reform,* 1955). Author characterizes League's program as a naive response to complex problems that were beyond the understanding of N.Dak. farmers. He attributes NPL's success to the charismatic personality of A. C. Townley and concludes that NPL exemplifies repressive nature of agrarian politics.

142. Boyle, James E. "Agrarian Movement in the Northwest." *American Economist* 8 (Sept. 1918): 505-21.
    Background of formation of NPL. Includes attempts to reform grain grading-laws and establish publicly owned grain elevators; information on N.Dak., Man., and Sask.

143. _____. "The Drive Against 'Big Biz'!" *The Nation's Business* 8 (Apr. 1920): 24-26.
    Describes N.Dak.'s state-owned industries.

144. Briley, Ronald. "Lynn J. Frazier and Progressive Reform: A Plodder in the Ranks of a Ragged Regiment." *South Dakota History* 7 (Fall 1977): 438-54.

Frazier's political career as N.Dak. governor and U.S. senator, focusing on Indian reform legislation and describing his role in NPL.

145. Brommel, Bernard J. "Kate Richards O'Hare: A Midwest Pacifist's Fight for Free Speech." North Dakota Quarterly 44 (Winter 1976): 5-19.
Includes an account of O'Hare's 1917 N.Dak. trial and conviction for obstructing enlistments and violating espionage law. O'Hare held NPL membership and her conviction was used against NPL in later campaigns.

146. Brown, R[ome]. G. "Disloyalty of Socialism." American Law Review 53 (Sept.-Oct. 1919): 681-710.
Denunciation of NPL program (called "Townleyism") in N.Dak. and Minn., with brief mention of Iowa.

147. Buell, C. J. "The Nonpartisan League in Minnesota." Single Tax Review 18 (May-June 1918): 78-80.
Favorable description of NPL program emphasizing its position on WWI.

148. Bullard, F. L. "People's Czar in North Dakota." Independent and Weekly Review 98 (Apr. 26, 1919): 148-50.
Firsthand account of NPL activities, focusing on A. C. Townley and NPL tactics and legislative program.

149. Burbank, Garin. "Agrarian Socialism in Saskatchewan and Oklahoma: Short-Run Radicalism, Long-Run Conservatism." Agricultural History 51 (Jan. 1977): 173-80.
Includes critical analysis of Seymour M. Lipset's comparison (see No. 65) of NPL with Canadian Cooperative Commonwealth Federation.

150. Burke, H. T. "Bankrupt North Dakota: Governor Nestos and Reconstruction." Outlook 135 (Sept. 12, 1923): 65-67.
Rangvold A. Nestos's actions after recall of Governor Lynn J. Frazier in 1921.

151. "Can You Beat It?" Oregon Voter 12 (Mar. 30, 1918): 401-3.
Gives details of organization and financing of Consumers United Stores Co. of N.Dak. Reprints contract signed by farmers who helped finance the venture.

152. Carroll, D. H. "Recall in North Dakota." National Municipal Review 11 (Jan. 1922): 3-5.
Reasons behind 1921 recall election. Author was chairman of N.Dak. Council of Defense.

153. Chrislock, Carl H. "Minnesota Politics in the World War One Period: From 'Consensus' to 'Conflict.'" Discourse 9 (Winter 1966): 3-32.
Covers 1914-18, with NPL figuring prominently. Discusses loyalty issue, political allegiance of German Americans, and role of organized labor, among other subjects.

154. "The Class in Minneapolis." Survey 46 (June 25, 1921): 428-29.
Discusses 1921 primary and general elections for mayor of Minneapolis, in which George E. Leach defeated Thomas Van Lear, whom NPL supported through Working People's Nonpartisan Political League.

155. "Class Movements in Politics." Public 21 (Jan. 11, 1918): 30-39.
Defends NPL against hostile article published in New York World.

156. Colegrove, Kenneth. "The Farmer and the Socialist." Unpopular Review 8 (Oct.-Dec. 1971): 287-301.
Discusses NPL in N.Dak., reviewing historical relationship between organized farmers and socialists.

157. "Confusing the Issue." Public 22 (Aug. 2, 1919): 814-15.
Defense of A. C. Townley.

158. "Continued Political Upheaval in the Northwest." Outlook 125 (June 2, 1920): 207-8.
NPL candidates in 1920 Minn. elections.

159. Cook, Gilbert W. "The North Dakota Rural Credit System." Journal of Land and Public Utility Economics 14 (Aug. 1938): 273-83.
History, details of administration, and statistical analysis of Farm Loan Department of Bank of N.Dak.

160. _____. "The North Dakota State Mill and Elevator." Journal of Political Economy 46 (Feb. 1938): 23-51.
Includes account of Populist campaign for a state elevator, its establishment under NPL, and its operation up to 1937. Gives production and financial statistics.

161. "The Cooperative Newspaper." Nation 109 (Oct. 4, 1919): 454-55.
Activities of newspaper unions and cooperative newspapers in the U.S., mentioning NPL's cooperatively owned newspapers.

162. "Counter Revolution in North Dakota." Independent and Weekly Review 105 (Mar. 5, 1921): 236-37.
Discusses controversies surrounding N.Dak. state-owned industries, particularly state bank.

163. "Country Gentleman on Non-Partisan League." Oregon Voter 13 (June 15, 1918): 373-80.

Reprints excerpts from a series of articles on NPL.

164. Courville, L. D. "The Conservatism of the Saskatchewan Progressives." Canadian Historical Association Papers, 1974, p. 157-81.
Thorough examination of local and provincial leadership of Sask. progressives, ca. 1919-30, with brief explanation of NPL's failure to take root in Sask. Disputes Seymour M. Lipset's analysis (see No. 65) of Canadian agricultural politics. Includes valuable diagram of chronology and relation ships of Canadian agricultural political groups of 1920s and 1930s.

165. Cravens, Hamilton. "The Emergence of the Farmer-Labor Party in Washington Politics, 1919-20." Pacific Northwest Quarterly 57 (Oct. 1966): 148-57.
Brief mention of NPL activities and leaders in Wash.

166. Creel, George. "Our 'Aliens'--Were They Loyal or Disloyal?" Everybody's Magazine 40 (Mar. 1919): 36-38, 70-73.
Discusses treatment of aliens during WWI, criticizing attacks by Minn. Commission of Public Safety on NPL and defending N.Dak.'s record of war support. Later refuted (see No. 219). Author was chief of U.S. government's Committee on Public Information.

167. ____. "What Do These Senators Want? Interview with L. J. Frazier." Collier's 71 (Mar. 10, 1923): 9-10.
Legislative plans of U.S. Senator Lynn J. Frazier. Explains causes of unrest in N.Dak. Mentions connections with senators Edwin F. Ladd (N.Dak.), Burton K. Wheeler (Mont.), Henrik Shipstead (Minn.), and Smith W. Brookhart (Iowa).

168. Currie, Barton W. "A Great Upheaval." Country Gentleman, Apr. 7, p. 4-5, Apr. 14, p. 4-5, 35, Apr. 21, p. 4-5, 29, Apr. 28, p. 6-7, 22, May 5, p. 6-7, May 12, p. 11-12, 1917.
A series of articles with good illustrations and photographs. (1) Early NPL history and legislative program. (2) NPL complaints about wheat-grading methods; questions results of E. F. Ladd's research. (3) NPL leadership and organizational structure. (4) Opponents of NPL and tactics used by NPL in 1917 N.Dak. legislative session. (5) Activities of N.Dak. Supreme Court Justice James E. Robinson. (6) NPL position on WWI. See also No. 506.

169. Davenport, Frederick M. "Farmers' Revolution in North Dakota." Outlook 114 (Oct. 11, 1916): 325-27.
Account of economic grievances that led to formation of NPL, along with description of

Nonpartisan League farmers grading their own wheat, ca. 1917

League's program and results of 1916 N.Dak. primary election.

170. ____. "Radicalism in the Making." Outlook 122 (Aug. 20, 1919): 599-600.
Account of A. C. Townley's trial at Jackson, Minn. (see No. 790), including background and outcome. Also covers reactions of Democratic and Republican parties to NPL. Author, a N.Y. state senator, traveled in the Northwest.

171. Davies, W. P. "The North Dakota Nonpartison League." American Cooperative Journal 11 (May 1916): 922.
Anti-NPL account of early organizing efforts. Author, editor of Grand Forks Herald, predicts NPL's demise in N.Dak. primary election of June 1916.

172. Devine, Edward T. "North Dakota, the Laboratory of the Nonpartisan League." Survey 43 (Mar. 6, 1920): 684-89.
Controversies surrounding NPL's legislative program, Public Library Commission scandal of 1919, dispute with state Superintendent of Public Instruction Minnie J. Nielson, and tax policies.

173. Dovre, Paul. "The Nonpartisan League: An Expression of Agrarian Protest." Discourse 4 (Autumn 1965): 319-29.
Study of rhetoric of NPL spokesmen and publications, summarizing author's Ph.D. dissertation (see No. 935).

174. Dyson, Lowell K. "The Red Peasant International in America." Journal of American History 58 (Mar. 1972): 958-73.
Account of the work of Alfred Knutson, an early NPL organizer in N.Dak. and Colo. and state NPL manager in Idaho and Wash. Discusses Knutson's later involvement in Farmer-

Labor party, United Farmers Education League, and Red Peasant International (sometimes called Farmers' International in the U.S.).

175. "Eastern Nonpartisan League." *Survey* 39 (Dec. 8, 1917): 325.
Describes meeting held in New York City to establish an NPL state chapter.

176. Ellsworth, Scott. "Organizing the Organized: The Origins of the Nonpartisan League." *The Organizer* 9 (Summer 1981): 4-15.
Important discussion of role played by American Society of Equity in development of NPL.

177. "The Exploited Farmer." *Nation* 122 (June 30, 1926): 712.
Editorial mentioning NPL's attempt to improve the farmer's economic standing and attributing NPL's demise to forces of big business. Later disputed (see No. 191).

178. "Farmer and the War." *New Republic* 13 (Nov. 3, 1917): 8-9.
Defense of NPL's position on WWI.

179. "Find It a Red Rag." *Oregon Voter* 12 (Mar. 30, 1918): 400-1.
Describes NPL reaction to disloyalty charges from the America First League.

180. Fite, Gilbert C. "John A. Simpson: The Southwest's Militant Farm Leader." *Mississippi Valley Historical Review* 35 (Mar. 1949): 563-84.
Discusses Simpson's long career in farm protest politics, including membership in Okla. NPL. Although discussion of NPL is brief, Simpson's career is probably typical of those of many NPL members and organizers.

181. _____. "The Nonpartisan League in Oklahoma." *Chronicles of Oklahoma* 24 (Summer 1946): 146-57.
NPL activities in Okla., 1917-21, and reasons for lack of success.

182. _____. "Peter Norbeck and the Defeat of the Nonpartisan League in South Dakota." *Mississippi Valley Historical Review* 33 (Sept. 1946): 217-36.
Argues that Norbeck helped defeat NPL by persuading S.Dak. Republican party to adopt much of NPL's program.

183. Frederick, John T. "A Legislature that Works." *New Republic* 14 (Feb. 23, 1918): 105-7.
Account of 1917 N.Dak. special legislative session, with reasons for its convening and relief measures passed.

184. Gaston, Herbert E. "Farmers Versus Labor." *New Republic* 40 (Sept. 3, 1924): 10-12.
Mentions NPL in general discussion of relationship between farmers and organized labor. Author was editor of *Minnesota Daily Star*.

185. Geiger, Louis G. "Conservative Reform and Rural Radicalism." *North Dakota Quarterly* 28 (Winter 1960): 1-9.
Analyzes NPL in context of competing reform traditions. Discusses differences between NPL supporters and N.Dak. progressives. Brief description of career of Edwin F. Ladd.

186. Gilbert, A. B. "The Farmers in the Northwest." *Intercollegiate Socialist* 7 (Feb.-Mar. 1919): 21-23.
NPL in N.Dak. and Minn., 1915-18, including election statistics, descriptions of plans, and an explanation aimed at Socialists who were impatient with NPL's progress. Author was an NPL organizer.

187. _____. "Municipal Policy of the Non-Partisan League." *National Municipal Review* 8 (Jan. 1919): 89-90.

188. _____. "Nonpartisan League." *National Municipal Review* 7 (July 1918): 379-83.
Method of organization, program, and ideology of NPL.

189. _____. "Nonpartisan League Politics." *Socialist Review* 8 (May 1920): 351.
Includes prospects for a national NPL ticket.

190. _____. "Out for a Solid West: The Coming Political Battle of the Nonpartisan League." *Forum* 60 (Dec. 1918): 727-37.
Short description of NPL activities in Minn., N.Dak., Idaho, S.Dak., Iowa, Nebr., and Colo., along with account of League's origins and programs.

191. _____. "Who Killed the Nonpartisan League?" *Nation* 123 (Aug. 18, 1926): 151.
Letter to editor responding to editorial (see No. 177). Author maintains that farmers' reluctance to pay dues, high cost of cooperative ventures, and untrustworthy politicians elected by NPL outside of N.Dak. caused NPL's demise.

192. Gillette, John M. "Agrarian Political Movements with Special Reference to the Nonpartisan League." *American Sociological Society Proceedings* 18 (1924): 194-98.
Reasons for rise of NPL including geographic and pioneer conditions, demands of N.Dak. farmers, and work of A. C. Townley. Also assesses influence of NPL legislative program.

193. _____. "North Dakota Harvest of the Non-partisan League." Survey 41 (Mar. 1, 1919): 753-60.
   Thorough discussion of NPL antecedents and legislative program, with several excellent photographs of NPL meetings and illustrations from NPL publications.

194. Glaab, Charles N. "The Failure of North Dakota Progressivism." Mid-America 39 (Oct. 1957): 195-209.
   Argues that progressivism failed in N.Dak. because it could not address issues of greatest interest to farmers and that NPL could do so.

195. "Glaring Example of Non-Partisan League's Abuse of Power." Oregon Voter 14 (Sept. 7, 1918): 301-3.
   Attacks moratorium on farm mortgage foreclosures passed by N.Dak. Council of Defense. Includes text of moratorium resolution and letter explaining the moratorium from N.Dak. Attorney General William Langer.

196. Godwin, Sidney. "The Farmers' Political League." Grain Growers' Guide 9 (Oct. 4, 1919): 17.
   NPL in Man. Not seen by compilers.

197. "A Goldbrick from North Dakota." Weekly Review 2 (June 16, 1920): 621-23.
   Unsympathetic description of NPL program in N.Dak., in response to Lynn J. Frazier's articles in the New York Times (May 16, 1920).

198. Gordon, F. C. R. "Farmers' Nonpartisan League." American Industries 18 (Feb. 1918): 14-15.
   Anti-NPL article, concentrating on NPL relationship with organized labor. Author claims that D. C. Coates, former lieutenant governor of Colo., was the "real power behind the Nonpartisan League."

199. Green, James R. "Tenant Farmer Discontent and Socialist Protest in Texas, 1901-17." Southwest Historical Quarterly 81 (Oct. 1977): 133-54.
   Brief mention of NPL leaders and activities.

200. Gregg, William C. "North Dakota Resents?" Outlook 129 (Nov. 9, 1921): 382-83.
   Answer to criticism published in N.Dak. newspapers of author's earlier article (see No. 201).

201. _____. "Political Storm in North Dakota." Outlook 129 (Oct. 12, 1921): 220-23.
   Unsympathetic analysis of NPL programs and N.Dak. state-owned industries. See also No. 200.

202. Haines, Austin P. "Adjournment of Common Sense." New Republic 16 (Sept. 7, 1918): 158-60.
   Emphasizes loyalty issue raised by NPL's stand on WWI. Covers Nebr., N.Dak., Minn., and Iowa.

203. _____. "Nonpartisan League and the Loyalty Issue." New Republic 16 (Sept. 14, 1918): 187-90.
   Includes discussion of statements concerning NPL's loyalty during WWI made by such national figures as George Creel and Woodrow Wilson.

204. Harger, C. M. "Farmers Organizing Politically." Financial World 30 (Mar. 23, 1918): 10-11.
   Brief description of NPL activities, program, and relationship with organized labor.

205. _____. "North Dakota's Financial Dilemma." Review of Reviews 63 (Apr. 1921): 414-16.
   Controversies surrounding NPL in 1921, particularly the investigation of state-owned industries.

206. Haug, Charles J. "The Industrial Workers of the World in North Dakota, 1913-17," and "The Industrial Workers of the World in North Dakota, 1918-25." North Dakota Quarterly 39 (Winter 1971): 85-102 and 41 (Summer 1973): 5-19.
   Two-part series. (1) Includes brief but detailed account of NPL's attempt to negotiate farm-labor agreement with IWW. (2) Briefly mentions NPL as ally of IWW. Includes two cartoons from Red Flame linking NPL and IWW.

207. Haynes, Fred Emory. "Third-Party Backgrounds." Independent 113 (Aug. 2, 1924): 71-74.
   Mentions NPL as a forerunner of Farmer-Labor party.

208. Hedges, M. H. "Where Democrats Vote Republican." New Republic 23 (Aug. 18, 1920): 334-35.
   Account of 1920 primary elections in Minn. and N.Dak.

209. Henke, Warren A. "Imagery, Immigration, and the Myth of North Dakota." North Dakota History 38 (Fall 1971): 412-91.
   State promotion of immigration, including discussion of NPL administrative policies.

210. Hicks, John D. "The Third Party Tradition in American Politics." Mississippi Valley Historical Review 20 (June 1933): 3-28.
   Argues in a brief mention that NPL acted as a third party despite its nonpartisan stance.

211. Hildreth, Melvin D. "Farmers Capture North Dakota." World's Work 32 (Oct. 1916): 678-89.
   NPL early history, with several excellent photographs of N.Dak. scenes and NPL political gatherings.

212. Hilton, O. A. "Public Opinion and Civil Liberties in Wartime 1917-1919." Social Science Quarterly 28 (Dec. 1947): 201-24.
   Brief discussion of problems encountered by NPL as a result of loyalty issue. Includes a well-documented account of campaign by Minn. Commission of Public Safety against the League.

213. "Hits Bank Stock Values." Oregon Voter 15 (Oct. 2, 1918): 40.
   Discusses problems facing Bank of N.Dak. and NPL cooperative ventures.

214. Holtan, Orley I. "A. C. Townley, Political Firebrand of North Dakota." Western Speech 35 (Winter 1971): 30-41.
   Examination of Townley as speaker and organizer.

215. Horwill, A. K. "Ideal State in the Northwest." World's Work 37 (Mar. 1919): 495-96.
   NPL legislative proposals.

216. ____. "Nonpartisan League." New Republic 18 (Apr. 5, 1919): 303-6.
   History and background of NPL. Includes account of NPL candidates' defeat in 1918 Minn. elections due to charges of disloyalty.

217. Huntington, Samuel P. "The Election Tactics of the Nonpartisan League." Mississippi Valley Historical Review 36 (Mar. 1950): 613-32.
   Briefly analyzes NPL election strategy (1916-22) in N.Dak., Minn., Colo., Idaho, Mont., Wash., Okla., Wis., Kans., and Nebr. Argues that NPL was more successful with balance-of-power tactics (endorsement of major party candidates within the two-party system) than with third-party campaigns. Useful discussion of the League's relationship with existing political parties.

218. "Idaho Oddity." Oregon Voter 15 (Nov. 16, 1918): 208.
   Evaluates 1918 Idaho general election and NPL influence on outcome. Mentions NPL lack of success in Oreg.

219. "The Illustrious Mr. Creel and the Facts." The Bellman 26 (Mar. 15, 1919): 285-87.
   Defends activities of Minn. Commission of Public Safety, including its attacks on NPL, from criticism by George Creel (see No. 166).

220. "Industrial Program of the Nonpartisan League Upheld by the Supreme Court of North Dakota." Law and Labor 2 (Mar. 1920): 68-71.
   Analysis of legal case (see No. 775) attempting to block the creation of N.Dak. state-owned industries.

221. Jenson, Carol. "Loyalty as a Political Weapon: The 1918 Campaign in Minnesota." Minnesota History 43 (Summer 1972): 42-57.
   Harassment of NPL in Minn.; drawn from author's Ph.D. dissertation (see No. 950).

222. Joachim, L. H. "Populism Today and Yesterday." Public 22 (Mar. 8, 1919): 234-36.
   Discusses similarities between NPL and 19th-century populists.

223. "The John Baer Story." Electrical Workers' Journal 66 (Jan. 1967): 53-55.
   Short biography. Includes details of Baer's career as illustrator and cartoonist, with reproductions of several political cartoons.

224. Johnson, C. R. "Conviction of Townley." New Republic 20 (Aug. 6, 1919): 18-20.
   Analysis of 1919 trial at Jackson, Minn. of A. C. Townley and Joseph Gilbert on charges of conspiring to discourage enlistments (see No. 790).

225. ____. "Is the Nonpartisan League Declining?" New Republic 24 (Sept. 22, 1920): 88-90.
   Analysis of NPL's showing in 1918 primary elections in Minn. and N.Dak., with estimate of general election prospects.

226. ____. "Minnesota and the Nonpartisan League." New Republic 20 (Oct. 8, 1919): 290-93.
   Emphasizes special Minn. legislative session of Sept. 1919.

227. ____. "Nonpartisan League Defeated." Nation 111 (Dec. 1, 1920): 614.
   Briefly details NPL's lack of success in 1920 elections in Minn., N.Dak., Wis., Mont., and Colo. Conclusions were later disputed (see No. 282).

228. ____. "Struggle in North Dakota." New Republic 26 (Mar. 9, 1921): 42-44.
   Effects of an IVA-supported initiative that allowed county and local government treasurers to move deposits from the Bank of N.Dak. to private banks. Later disputed (see No. 359).

229. Johnson, Claudius Osborne. "William E. Borah: The People's Choice." Pacific Northwest Quarterly 44 (Jan. 1953): 15-22.
   Briefly covers NPL activities in Idaho, including its endorsement of Borah for U.S.

senator in 1918, his acceptance of the endorsement, and his defense of NPL against charges of disloyalty.

230. Johnson, Roger T., and Lawrence H. Larsen. "The Story that Never Was: North Dakota's Urban Development." *North Dakota History* 47 (Fall 1980): 4-10.
   Attributes N.Dak.'s lack of urban development, in part, to an anti-business attitude typified by NPL.

231. Kennedy, John C. "The Outlook for a Labor Party." *American Labor Monthly* 2 (June 1923): 17-23.
   Author was secretary of Wash. Farmer-Labor party. Summarizes 1920-22 activities.

232. King, Judson. "Big Business and the Background of the Townley Trial," "Banking and Steel Interests and the Townley Trial," and "Millers, Packers, Politicians, and the Townley Trial." *Public* 22 (Nov. 15, 22, 29, 1919): 1071-73, 1089, 1113-15.
   Three-part series on background of A. C. Townley's trial at Jackson, Minn., in 1919 for conspiring to discourage enlistments (see No. 790). Favorably address NPL's attempts to reform banking, steel, milling, and packing industries in Minn.

233. ____. "Nonpartisan Victory." *Public* 22 (July 5, 1919): 706-8.
   N.Dak. primary election of 1920.

234. ____. "The Prosecution of Mr. Townley." *Nation* 109 (Aug. 2, 1919): 143-44.
   Sedition trial of A. C. Townley and Joseph Gilbert held at Jackson, Minn. (see No. 790), in 1919. Includes legal details and excerpts from trial transcripts.

235. Korth, Philip A. "The American Yeoman vs. Progress and the Nonpartisan League." *North Dakota History* 37 (Spring 1970): 125-37.
   Discussion of NPL's attacks on nostalgic image of yeoman farmer. Based primarily on articles from *Nonpartisan Leader*.

236. "Labor and the North Dakota Drive." *Socialist Review* 10 (Apr.-May 1921): 58-59.
   Difficulties encountered by Bank of N.Dak. in its attempt to sell bonds. Also discusses N.Dak. coal strike.

237. "Labor's Newspapers." *Nation* 117 (Sept. 12, 1923): 258.
   Mentions *Minnesota Daily Star* in discussing current status of U.S. labor newspapers.

238. Lamb, Charles R. "The Nonpartisan League and Its Expansion into Minnesota." *North Dakota Quarterly* 49 (Summer 1981): 108-43.
   Uses NPL membership file (see No. 864), census material, and tax records to examine economic and cultural background of NPL members in Minn. Analyzes effect of changes in membership on League's ability to survive in Minn. Based on unpublished paper (see No. 959).

239. Larson, Bruce L. "Kansas and the Nonpartisan League: The Response to the Affair at Great Bend." *Kansas Historical Quarterly* 34 (Spring 1968): 57-71; also in Burton J. Williams, ed., *Essays on Kansas History in Honor of George L. Anderson* (Lawrence, Kans.: Coronado Press, 1977).
   NPL activities in Kans., focusing on harassment of NPL supporters and organizers at Great Bend, Kans., on Mar. 12, 1921, and on response of the press.

240. ____. "A Kansas Newspaper and the Nonpartisan League, 1919-1920." *Journalism Quarterly* 49 (Spring 1972): 98-106.
   History and analysis of *Ellsworth County Leader* (see No. 721). Provides details of NPL activities in Kans.

241. "Lawlessness in Minnesota by Public Officials." *Public* 21 (July 13, 1918): 876-78.
   Reports incidents of harassment of NPL members in Minn. and defends NPL against disloyalty charges.

242. "League Gains in Elections." *Oregon Voter* 15 (Nov. 30, 1918): 291-92.
   Lists NPL gains in 1918 general elections in N.Dak., Minn., S.Dak., Mont., Idaho, Colo., and Nebr.

243. "League Slate Forming." *Oregon Voter* 35 (Oct. 20, 1923): 98-99.
   Lists proposed NPL candidates for Oreg.'s 1924 state and county elections from Clackamas, Yamhill, and Washington counties.

244. "League Wins Big." *Oregon Voter* 15 (Nov. 16, 1918): 208.
   Discusses passage of constitutional amendments allowing establishment of state-owned industries in 1918 N.Dak. general election. Mentions NPL inability to gain support in Oreg.

245. Le Sueur, Arthur. "The Nonpartisan League: A Criticism." *Socialist Review* 9 (Nov. 1920): 193-95.
   Criticizes NPL plan to have state officials manage state-owned industries; advocates appointing managing boards to assure continuity and avoid intrusion of political considerations.

246. Levine, Louis. "Politics in Montana." *Nation* 107 (Nov. 2, 1918): 507-8.
   Discusses NPL role in Mont.'s 1918 election

campaign, including activities of Jeannette Rankin and Burton K. Wheeler.

247. Liggett, Walter W. "North Dakota and the United States." Searchlight 5 (Oct. 1920): 7-10.
Theories of government intervention in the economy with reference to N.Dak.'s state-owned industries.

248. "Line Up the Firing Squad." The Bellman 24 (Apr. 6, 1918): 371.
Recounts and applauds efforts to suppress NPL and other groups.

249. Locke, Walter. "The Irrepressible Farmer." New Republic 25 (Dec. 22, 1920): 99-101.
Analysis of NPL showing in 1920 general elections in N.Dak., Minn., Nebr., Colo., and Mont. Later disputed (see No. 283).

250. "Lombard Is Right." Oregon Voter 15 (Oct. 2, 1918): 41.
Reaction to letter from Norman Lombard, president of the Western Farm Credit Co., suggesting that most effective opposition to NPL would be enactment of remedies to economic problems facing Oreg. farmers.

251. Long, Andrew. "The Federated Press." Survey 45 (Oct. 23, 1920): 126-27.
Describes attempt by reformist and radical editors (including NPL members) to establish their own news service in Chicago in Nov. 1919.

252. Lovin, Hugh. "Disloyalty, Libel, and Litigation: Ray McKaig's Ordeal, 1917-1920." Idaho Yesterdays 27 (Summer 1983): 13-24.
Account of libel suit (see No. 777) brought by McKaig (NPL leader and organizer) against Frank Gooding (Idaho governor and U.S. senator) and a Boise newspaper company that published Idaho Statesman. Article also gives a brief account of NPL activities in Idaho, including membership estimates.

253. _____. "The Farmer Revolt in Idaho, 1914-1922." Idaho Yesterdays 20 (Fall 1976): 2-15.
Activities of NPL in Idaho.

254. _____. "Idaho and the 'Reds,' 1919-1926." Pacific Northwest Quarterly 69 (July 1978): 107-15.
Discusses attacks on Idaho NPL, 1919-20, in context of post-WWI anti-communism.

255. _____. "Ray McKaig: Nonpartisan League Intellectual and Raconteur." North Dakota History 47 (Summer 1980): 12-19.
Political career of NPL organizer in Idaho. Analyzes McKaig's unpublished novel about NPL. This article is the first study of McKaig to make use of his papers (see No. 846).

256. _____. "The Red Scare in Idaho, 1916-1918." Idaho Yesterdays 17 (Fall 1973): 2-13.
History of Idaho NPL in context of WWI anti-communism. Mentions Ray McKaig as early NPL organizer.

257. Lundberg, George A. "The Demographic and Economic Basis of Political Radicalism and Conservatism." American Journal of Sociology 32 (Mar. 1927): 719-32.
Case study using quantitative analysis of N.Dak. and Minn. election results, 1916-22.

258. MacDonald, William. "North Dakota's Experiment." Nation 108 (Mar. 22, 1919): 420-22.
Background, early history, and current activities of NPL as reported during author's trip to Bismarck.

259. McGuire, Patrick. "Death of a Myth: The Non-Partisan League and the Socialist Party of America 1912-20." In Herbert Blakely, ed., Proceedings of the Dakota History Conference 13 (1982): 598-623.
Describes NPL as a pragmatic political movement, rather than a socialist organization. Discusses N.Dak. Socialist party.

260. McKaig, Ray. "Farmers Mob the Mobbers." Public 21 (Sept. 28, 1918): 1241-42.
Describes incident in Boise, Idaho, in which NPL supporters turned back an attempt to disrupt an NPL gathering. Author was an NPL organizer.

261. _____. "The New Minnesota Despotism." Public 21 (Apr. 13, 1918): 465-67.
Offers evidence of support for NPL from

Organizer E. A. Young "writing up" a member, undated

Woodrow Wilson, George Creel, and other national figures. Discusses loyalty issue.

262. ____. "The Nonpartisan Champion." Public 22 (May 17, 1919): 518-20.
Profile of A. C. Townley.

263. ____. "Nonpartisan League and Its Independent Press." Public 22 (Jan. 4, 1919): 13-15.
Brief account of NPL activities in Idaho, Mont., S.Dak., Minn., Colo., Nebr., and N.Dak. Also recounts establishment of NPL newspapers in N.Dak.

264. ____. "The Townley Mistrial." Public 22 (Aug. 9, 1919): 855-57.
Firsthand account of Townley's trial at Jackson, Minn. (see No. 790) for conspiring to discourage enlistments.

265. McMillan, James. "The Macdonald-Nielson Imbroglio: The Politics of Education in North Dakota, 1918-1921." North Dakota History 52 (Fall 1985): in press.
Thorough treatment of 1918-19 controversy surrounding the office of N.Dak. state superintendent of public instruction. Includes biographies of Neil C. Macdonald and Minnie J. Nielson; discussion of dismissal of George McFarland as president of Valley City State College (1918); description of board of administration (created by NPL); and an analysis of the role that the dispute played in NPL's decline.

266. McNally, Winnifred. "The History of the Non-Partisan League with Specific Reference to the Direct Primary." Ariston (St. Catherine's College, St. Paul), Spring 1923, p. 10-13.
Brief history of NPL, concentrating on election strategy. Discusses NPL's effect on existing N.Dak. political parties. Offers a brief account of direct primary reform.

267. Mader, Joseph H. "The North Dakota Press and the Nonpartisan League." Journalism Quarterly 14 (Dec. 1937): 321-32.
Analysis of NPL publications and newspaper legislation. Based on author's master's thesis (see No. 966).

268. Manley, Robert N. "The Nebraska State Council of Defense and the Non-Partisan League." Nebraska History 43 (Dec. 1962): 229-52.
Activities 1918-19.

269. Markusen, Ann. "Who Were Your Grandfathers, John Hanson?" Quest: A Feminist Quarterly 5 (Summer 1980): 25-35.
A feminist critique of the film "Northern Lights" (a fictional account of NPL). Using recent scholarship on farm women and her own family history as background, author raises important questions about role of women in NPL and in farm life in general. Also published in No. 50.

Doily crocheted by Mrs. E. A. Meyer of Kalispell, Mont., ca. 1917. Her husband was a League organizer.

270. Martin, Michael J., and Glenn H. Smith. "Vice and Violence in Ward County, North Dakota, 1905-1920." North Dakota History 47 (Spring 1980): 10-21.
Includes discussion of William Langer's raid on criminal elements in Minot in 1917.

271. Martinson, Henry R. "'Comes the Revolution . . .' A Personal Memoir." North Dakota History 36 (Winter 1969): 40-109.
Account of Socialist party of N.Dak. by a former member, who was also an NPL organizer and officeholder (deputy commissioner of labor, 1937-65). Discusses relationship of Socialist party with NPL.

272. ____. "Some Memoirs of a Nonpartisan League Organizer." North Dakota History 42 (Spring 1975): 18-21.
Firsthand account of the life of an NPL organizer. Discusses harassment of organizers, organizing strategies, and the Consumers United Stores Co. Brief information on two other organizers, R. H. Walker and L. L. Griffith.

273. "Menace of the Non-Partisan League." Iron Age 101 (May 2, 1918): 1141.
Summary of speech by W. H. Barr, president of National Founder's Assn., discussing threat to business interests of organized labor and NPL.

274. Merz, Charles. "Nonpartisan League: A Survey." New Republic 22 (May 12, 1920): 333-38.
Defense of NPL conduct in struggle with Minnie Nielson for control of schools and in Scandinavian-American Bank scandal. Includes

account of NPL success in implementing its legislative program.

275. _____. "Political Revolt in the Northwest." New Republic 13 (Nov. 3, 10, 17, Dec. 1, 1917): 15-17, 44-46, 71-73, 121-23.
A series of four articles. (1) Political and economic background of NPL, with details of early organizing; emphasizes important roles played by American Society of Equity, Grange, and Farmers Union in success of NPL. (2) Account of 1917 N.Dak. legislative session. (3) NPL's attempt to reform N.Dak. educational system. (4) Prospects for further NPL success, including League expansion into other states and work with organized labor.

276. Mikolasak, V. F. "'Co-operation' under the Nonpartisan League." Co-operation 9 (Feb. 1923): 35.
Letter to editor assessing NPL legislative program in N.Dak.

277. "Minneapolis to Have Non-Partisan Daily." Editor and Publisher 51 (June 26, 1919): 6.
An account of establishment of Minneapolis Star. Discusses other NPL newspapers and gives details of NPL activities in Nebr.

278. "Minnesota, the Nonpartisan League and the Future." Nation 117 (Aug. 1, 1923): 102.
Explanation of rise of Farmer-Labor party in Minn. Analyzes reasons behind NPL's demise.

279. "Mr. Townley and Fargo's Bank Blow-Up." Literary Digest 63 (Nov. 1, 1919): 44-50.
Account of investigation of Scandinavian-American Bank in Fargo. Includes details of A. C. Townley's bankruptcy as a flax farmer.

280. Moorhead, F. G. "Nonpartisan League in Politics." Nation 107 (Oct. 5, 1918): 364-65.
Details of NPL activities--particularly 1916 election results--in Idaho, Nebr., Kans., Wash., N.Dak., S.Dak., Minn., Mont., and Iowa. Includes membership estimates.

281. Morlan, Robert L. "The Nonpartisan League and the Minnesota Campaign of 1918." Minnesota History 34 (Summer 1955): 221-32.
Basis for chapter entitled "A New National Party?" in author's book (see No. xx).

282. Morris, Oliver S. "Nonpartisan League." Nation 111 (Dec. 22, 1920): 733.
Letter from editor of Nonpartisan Leader refuting an earlier article (see No. 227). Outlines NPL's success in Wis., N.Dak., Wash., S.Dak., Mont., Colo., and Nebr.

283. _____. "Nonpartisan League and the Cooperative Movement." New Republic 25 (Jan. 19, 1921): 229-30.
Letter criticizing Nation's contention that NPL was declining (see No. 249). Author disputes earlier article's claim that NPL was successful only in state that had no existing cooperative movement.

284. _____. "The Vote of North Dakota Farmers." Nation 113 (Nov. 9, 1921): 535-36.
Background and results of N.Dak.'s 1921 recall election.

285. _____. "What Is Happening in North Dakota." Nation 112 (Mar. 9, 1921): 367-69.
Gives details of N.Dak.'s attempts to sell revenue bonds for state industries; discusses difficulties facing state bank because of poor sales.

286. Morton, W. L. "Western Progressive Movement and Cabinet Domination." Canadian Journal of Economic and Political Science 12 (May 1946): 136-47.
Briefly describes NPL difficulties in adapting to Canadian political system. Also discusses NPL relationship with United Farmers of Alba.

287. Moum, Kathleen. "Social Origins of the Nonpartisan League." North Dakota History 53 (Spring 1986): in press.
Offers profile of N.Dak. NPL members, concentrating on ethnicity, economic standing, and geographic factors. Sources used include nominating petitions, records of Consumers United Stores Co., and 1910 federal census. Author's research will be expanded in Ph.D. dissertation (University of California, Irvine) to be completed June 1986.

288. "National Nonpartisan League." American Labor Yearbook 5 (1923-24): 153-57.
Discusses decline of NPL and rise of Farmer-Labor party in S.Dak., Idaho, Wash., Minn., and N.Dak.

289. Nelson, Harold L. "The Political Reform Press: A Case Study." Journalism Quarterly 29 (Summer 1952): 294-302.
NPL background, finances, and circulation statistics of Minnesota Daily Star and its successor, Minneapolis Star.

290. "A New National Party." Literary Digest 55 (Aug. 11, 1917): 13-14.
Comment on national status of NPL after 1917 election of John M. Baer to Congress from N.Dak. Includes congressional and national press reaction.

291. "New Party in Oregon." Oregon Voter 20 (Feb. 7, 1920): 220.
Account of a farmer-labor convention held in Salem, Oreg., organized by Walter Thomas Mills. Discusses NPL organizing attempts.

292. "Newspaper Case before the Court." North Dakota Press Association Bulletin 3 (Apr. 1920): 1.
   Brief account of case before N.Dak. Supreme Court challenging NPL-backed newspaper legislation passed by 1919 legislature.

293. "Newspaper Law Being Tried in Supreme Court." North Dakota Press Association Bulletin 3 (Feb. 1920): 1, 3.
   Brief account of case before N.Dak. Supreme Court challenging NPL-backed newspaper legislation passed by 1919 legislature.

294. Nicholas, E. H. "Mr. Creel and the Nonpartisan League." Review 1 (June 14, 1919): 101.
   Evidence for charges against A. C. Townley in trial at Jackson, Minn. (see No. 790); author was Jackson County Attorney. Response to an earlier article (see No. 166).

295. "Non-Partisan League." The Bellman 24 (Mar. 23, 1918): 314.
   Condemnation of NPL.

296. "Non-Partisan League." Oregon Voter 10 (Sept. 8, 1917): 315.
   Gives an account of NPL activities in Nebr. and Oreg. Discusses NPL's endorsement by Oreg. Farmers Union and Oreg. State Grange. Reprints a statement by Nebr. Farmers Union, which declined to endorse NPL.

297. "The Nonpartisan League." Weekly Review 1 (July 19, 1919): 207-9.
   Attacks A. C. Townley; calls NPL program socialist.

298. "Nonpartisan League Fights On." Nation 114 (June 14, 1922): 711.
   Activities of NPL before 1922 N.Dak. elections. Analyzes implications of A. C. Townley's retirement as national NPL president.

299. "Nonpartisan League Gains." Literary Digest 67 (Dec. 11, 1920): 21-22.
   National press reaction to NPL victories in 1920 N.Dak. general election. Includes an anti-NPL cartoon.

300. "Non-Partisan League Here." Oregon Voter 33 (May 5, 1953): 152-53.
   Report on a meeting of Pomona Grange of Yamhill Co. (McMinnville, Oreg.), which endorsed NPL program. Discusses relationship between NPL and Walter M. Pierce (Democratic governor of Oreg., 1923-27).

301. "Nonpartisan League Meeting at St. Paul." Agricultural Digest 2 (Oct. 1917): 647-48, 676.
   Discusses press reaction to NPL's Producers and Consumers Convention held in St. Paul, Sept. 1917.

302. "Non-Partisan News." Oregon Voter 14 (Aug. 17, 1918): 210-11.
   An account of NPL activities in N.Dak., Minn., Idaho, and Wash. Mentions lack of NPL success in Oreg. Discusses indictment of A. C. Townley and Joseph Gilbert at Jackson, Minn. (see No. 790).

303. "Nonpartisan Partisanship." Outlook 123 (Dec. 3, 1919): 411-12.
   General report on NPL covering A. C. Townley's trial at Jackson, Minn.; failure of Scandinavian-American Bank; N.Dak. coal strike of 1919.

304. "Non-Partisan Program." Oregon Voter 12 (Mar. 16, 1918): 354-56.
   NPL program as put forth in Idaho.

305. Nord, David Paul. "Minneapolis and the Pragmatic Socialism of Thomas Van Lear." Minnesota History 45 (Spring 1976): 2-10.
   Discusses reasons for Van Lear's victory in 1916 campaign for mayor of Minneapolis as a Socialist; argues that organized labor left Socialist party by late 1918 (because of Socialist opposition to WWI) to form Municipal Nonpartisan League, which later became Working People's Nonpartisan Political League.

306. "North Dakota." Oregon Voter 25 (June 18, 1921): 460-77.
   Reprints a history of NPL originally published by National City Co. (a bank in Portland). Primarily a discussion of Bank of N.Dak.

307. "North Dakota and the Banks." Nation 112 (Mar. 2, 1921): 330.
   Discusses difficulties N.Dak. faced in selling state revenue bonds and problems facing state bank.

308. "North Dakota Coalition." Weekly Review 1 (July 12, 1919): 180-81.
   Comparison of NPL with Liberal-Labor party of New Zealand. Discusses NPL alliance with organized labor in N.Dak.

309. "North Dakota Farmers." Public 22 (Mar. 29, 1919): 318-19.
   Discussion of British government's refusal to visa passports issued by U.S. Dept. of State to NPL officers.

310. "North Dakota Financial Crisis." Literary Digest 68 (Mar. 5, 1921): 13-14.
   Account of financial crisis precipitated by N.Dak.'s inability to sell bonds to finance state bank. Includes excerpts from several newspapers and two anti-NPL cartoons from N.Y. newspapers.

311. "North Dakota Five Years After." New Republic 46 (Apr. 28, 1926): 292-93.
   Analysis of economic impact of earlier NPL legislation on N.Dak. economy of 1926.

312. "North Dakota Goes to the People." Nation 112 (Apr. 13, 1921): 530-31.
   Discusses N.Dak.'s attempt to sell state revenue bonds directly to the people.

313. "North Dakota near the Rocks." Outlook 127 (Mar. 2, 1921): 328.
   Problems facing N.Dak. and NPL, particularly difficulty encountered by Bank of N.Dak. in selling bonds to finance its operation.

314. "North Dakota Pays the Price." Weekly Review 4 (Mar. 30, 1921): 290-91.
   Unsympathetic analysis of NPL's record in N.Dak. Especially critical of Bank of N.Dak.

315. "North Dakota Primaries." Independent 109 (July 8, 1922): 573-74.
   Analysis of 1922 N.Dak. primary elections.

316. "North Dakota Publishers Should Get Busy." North Dakota Press Association Bulletin 3 (June 1919): 1-3.
   Calls for defeat of N.Dak. House Bill No. 157 (the "Printing Bill") in June 1919 referendum election. Bill provided for the choosing by popular election of one official newspaper per county, to receive all public advertising, legal notices, etc.

317. "North Dakota Wins Her Fight." Nation 113 (Oct. 19, 1921): 438.
   Report on events leading to 1921 recall election in N.Dak., including sale of state bonds to finance state industries and legal cases challenging NPL's program (see No. 775).

318. "'North Dakotaism's' Victory." Literary Digest 62 (July 19, 1919): 15-16.
   Reaction of national press to N.Dak. referendum of June 1919 ratifying NPL legislative program.

319. "North Dakota's Farmer Revolt." Literary Digest 54 (Jan. 20, 1917): 115-16.
   Excerpts from stories on NPL printed in various U.S. newspapers during 1916 N.Dak. campaign and general election.

320. "North Dakota's Political Twister." Literary Digest 71 (Oct. 22, 1921): 12-13.
   National and N.Dak. press discussions of forthcoming 1921 N.Dak. recall election.

321. "North Dakota's Rash Adventure." Outlook 122 (July 19, 1919): 396-97.
   Analysis of NPL legislative program.

322. "North Dakota's 'Recall' Puzzle." Literary Digest 71 (Nov. 19, 1921): 10.
   The 1921 N.Dak. recall election. Includes a photograph of A. C. Townley speaking.

323. "North Dakota's 'Revolution.'" Literary Digest 60 (Mar. 29, 1919): 11-14.
   Reaction of national press to enactment of NPL program in N.Dak. Includes two NPL cartoons and a photograph of an NPL meeting.

324. Nye, R. B. "Political Prairie Fire by R. L. Morlan, Review." Saturday Review 39 (July 7, 1956): 8-9.

325. "O.A.C. [Oregon Agricultural College] and League." Oregon Voter 10 (Aug. 11, 1917): 186.
   Mentions support given NPL by Edwin F. Ladd and the N.Dak. Agricultural College. Discusses NPL attempts to gain support of Oreg. Agricultural College.

326. O'Hara, F. "Grievances of the Spring Wheat Growers." Catholic World 106 (Dec. 1917): 380-87.
   General discussion of NPL, including Robert M. LaFollette's controversial speech to Producers and Consumers Convention in St. Paul, Sept. 1917.

327. "Oregon Free So Far." Oregon Voter 18 (Aug. 2, 1919): 173.
   Report on vote by NPL membership to re-elect A. C. Townley as president. Brief mention of League plans to begin organizing in Oreg.

328. Packard, Frank E. "Farmer's Movement in North Dakota." National Tax Association Proceedings, 1917, p. 166-74.
   Brief account of NPL's early days, emphasizing League's proposals for tax legislation. Author was a member of N.Dak. State Tax Commission.

329. Patterson, Robert George. "North Dakota: A Twentieth Century Valley Forge." Nation 117 (Aug. 8, 1923): 134-36.
   Radical politics in N.Dak. from territorial days to NPL.

330. Pickett, John E. "A Prairie Fire." Country Gentleman, May 18, p. 3, 4, 30, 31, May 25, p. 13, 14, 31, June 1, p. 13, 14, 23, June 8, p. 13, 14, 23, June 15, p. 13, 14, 22, June 22, p. 13, 14, 23, 1918.
   A series of six articles, accompanied by good illustrations and photographs. (1) Brief history of NPL with emphasis on its organizing tactics and relationship with organized labor. (2) Questions results of Edwin F. Ladd's research into wheat-grading methods. Gives an account of attempt by NPL's Consumers United Stores Co. to negotiate labor agreement with IWW. (3) Loyalty

issue in Minn., with details of several confrontations between NPL members and their opponents. (4) Opposition to NPL by Jerry Dempster Bacon, editor of Grand Forks Herald. (5) Explores populist background of NPL and League efforts to organize in other states—primarily Kans., Nebr., and Iowa. (6) Analyzes NPL's relationship with other farm organizations, including American Society of Equity and Farmers Union. Also discusses NPL organizing in Kans. and Nebr. (see also No. 506).

331. "Pierce and Non-P. League." Oregon Voter 13 (May 11, 1918): 203-4.
Discusses Walter M. Pierce's relationship with NPL and raises loyalty issue.

332. Plachy, Frank, Jr. "Nonpartisan League." Nation 107 (July 27, 1918): 92-93.
Economic and political background of NPL. Details of expansion into Minn. and relationship with organized labor in Minn. and N.Dak. Short discussion of loyalty issue.

333. "Platform of Independent Publishers." North Dakota Press Association Bulletin 6 (Sept. 1922): 1, 3.
Resolution of anti-NPL newspaper publishers endorsing J. F. T. O'Connor for U.S. Senate.

334. "Politics, Bank Explosions, Lawsuits, and Other Live Matters in North Dakota." Literary Digest 64 (Mar. 20, 1920): 62-66.
Account of investigation of Scandinavian-American Bank of Fargo and its political aftermath.

335. Pratt, William C. "Radicals, Farmers, and Historians: Some Recent Scholarship on Agrarian Radicalism in the Upper Midwest." North Dakota History 52 (Fall 1985).
Places NPL within context of 19th- and 20th-century agrarian radicalism. Includes a discussion of recent NPL historiography; a review of recent accounts of NPL's relationship with American Society of Equity and Farmers Union; a comparison of NPL history with history of Socialist party; an assessment of A. C. Townley's role within NPL; and a call for more scholarly attention to the link between NPL and later farm movements such as Farm Holiday.

336. "Press Executives Hold Conference." North Dakota Press Association Bulletin 4 (Mar. 1921): 1, 4.
Account of meeting to draft bill to submit to legislature concerning NPL-sponsored newspaper legislation.

337. "The Press Meeting." North Dakota Press Association Bulletin 3 (Sept. 1919): 4, 6.
Account of annual meeting of N.Dak. Press Assn., including a discussion of NPL-sponsored newspaper legislation of 1919.

338. Preus, Jacob A. O. "A Government Experiment vs. Life Insurance Principles, with Specific Reference to the Rights of the Nonpartisan League." Economic World 22 (Dec. 17, 1921): 885-89.
Address delivered by Minn. governor to annual convention of Assn. of Life Insurance Presidents (New York City, 1921). Primarily analyzes socialist tendencies of NPL and urges a cooperative marketing system as answer to farmers' problems.

339. "Protest against Townley Autocracy." Oregon Voter 14 (Sept. 27, 1918): 314, 316.
Account of objections made by NPL organizers over lack of democratic procedures in NPL administration. Includes excerpts from protest letter written by NPL organizers.

340. Putnam, Jackson. "The Role of the North Dakota Socialist Party in North Dakota History." North Dakota Quarterly 24 (Fall 1958): 115-22.
Discusses assimilation of socialist organizers and members into NPL after 1915.

341. Quigley, Harold S. "Nonpartisan League." Unpartizan Review 14 (July-Dec. 1920): 55-75.
Discussion of N.Dak. state-owned industries, NPL organizing efforts, and membership estimates for N.Dak., Minn., S.Dak., Mont., Nebr., Colo., Wash., Wis., and Idaho.

342. Ratliff, Beulah Amidon. "Cream Lady." New Republic 28 (Oct. 26, 1921): 240-42.
One woman's experiences as an NPL member.

343. Reid, Bill G. "Arthur C. Townley: A Study in Success and Failure." Red River Valley Historian, Fall 1980, p. 18-22.
Brief biography including details of Townley's life before and after NPL days. Interesting discussion of speaking style, personality, and the image he projected to N.Dak. farmers and city dwellers.

344. _____. "John Miller Baer: Nonpartisan League Cartoonist and Congressman." North Dakota History 44 (Winter 1977): 4-13.
Short biography of Baer and analysis of his political cartoons and role in NPL, with several of his drawings (see p. 26).

345. Remele, Larry. "Farmers Have Sought Market Power since Statehood." Onlooker (Mandan, N.Dak.) 2 (Apr. 12, 1976): 9-10.
Analysis of N.Dak. farmers' attempts to control marketing of their crops. Discusses NPL as cumulation of efforts of earlier groups, including Farmers Union and American Society of Equity.

"Politician Equipped for the 1918 Campaign," cartoon by John M. Baer published in Nonpartisan Leader, March 11, 1918.

346. _____. "The Immaculate Conception at Deering." North Dakota History 47 (Winter 1980): 28-31.
  Detailed investigation of various versions of NPL origins.

347. _____. "The Nonpartisan League and the North Dakota Press: Organization Period, 1915-1916." North Dakota Quarterly 44 (Autumn 1976): 30-46.
  Reactions of N.Dak. press to early NPL organizing, based on random sample of 205 N.Dak. newspapers. Author finds more favorable early reaction than scholars had previously recognized.

348. _____. "North Dakota Farmers Union and the Nonpartisan League." North Dakota Quarterly 46 (Autumn 1978): 40-50.
  History of Farmers Union in N.Dak.; describes its split with NPL over ideological differences involving cooperatives.

349. _____. "The North Dakota State Library Scandal of 1919." North Dakota History 44 (Winter 1977): 21-29.
  Thorough examination of scandal that erupted when Public Library Commission--under NPL administration--was accused of circulating books that advocated socialism.

350. _____. "North Dakota's Forgotten Farmers Union: 1913-1920." North Dakota History 45 (Spring 1978): 4-21.
  History of N.Dak. branch of Farmers Union, including discussion of how its relationship with NPL divided Union's membership and finally led to its demise. Addresses role of Consumers United Stores Co.

351. _____. "Political Charisma in North Dakota: An Interpretation of an Evolution." Onlooker (Mandan, N.Dak.) 2 (Dec. 26, 1976): 5-8.
  Includes discussion of A. C. Townley and William Langer.

352. _____. "This Dirty Campaign: 1918 and 1980." Prairie Fire (Bismarck) 9 (Oct. 31, 1980): 1, 3.
  Comparison of N.Dak. election campaigns.

353. _____. "The Tragedy of Idealism: The National Nonpartisan League and American Foreign Policy, 1917-1919." North Dakota Quarterly 42 (Autumn 1974): 78-112.
  Thorough examination of NPL views, including U.S. involvement in WWI, Versailles Conference, League of Nations, Russian Revolution, and Mexican-American relations.

354. "Reveille in North Dakota." Survey 49 (Oct. 15, 1922): 110.
  Discussion of the State Board of Health.

355. "Revolt of the Farmers: The National Nonpartisan League." Social Service Bulletin 9 (July 1919): 1-2.
  Brief account of NPL origin and accomplishments. Discusses loyalty issue and Lynn J. Frazier's appointment to board of governors for a nationwide campaign against anarchy.

356. Rice, Hazel F. "A Memo from Memory: Working with the North Dakota Workman's Compensation Bureau, 1919-1922." North Dakota History 46 (Spring 1979): 22-29.
  An account of author's employment with Bureau, established by NPL. She investigated wages, hours, and working conditions of females and minors in towns of 500 or more people.

357. Rice, Stuart Arthur. "Farmers and Workers in American Politics." Columbia University Studies 113 (1924): 327-551.
  General study of farmer-labor parties and alliances with brief account of NPL history. Includes quantitative analysis of elections and legislative votes that pertain to NPL in Minn. and N.Dak. Based on Ph.D. dissertation (see No. 988).

358. Rippley, La Vern J. "Conflict in the Classroom: Anti-Germanism in Minnesota Schools,

1917-19." *Minnesota History* 47 (Spring 1981): 171-83.
    Attack by Minn. Commission of Public Safety on teachings of German in public schools. Mentions NPL's relationship with Commission.

359. Rockwell, J. E. "Struggle in North Dakota; Reply to C. R. Johnson, with Rejoinder." *New Republic* 26 (Apr. 20, 1921): 238-39.
    Letter to editor disputing Johnson's analysis of controversies surrounding Bank of N.Dak. (see No. 228), with Johnson's reply.

360. Rowell, Chester H. "Why the Middle West Went Radical," "Political Cyclone in North Dakota," "La Follette, Shipstead, and the Embattled Farmers," "Brookhart, Howell, and 'Brother Charley' Bryan," "Is Middle West Radicalism Here to Stay?" *World's Work* 46 (June, July, Aug., Sept., Oct. 1923): 157-65, 265-74, 408-20, 478-85, 655-58.
    Series of five articles. (1) Includes discussion of NPL in N.Dak., Wis., Minn., Iowa, Kans., and Nebr. Concentrates on NPL's relationships with established parties in these states. (2) Standard but comprehensive history of NPL. (3) NPL is briefly discussed in connection with 1922 elections in Minn. and Wis. (4) Brief description of 1922 elections in Iowa and Nebr. Discusses Smith W. Brookhart of Iowa, R. B. Howell of Nebr.--both elected to U.S. Senate--and Charles W. Bryan (William Jennings Bryan's younger brother), who was elected governor of Nebr. (5) Discusses long-term political power of NPL and Farmer-Labor party.

361. Roylance, W. G. "Americanism in North Dakota." *Nation* 109 (July 12, 1919): 37-39.
    Defense of NPL's activities and programs as logical outgrowths of American democracy. Reaction to an article by Emerson Hough (published in *Saturday Review,* ca. June 1919) that attacked NPL as a form of European radicalism.

362. Rude, Leslie G. "The Rhetoric of Farmer-Labor Agitators." *Central States Speech Journal* 20 (Winter 1969): 280-85.
    Analysis of organizing methods of NPL and later farmer-labor groups. Focuses on speaking styles and strategies of leaders and organizers. Includes descriptions of NPL rallies and meetings.

363. Ruhl, Arthur. "North Dakota Idea." *Atlantic Monthly* 123 (May 1919): 686-96.
    An on-the-scene report that includes discussion of farmers' economic grievances, A. C. Townley, NPL legislators, and early NPL history.

364. Russell, Charles Edward. "Farmers' Battle." *Pearson's Magazine* 33 (May 1915): 516-27.
    Grain trade and farmers' attempt to reform it by establishing cooperative marketing and milling enterprises. NPL members received this publication in 1915.

365. _____. "Grain and the Invisible Government." *Pearson's Magazine* 34 (Dec. 1915): 515-27.
    Outline of farmers' grievances against grain traders, focusing on dispute between American Society of Equity and Minneapolis Grain Exchange.

366. _____. "The Nonpartisan League." *American Sociological Society Proceedings* 11 (1917): 31-36.
    Economic background of NPL and results of 1916 N.Dak. elections.

367. _____. "Nonpartisan League Growing So Rapidly that It Might Decide Next Presidency." *Reconstruction* 1 (Aug. 1919): 228-30.
    Not seen by compilers.

368. _____. "Origin and Aim of the Farmers' Nonpartisan League." *Community Center* 3 (Mar. 17, 1917): 20-21.
    Early history of NPL with discussion of conditions that led to its rise.

369. _____. "Revolt of the Farmers." *Pearson's Magazine* 33 (Apr. 1915): 417-27.
    Analysis of grain trade and attempts to reform it.

370. Saby, Rasmus S. "The Nonpartisan League in North Dakota." *The Northstar* 1 (Jan. 1920): 11-15.
    Account of NPL background, program, and tactics. Author was on faculty of Cornell University.

371. Saloutos, Theodore. "The Montana Society of Equity." *Pacific Historical Review* 14 (Dec. 1945): 393-408.
    Includes some details of NPL activity in Mont., 1914-19.

372. _____. "The Rise of the Equity Cooperative Exchange." *Mississippi Valley Historical Review* 32 (June 1945): 31-62.
    Detailed history of Exchange, with a brief mention of NPL. Demonstrates importance to NPL's success of groundwork laid by Exchange.

373. _____. "The Rise of the Nonpartisan League in North Dakota, 1915-1917" and "The Expansion and Decline of the Nonpartisan League in the Western Middle West, 1917-1921." *Agricultural History* 20 (Jan., Oct. 1946): 43-61, 235-52.

A two-part series. (1) Early NPL history, emphasizing relationships with Socialist party of N.Dak. and organized labor. Deals primarily with NPL in N.Dak. (2) Good discussion of Arthur Le Sueur and formulation of N.Dak. legislative program, relationship with Socialist Party of America, and other points of NPL history, 1917-21, in N.Dak., Minn., Wis., S.Dak., Kans., and Mont.

374. Schmidt, Paul C. "The Press in North Dakota." North Dakota History 31 (Oct. 1964): 216-22.
General history emphasizing N.Dak. Press Assn. Discusses NPL's newspaper legislation and People's Press Assn. (later Progressive Press Assn.), an organization of newspaper editors who supported NPL.

375. Schrader, Frederick. "Non-Partisan League Wins." Issues and Events 7 (July 21, 1917): 35.
Significance of the election of John M. Baer to U.S. Congress from N.Dak. in 1917.

376. Scott, Frank R. "North Dakota." Banking 14 (Feb. 1921): 533.
Short description of economic conditions in N.Dak. in 1921, with special reference to economic effects of NPL legislation, predicting bleak prospects for Bank of N.Dak.

377. "Self Government in North Dakota." Christian Science Monitor, May 10, 1920, p. 5.
Interview with N.Dak. Governor Lynn J. Frazier concerning NPL accomplishments and plans.

378. Shimmons, Earl W. "The Labor Dailies." American Mercury 15 (Sept. 1928): 85-93.
Brief account of Minnesota Daily Star and its NPL origins.

379. Simons, A. M. "Uselessness of Protest Parties." American Federationist 27 (Apr. 1920): 331.
Primarily concerned with third parties that attempted to attract labor support. Mentions NPL as example of a "useful" protest party.

380. Slosson, Edwin E. "Kansas Freedom." Independent 105 (Apr. 16, 1921): 399.
Condemns harassment of NPL leaders in Great Bend, Kans.

381. Smith, Glenn H. "The State Experimental Creamery: A Footnote to Nonpartisan League History." North Dakota Quarterly 49 (Summer 1981): 57-63.
Examination of state-owned creamery set up under NPL legislation.

382. Smith, Robert E. "The Farmers' Non-Partisan League." Oregon Voter 11 (Oct. 20, 1917): 80-81.
Brief account of NPL and a forecast of its activities in Oreg.

383. "Socialism and Single Tax." Oregon Voter 12 (Mar. 30, 1918): 400.
Reprints very brief excerpts from NPL national platform.

384. "Some Apologies to Mr. Rockwell of Fargo." New Republic 25 (Jan. 19, 1921): 229.
Editorial comment on a letter (published in the New York Times, Jan. 4, 1921) from James E. Rockwell, who disputed magazine's claims for 3,000,000 NPL votes in nine states in 1920 general elections. Comment states that figure was report of NPL claim.

385. Spafford, D. S. "'Independent' Politics in Saskatchewan before the Nonpartisan League." Saskatchewan History 18 (Winter 1965): 1-9.
Discussion of third-party movements, ca. 1905-13, that set stage for NPL's brief appearance.

386. "Stallard Defends N.P.L." Oregon Voter 36 (Feb. 9, 1924): 166-67.
Letter to editor from H. H. Stallard of Portland. Discusses NPL activities in Oreg.

387. "Star Shines at Last in Minneapolis." Editor and Publisher 53 (Aug. 28, 1920): 24.
Brief account of beginning of Minnesota Daily Star, including subscription details and lists of officers and advertising representatives.

388. Starr, Karen. "Fighting for a Future: Farm Women of the Nonpartisan League." Minnesota History 48 (Summer 1983): 255-62.
Analysis of role of women in NPL activities. Includes discussion of farm family, woman suffrage, and reasons for decline of NPL.

389. "State of North Dakota Goes into the Banking Business." Bankers Magazine 98 (Apr. 1919): 417-19.
Analysis of legislation that created Bank of N.Dak., with warning about problems of banks under political control.

390. "State Socialism Constitutional." Literary Digest 65 (June 26, 1920): 20-21.
National press reaction to U.S. Supreme Court's decision upholding NPL's legislative program of state-owned industry in N.Dak. (see No. 775).

391. Steele, H. H. "Tax Program of the Nonpartisan League of North Dakota." National Tax Association Proceedings, 1919, p. 517-28.
Detailed explanation of tax legislation

passed by 1919 N.Dak. legislature. Author was chairman of N.Dak. State Tax Commission.

392. Stolberg, Benjamin. "Third Party Chances, I: Background, 1918-1923" and "Third Party Chances, II: 1923 and After." Nation 118 (Apr. 2, 16, 1924): 364-67, 422-24.
   Two-part series. (1) NPL history and influence on organized labor's attempt to form a third party. (2) Organized labor's attempt to form a third party. Mentions NPL's participation in conference sponsored by Minn. Farmer-Labor party, Nov. 1922.

393. "Straddling on League." Oregon Voter 13 (June 29, 1918): 442.
   Attacks Bruce Dennis, editor of La Grande (Oreg.) Observer, for his defense of NPL against disloyalty charges.

394. Taft, Philip. "The IWW in the Grain Belt." Labor History 1 (Winter 1960): 53-67.
   Detailed account of IWW organizing among agricultural workers ca. 1910-20. Although NPL is mentioned only briefly, gives important background information on its attempt to negotiate labor agreement between IWW and N.Dak. farmers.

395. Taft, William Howard. "North Dakota's Fight against the Townleyites." Public Ledger (Philadelphia), July 1, 19, Dec. 13, 1920.
   Series of anti-NPL newspaper articles by former U.S. president. (1) Briefly describes NPL, focusing on 1920 N.Dak. primary campaign for U.S. Senate between Edwin F. Ladd and Asle J. Gronna. (2) Discusses results of 1920 N.Dak. primary elections and possibility of fusion between Democrats and Republicans to defeat NPL in general election. (3) Reports on results of 1920 N.Dak. general election, including the laws passed by referendum.

396. Talbot, Ross B. "North Dakota--A Two Party State?" North Dakota Quarterly 25 (Fall 1957): 93-104.
   N.Dak. elections of 1948-56 and merger of Democratic party and NPL in 1956. Briefly mentions NPL election tactics from 1916 to 1922.

397. Taylor, Eleanor. "Farmers and Factory-Hands: The New Alliance of Organized Producers and Organized Labor." Survey 38 (Sept. 29, 1917): 564-65.
   Coverage of NPL's Producers and Consumers Convention held in St. Paul, Sept. 1917. Summarizes convention's sentiments on loyalty issue and alliance with organized labor.

398. "Technique of Revolution." Nation 108 (Mar. 22, 1919): 417-18.
   Editorial asserting need for more states to adopt reforms urged by NPL, if U.S. were to avoid more radical changes like those brought to Russia by the 1917 revolution.

399. Teigan, Henry G. "Fight in North Dakota." Socialist Review 10 (Apr.-May 1921): 55-58.
   NPL accomplishments, especially early operation of Bank of N.Dak. Discusses difficulties bank encountered in its sale of bonds. Author was NPL executive secretary (1916-23).

400. _____. "Minnesota's Political 'Why.'" Labor Age 12 (Feb. 1923): 10-12.

Nonpartisan League candidates campaigning by airplane, undated

Analysis of 1922 election of Henrik Shipstead to U.S. Senate as a Farmer-Labor party member from Minn. Gives history of NPL, emphasizing relationship with organized labor. Describes Working People's Nonpartisan Political League.

401. ____. "The National Nonpartisan League." *American Labor Yearbook* 3 (1919-20): 280-89.
Economic background and history of NPL. Includes membership estimates for Minn., N.Dak., S.Dak., and Mont.; lists number of NPL state legislators elected in S.Dak., Minn., N.Dak., Mont., and Idaho.

402. ____. "The National Nonpartisan League." *American Labor Yearbook* 4 (1921-22): 421-26.
Discusses controversies surrounding N.Dak. state-owned industries. Includes number of state legislators elected in N.Dak., S.Dak., Nebr., Colo., Wis., Wash., Mont., Minn., and Idaho.

403. ____. "The Revolution in North Dakota." *Western Comrade*, Oct., p. 10, 11, 30, Nov., p. 12, 13, 26, Dec., p. 10--all 1917.
Series of articles. (1) NPL economic background, birth, and early organizing activities. (2) N.Dak. campaign of 1916. (3) Brief account of organizing efforts outside of N.Dak. Discusses 1917 election of John M. Baer to U.S. Congress.

404. "That Unsuccessful 'Bank Blow-Up' in Fargo." *Literary Digest* 63 (Dec. 20, 1919): 48-52.
Details of investigation of Scandinavian-American Bank, with account of NPL mass meeting held in Fargo on Oct. 19, 1919, to discuss bankruptcy.

405. Thompson, J., and W. H. Hunter. "National Nonpartisan League." *Review of Reviews* 57 (Apr. 1918): 397-401.
Debate on merits of NPL between Thompson (pro) and Hunter (con).

406. Tighe, Ambrose. "The Legal Theory of the Minnesota Safety Commission Act." *Minnesota Law Review* 3 (Dec. 19, 1918): 1-19.
Based on address delivered to Minn. State Bar Assn. Author was legal counsel for Minn. Commission of Public Safety.

407. Tostlebe, Alvin Samuel. "The Bank of North Dakota: An Experiment in Agrarian Banking." *Columbia University Studies* 114 (1924): 1-210.
Political and economic background of bank and detailed history of its operation to ca. 1923. Based on Ph.D. dissertation (see No. 1002).

408. "Townley Campaigns in the East." *Agricultural Digest* 2 (Dec. 1917): 738-39.
Discusses meeting to organize NPL chapter in New York and reaction of *New York Times.*

409. "Townley in Kansas." *Literary Digest* 68 (Mar. 12, 1921): 17-18.
Reaction of Kans. newspapers to NPL attempt to expand into Kans. Includes an anti-NPL cartoon.

410. "Townley's Supreme Court." *Oregon Voter* 18 (Aug. 2, 1919): 183-84.
Attacks N.Dak. Supreme Court decision that upheld the passage of constitutional amendments (allowing the establishment of state-owned industries) in 1918 N.Dak. general election (see No. 788).

411. "Trial of Townley and Gilbert." *Weekly Review* 1 (July 26, 1919): 230.
Account of trial at Jackson, Minn. (see No. 790). Includes excerpts from speeches that led to charges of discouraging enlistments.

412. Tselos, George. "The Farmer-Labor Party in Minnesota: 1918-1944." *International Socialist Review* 32 (May 1971): 14-19, 26-27.
History of Farmer-Labor party emphasizing labor's involvement and role of Communist party. Brief account of NPL in N.Dak. and Minn.

413. "Turning Down the N.P.L." *Oregon Voter* 36 (Feb. 2, 1924): 132.
Reports on an Oreg. Agricultural Economic Conference that defeated a resolution supporting state-owned industries.

414. Villard, Oswald Garrison. "Newspaper with Six Thousand Owners." *Nation* 116 (June 6, 1923): 648-50.
History and operation of *Minnesota Daily Star*, published by the Northwest Publishing Co. Discusses roles of Herbert F. Gaston (officer and editor) and Thomas Van Lear (officer).

415. Vindex, Charles. "Radical Rule in Montana." *Montana the Magazine of Western History* 18 (Jan. 1968): 3-18.
Socialist rule in Plentywood, Mont., during 1920s and 1930s. Background information includes discussion of NPL activities in Mont. and NPL's relationship to socialists.

416. Vivian, James F. "'Not a Patriotic American Party': William Howard Taft's Campaign against the Nonpartisan League, 1920-1921." *North Dakota History* 50 (Fall, 1983): 4-10.
Account of Taft's lecture tour of N.Dak. and his series of anti-NPL articles (see No.

395). Includes an analysis of NPL's relationship to national Republican party.

417. Wallace, Henry. "Report on the Farmers." New Republic 116 (June 30, 1947): 12-13, 37-38.
Analysis of U.S. farm economy and politics. Discusses NPL history in an account of formation of Farmers' Union Progressive Alliance in N.Dak. in 1947.

418. Wannamaker, Olin D. "A Nonpartisan League for the South." Nation 110 (May 15, 1920): 648-49.
Discusses southern agriculture and economics in reference to possible NPL organizing efforts.

419. Warner, Arthur. "Enter the Labor Press." Nation 112 (June 1, 1921): 785-87.
Mentions Minnesota Daily Star, Nonpartisan Leader, and Fargo Courier-News. Discusses relationship between farmers and organized labor.

420. ____. "Farmer Butts Back." Nation 111 (Aug. 28, 1920): 240-41.
Background and early history of NPL, with brief analysis of its stand on woman suffrage, split between rural and urban voters in N.Dak., and relationship with organized labor.

421. ____. "When Farmers Turn Politicians." Nation 111 (Aug. 14, 1920): 183.
NPL reaction to formation of a national Farmer-Labor party with brief description of NPL activities in Minn. and N.Dak. before 1920 elections.

422. "Washington Notes." New Republic 92 (Aug. 25, 1937): 74-75.
Account of labor's attempt to form a Nonpartisan League, focusing on E. L. Oliver, an NPL organizer in Minn. harassed for alleged disloyalty in 1919.

423. "We Are Coming!" Oregon Voter 9 (June 23, 1917): 426-28.
Account of NPL attempts to organize Oreg. farmers. Mentions an appearance by NPL organizer Ray McKaig at an Oreg. State Grange convention at Astoria, Oreg.; discusses relationship between NPL and Oreg. Grange.

424. Wells, Merle W. "Fred T. DuBois and the Nonpartisan League in the Idaho Election of 1918." Pacific Northwest Quarterly 56 (Jan. 1965): 17-29.
Comprehensive history of NPL activities in Idaho focusing on complicated political maneuvering that surrounded 1918 election.

425. "What a 74-Year-Old Farmer-Soldier-Patriot Thinks of League Organizers." Oregon Voter 13 (June 29, 1918): 444-45.
Facsimile reproduction of handwritten letter from Daniel Shamer of Lewis Co., Wash., who condemns NPL.

426. "When Chickens Come Home to Roost." North Dakota Banker 4 (Sept. 1916): 14.
Short account of N.Dak. farmers' reaction to IWW and attempts to organize farm workers.

427. Wilcox, Benton H. "An Historical Definition of Northwest Radicalism." Mississippi Valley Historical Review 26 (Dec. 1939): 377-94.
Defense of participants in northwest agrarian protest movements such as Grange, Populist party, and NPL as "ordinary businessmen" attempting to correct economic injustice. Discusses NPL's program; anticipates later attempts to characterize agrarian protest as irrational.

428. Wilkins, Robert P. "The Non-Ethnic Roots of North Dakota Isolationism." Nebraska History 44 (Sept. 1963): 205-21.
Analysis of isolationism of N.Dak. politicians, 1914-56. Includes views of NPL and its spokesmen on foreign affairs.

429. ____. "The Nonpartisan League and Upper Mid-west Isolationism." Agricultural History 39 (Apr. 1965): 102-9.
Examination of NPL attitudes toward foreign policy questions, 1915-ca. 1960.

430. ____. "Referendum on War? The General Election of 1916 in North Dakota." North Dakota History 36 (Fall 1969): 296-335.
Analysis of war issue in N.Dak. 1916 presidential campaign, with discussion of NPL attempts to remain neutral in national races.

431. "W[illamette] V[alley] Farmer Not Gullible." Oregon Voter 12 (Mar. 30, 1918): 407.
Reprint of article from Cottage Grove Sentinel (Oreg.), giving NPL little chance for success in Oreg.

432. Willis, Hugh E. "North Dakotas's Industrial Program and the Law." Survey 45 (Dec. 18, 1920): 418-19.
Discussion of U.S. Supreme Court decision (see No. 775) that gave N.Dak. the right to establish state-owned industries.

433. "Won't Work in Oregon." Oregon Voter 12 (Feb. 23, 1918): 240.
Brief account of NPL organizing attempts. Concentrates on commission paid to NPL organizers for signing new members.

Pamphlets and Ephemera

For more information on the entries in this section, see Introduction.

434. Aberdeen Daily American. <u>Story of the Non-Partisan League of North Dakota</u>. Aberdeen, S.Dak., [1916]. 23 p. MHS.
 Reprint of eight articles first published in <u>Aberdeen Daily American</u>, Dec. 3-16, 1916.

435. Ambrose, Rev. F. Halsey. <u>A Sermon on Socialism Preached by . . . in the First Presbyterian Church, Grand Forks, N.D., at Evening Services Sunday, March 2, 1919, in Which Is Shown Its Relationship to the Non-Partisan League</u>. Grand Forks, [1919]; Grand Forks: Grand Forks Herald, 1919. 18, 20 p. MHS.
 Quotes Rome G. Brown extensively (see Nos. xxx and xxx). NPL materials on pages 12-18. Title page of 18-page edition stamped "Paid for and distributed by Independent Voters Ass'n."

436. America First Association. <u>The America First Association: Its Aims and Purposes</u>. St. Paul, [1917]. 4 p. MHS.
 Aims, purposes, and constitution as adopted at Northwest Loyalty Meetings at St. Paul, Nov. 16, 1917.

437. American Committee of Minneapolis. <u>Breaking Up the Family</u>. Minneapolis, [1919]. 4 p. MHS.
 Published to respond to a picnic meeting at which Arthur Le Sueur and Delbert Early spoke and a handbill of the same title (not located by compilers) was distributed. The Minneapolis Trades and Labor Assembly sponsored the event to protest the U.S. government's sending an unnamed Socialist back to Russia without his wife and children. The Committee was formed after the Russian Revolution to counter agitation by NPL, IWW, and other labor and radical organizations.

438. _____. <u>Fall In!!! The United States Needs You</u>. Minneapolis, [1919]. 4 p. MHS.
 Lists James H. Ellison, chairman; F. A. Chamberlain, treasurer; James F. Gould, secretary. Includes "Declaration of Principles."

439. <u>Are You Ready to Hand Over Your Farm to a Bunch of Socialist Adventurers?: That Is What Townleyism Means, Mr. Farmer</u>. N.p., [1918?]. 11 p. MHS.
 Material on IWW and extract from Minn. Socialist party's platform, 1918. Includes facsimile reproduction of a registration form, probably for voting, listing A. C. Townley as a Socialist.

440. Bacon, Jerry Dempster. <u>A. C. Townley, Pretending to Be the Farmer's Friend, Plays into the Hand of Socialists and I.W.W.'s by Assisting in Keeping the Price of Wheat Down. . . .</u> N.p., [1919?]. 12 p. MHS.
 Author was editor of <u>Grand Forks Herald</u>.

441. _____. <u>Carry the Truth to the People: A.fter C.ash Townley Smoked Out, A Companion Volume to "The Farmer and Townleyism": Being the Second Volume of an Expose and Inside Story of the Methods, Personnel and Menace . . . House Bill 44 Explained</u>. Grand Forks: Bacon, 1918. 96 p. MHS.
 The cover title reads: "A.fter C.ash Townley Smoked Out. Whistles a New Tune, But Only to Aid His Huge Profiteering Schemes. Carry the Truth to the People. Beware of 'Poison Gas' Behind the Lines!" Second in series (see also Nos. 444, 445, and 446).

442. _____. <u>North Dakota's Reward for Electing Non-Partisan League Officers</u>. [Fargo: Independent Voters Association, 1920?]; Grand Forks: Bacon, [1921?]. 16, 18 p. MHS.
 Urges support of initiated laws in 1920 election. Title page of first edition stamped "Paid for and distributed by Independent Voters Ass'n"; second edition contains results of election.

443. _____. Resume of the Nonpartisan League: Their Officers, Methods, Laws and the Effect on Economic Conditions in North Dakota. N.p., [1918].
   Not located by compilers.

444. _____. Sovietians: Wreckers of Americanism. Grand Forks: Bacon, 1920. 96 p. MHS.
   Anti-NPL. Lists "Townley's Workers" (p. 78-79). Fourth in series (see also Nos. 441, 445, and 446). Indexed.

445. _____. Townleyism Unmasked! Now Stands Before the World in Its True Light as Radical Socialism! . . . Grand Forks: Bacon, [1919]. 68 p. MHS.
   Third in series (see also Nos. 441, 444, and 446).

446. _____. A Warning to the Farmer against Townleyism as Exploited in North Dakota: An Expose and Inside Story of the Methods, Personnel and Menace of the Most Remarkable Phenomenon of Fifty Years in American Political History. Grand Forks: [Bacon, 1918]. 98 p. MHS.
   Attacks every aspect of NPL, especially loyalty. Cover title: "The Farmer and Townleyism: Carry the Truth to the People. The Inside Story of the National Non-partisan League under Townley Dictatorship." Indexed. First in series (see also Nos. 441, 444, and 445). Reprinted in No. 82.

447. Bankers Resolution. N.p., [1921]. 1 p. SHSND.
   Anti-NPL resolution adopted by N.Dak. bankers at Grand Forks, Dec. 1920.

448. Barnes, C. W. What Will You Do about This? St. Paul, [1918]. 4 p. MHS.
   Literature for campaign of Charles A. Lindbergh, Sr., in his 1918 NPL-backed bid for Minn. governor. Urges farmers to reverse conditions that allow price-fixing; attacks Governor J. A. A. Burnquist and Minn. Commission of Public Safety.

449. _____. Why Burnquist Cannot Run on His Record. It Won't Bear Inspection, Look at It. St. Paul: Barnes, [1918]. 8 p. MHS.
   Attacks J. A. A. Burnquist and Minn. Commission of Public Safety; defends Charles A. Lindbergh, Sr. Connects Burnquist with the "big interests against the workers."

450. Bear This in Mind. N.p., [1920]. 2 p. MHS.
   "Anti-socialist anti-Townley Ticket" for N.Dak. Republican ballot, June 30, 1920. Includes paragraph addressed "To Women Voters."

451. Berger, Victor. Answering the Socialist Charge. N.p., n.d. 1 p.
   Deals with relationship between NPL and Socialist party of America; points out that NPL congressmen proved themselves anti-socialist by voting not to seat Berger in Congress. Not located by compilers.

452. The Black Flaggers: Why the Financial Pirates Are Trying to Scuttle the State Bank, the Dockage Law, and Get Away with the Railroad Loot. N.p., 1920. 16 p. MHS.
   NPL campaign literature published as a supplement to Fargo Courier-News, North Dakota Leader (Fargo), and possibly other newspapers to promote election of NPL candidates and defeat five initiated measures.

453. Borner, Florence. A Modern Hiawatha. St. Paul, [1920?].
   Pro-NPL poem also published in Borner's book (see No. 6). Not located by compilers.

454. Brinton, J[ob] W[ells]. The Nonpartisan League and the Society of Equity or John Burke the Politician? N.p., [1916?]. 12 p. SHSND.
   A pro-NPL pamphlet attacking John Burke, former N.Dak. governor.

455. _____, and J. R. Waters. A. C. Townley, Dreamer, Promoter and Boss Politician: His Failures and Defeat of the Non-Partisan League. Bismarck: J. W. Brinton & Co., 1920. 40 p. MHS.
   Reprint of series of articles first published under the same title in Grand Forks Herald. Caused dissent and defection in NPL by charging that Townley was concerned with schemes to get rich and was not democratic. Both authors had been prominent in NPL.

456. Brown, Robert L. How About the City Council? Minneapolis, [1921]. 4 p. MHS.
   Campaign literature for anti-NPL Alderman James F. Wallace. Edward W. Hawley, his opponent, was supported by Minnesota Daily Star, which was established by NPL and organized labor.

457. Brown, Rome G. Americanism vs. Socialism: Address before the Middlesex County Bar Association at Youngs Hotel, Boston, Massachusetts, December 23, 1919. N.p., [1919?]; Washington, D.C.: Government Printing Office, 1920. 32, 23 p. MHS.
   Tells New Englanders to see West as a nursery of socialism; urges Democrats and Republicans to combine to defeat socialism. Includes summary of contents. Author was an attorney, president of Minneapolis Tribune, and chairman of American Bar Assn. Committee to Oppose Judicial Recall. MHS Library holds other pamphlets by this author that do not mention NPL.

458. _____. The Disloyalty of Socialism: Annual Address before Iowa State Bar Association at Des Moines, Iowa, June 28, 1918. N.p., [1918]. 28 p. MHS.
   Includes section on "Townleyism."

459. Burnquist, J[oseph] A. A. Aiding the Enemies of Our Nation!: A Timely Warning. N.p., [1918?]. 5 p. MHS.
   Response to Arthur Le Sueur's invitation to address NPL convention in St. Paul, 1918.

460. _____. Governor Burnquist to Non-Partisan Leaders: Sharp Rebuke Administered to Breeders of Class Hatred and Discontent during the National Crisis. [St. Paul, 1918]. 3 p. MHS.
   Response to Arthur Le Sueur's invitation to adddress NPL convention in St. Paul, 1918.

461. _____. Quotations from Governor's Addresses Delivered during 1917 Prior To and Since the Declaration of War and Address at Dassel, Minn., October 5, 1918. . . . N.p: Republican State Central Committee, [1918?]. 24 p. MHS.
   Includes section on "Leaders of the Non-partisan League" (p. 13-14) and other material on NPL's radical activities.

462. Buttree, J. Edmond. The Psychology of Suspicion. 1918.
   Reprinted in Chapters 1 and 2 of Buttree's book (see No. 12). Not located by compilers.

463. Canadian Reconstruction Association. The Nonpartisan League in North Dakota: A Study of a Class War and Its Disastrous Consequences, together with a Comparison of Bank Services in Canada and Western States. Toronto, Ont., 1921. 96 p. MHS.
   An attempt to dissuade Canadians from engaging in "dangerous government experiments" as did NPL. Preface by S. Roy Weaver of the CRA's Investigation Departments.

464. Cathro, F. W. How About Your Taxes? Fargo, 1919.
   Author was director general of Bank of N.Dak. Not located by compilers.

465. Certificate of Enlistment of Local Worker (Men) and Certificate of Enlistment of Local Worker (Women). N.p., 1921. 2 p. and 2 p. SHSND.
   Recruiting local help and precinct captains for defeat of NPL's 9-point program.

466. Charges against the League Leaders in Connection with Our Schools. N.p., [1920?]. 7 p. MHS.
   Attacks NPL's programs for education in N.Dak. Includes references to Bill 134, firing of Minnie J. Nielson, and hiring of Socialists for library and educational jobs.

467. Charley and Sandy: They Discuss Durum Wheat, Religion, Jefty O'Connor, etc., in the Elevator Office. N.p., [1920?]. 8 p. MHS.
   Fictional conversation attacking NPL and its leaders A. C. Townley, William Lemke, Lynn J. Frazier. Handwritten note on cover reads, "Written by [J. G. Halland?]."

468. Clancy, James M., et al. The Truth About the Street Car Trouble. St. Paul: St. Paul Trades and Labor Assembly, [1918]. 8 p. MHS.
   Discussion of strike against Twin City Rapid Transit Co. and opposition posed by the company and the St. Paul Assn. Includes an account of the meeting at Rice Park on Dec. 2, 1917, at which James Manahan offered NPL support to the strikers.

469. Clergymen Endorse Farmers Government of North Dakota. Fargo, 1920. 31 p. SHSND.
   Contributions by religious leaders Father Martin O'Donoghue and others in sympathy with NPL ticket in 1920 primary.

470. Clifford L. Hilton for Attorney General: Editorials and News Comment. St. Paul: Personal Campaign Committee for Clifford L. Hilton, [1918]. 1 p. MHS.
   Supports Republican candidate for Minn. attorney general; attacks Thomas V. Sullivan, NPL candidate.

471. Coates, W. C. A Correction: Note the Date of the Newspaper Meeting to be Held at Verndale, Sunday, February 9, at 2:00 p.m. Long Prairie, Minn., [1919]. 1 p. MHS.
   Advertises meeting to set up farmer-owned newspaper in Wadena. May have resulted in Progressive News (Wadena), first published June 26, 1919.

472. Collins, Peter W. What Is Socialism? Minneapolis: American Committee of Minneapolis, [1919]; Fargo: Independent Voters Assn., 1919. 16 p. MHS.
   Anti-socialist pamphlet used by opponents of League; does not specifically deal with NPL.

473. _____. Why Socialism Is Opposed to the Labor Movement. Minneapolis: American Committee of Minneapolis, [1919]; Fargo: Independent Voters Assn., 1919. 16 p. MHS.
   Anti-socialist pamphlet used by opponents of League; does not specifically deal with NPL.

474. Colorado State Federation of Labor. Official Proceedings of the 26th Annual Convention . . . Colorado Springs August 8-11, 1921. N.p., [1921]. Archives of the Colorado State Federation of Labor, Western Historical Collec-

tions, University of Colorado at Boulder. Reports of Vice-President Durham and Secretary-Treasurer Ed Anderson concerning NPL resolution No. 22, "upon the subject of political action by the workingmen and women of Colorado"; urges cooperation with NPL. Not seen by compilers.

475. ____. Proceedings from the Annual Meeting of the Executive Board, Jan. 5-6, 1920. N.p., [1920]. Archives of the Colorado State Federation of Labor, Western Historical Collections, University of Colorado at Boulder.
Contains endorsement of NPL principles and policies and directive to the president and secretary of the board to maintain contact with NPL's state committee. Not seen by compilers.

476. A Constructive Criticism of North Dakota's New Laws as Passed by the Sixteenth Legislative Assembly in Session at Bismarck, North Dakota, January and February, 1919. Minot: Dakota State Journal, [1919]. 11 p. SHSND.
Discussion of 1919 N.Dak. legislative session published by anti-NPL newspaper.

477. Consumers United Stores Company of North Dakota Incorporated: A Cooperative Chain Store System Established for Service, Not Profit or Dividends, a North Dakota Company for North Dakota People. N.p., [1918?]. 11 p. MHS.
Store, managed by J. W. Brinton, was incorporated by former NPL officials. Illustrated.

478. Dale, Alfred S. Public Ownership in North Dakota. N.p., [1929]. 2 p. SHSND.
Possibly reprinted from New Republic. Supports NPL programs; states that they still work in spite of management by anti-NPL forces.

479. Dangers That Lurk in the Bank of North Dakota. N.p., [1920]. 6 p. MHS.
Laments lack of "safeguards against the abuse of the power granted" to state bank. Discusses Scandinavian-American Bank scandal. Title page stamped "Paid for and Distributed by the Independent Voters Ass'n."

480. Dare You Read This? Do You Think for Yourself? St. Paul, [1918]. 2 p. MHS.
Two-sided poster distributed through the mail. Attacks A. C. Townley, Arthur Le Sueur, IWW, and NPL.

481. Dean, Ezra C. Did Townley Have a Fair Trial?: A Straight Forward Statement Worth Considering. N.p., [1919]. 10 p. MHS.
Author presided at trial of Joseph Gilbert and A. C. Townley at Jackson, Minn.

482. Democratic Party (Minn.). State Central Committee. The Loyalty Record of a Fifty-fifty Official: Compiled from a Testimony of His Friends. St. Paul: The Committee, [1918]. 9 p. MHS.
Questions Minn. Governor J. A. A. Burnquist's loyalty by comparing his war record to that of Governor Alexander Ramsey. Supports crossover vote; charges Republicans with encouraging League members to run their own candidates rather than voting for Democrats.

483. Durocher, Leon. Life and Exploits of A. C. Townley. Minneapolis: Appreciation Committee, 1923. 3 p. MHS.
Contains photo of Townley and one page of satyrical text ("Me and Public Welfare, by A. C. Townley").

484. The Easy Way to Vote. N.p., [1922]. 2 p. SHSND.
Sample ballot listing IVA candidates in 1922 N.Dak. election.

485. Effect of Townleyism on State and Individual Credit. N.p., [1920?]. 13 p. MHS.
Explanation of how A. C. Townley "destroyed" credit in N.Dak. Cover carries IVA stamp and handwritten note, "Written by [J. G. Halland?]."

486. An Enemy of the Christian Church. Fargo: Republican Headquarters, [192-?]. 6 p. MHS.
Contains letter to the editor reprinted from Minneapolis Tribune; handwritten note on cover reads "compiled and written by [J. G. Halland?]."

487. Equity Co-operative Exchange. What Is the Equity Co-operative Exchange? A Self-answered Questionnaire about a Great Farmers' Organization. Fargo: Exchange Publishing Co., 1919. 16 p. MHS.
Information on a group that worked with NPL.

488. Facts about North Dakota's New Laws: As Passed by the Sixteenth Legislative Assembly in Session at Bismarck, North Dakota, January and February, 1919. Various places, 1919. 32 p. MHS; N.Dak. NPL Collection 1, UND.
Explanation and defense of NPL program printed as supplement to Grand Forks American, Apr. 26, 1919 (UND; not seen by compilers); North Dakota Leader, Apr. 26, 1919 (UND; credits Walter W. Liggett with authorship); Fargo Courier-News, Apr. 27, 1919, and Farmers Sentinel, May 15, 1919 (both MHS); and perhaps elsewhere.

489. "Farmer John." Bill and the Menckens. N.p., [1922?]. 7 p. MHS.
Supports J. F. T. O'Connor, Rangvold A. Nestos, and IVA ticket in N.Dak. election of 1922.

490. Farmer-Labor Federation of Minnesota. Constitution . . . The Instrument of Farmers and Workers, United for Their Mutual Political Welfare. St. Paul: The Federation, [1924?]. 8 p. MHS.
   Membership of proposed organization to comprise NPL, Working People's Nonpartisan Political League, farmers' economic and cooperative organizations. District committeemen listed on back cover; William Mahoney was chairman.

491. _____. Minnesota Farmer-Labor Convention Proceedings, 1923. [Minneapolis: Cole & Wickham Co., 1923]. 68 p. MHS.
   Contains constitution and bylaws of proposed organization, list of NPL delegates, and speeches by William Mahoney (president of Working People's Nonpartisan Political League) on farmer-labor movement in Minn.; Henry G. Teigan (NPL secretary) detailing transition from NPL to Farmer-Labor party; A. C. Townley on his new organization, National Producers' Alliance; Joseph Gilbert, Charles A. Lindbergh, Sr., Susie Stageberg, and others.

492. Die Farmer-Regierung von North Dakota: Indossement von Geistlichen. Fargo: Allied Printing, n.d. 16 p. North Dakota NPL Collection 1, UND.
   German-language pamphlet supporting NPL (The Farmer-Government of North Dakota: Indorsement by Religious People). Not read by compilers.

493. Farmers Prove Friendship for Labor: Being a Summary of the Laws Passed by the 16th Legislative Assembly (Non-Partisan League Farmers) of North Dakota, in the Interests of All Industrial Workers of the State. Bismarck: Burleigh City Farmers Press, n.d. 11 p. UND.
   NPL attempt to attract labor support.

494. For Home and Country League. Will You Vote for Socialism or Will You Vote for Americanism? . . . St. Paul: The League, [1920]. 1 p. MHS.
   Campaign mailer for St. Paul's Mayor Larry Hodgson. Claims that William Mahoney, Julius Emme, A. E. Smith, H. C. Wenzel, and J. M. Clancy are not the "labor ticket," but a "Socialist ticket." Points to role of Mahoney and Smith in forming Working People's Nonpartisan Political League.

495. Frank and Tom Discuss Primary Election. N.p., [1922?]. 8 p. MHS.
   Supports Rangvold A. Nestos and IVA in 1922 N.Dak. election.

496. Fraud! Vote for Frazier, Lemke and Hagan. Fargo: Elliot Printing Co., [1921]. 1 p. MHS.
   Disputes legality of IVA petition for recall; charges that too few signatures were gathered.

497. [Frost, James]. Townley & Co. and the Non-Partisan League. Beach, N.Dak.: Beach Publicity Assn., 1918. 46 p. MHS.
   Short history attacking NPL and emphasizing roles of A. C. Townley and J. W. Brinton. Charges that NPL "appeals to all tastes. . . . It is pork to the gentile, and beef to the Jew, potheen to the Irish, and beer to the German . . . Ludefisk to the Scandinavian, and tamale to the Greaser." Beach Publicity Assn. was also known as Farmers' Publicity Assn.

498. Fussell, E. B. League Indorsed by Federal Court: Year's Investigation Shows "Honest Record of Honest Stewardship." St. Paul, [Jan., 1919]. 1 p. MHS.
   Report on N.Dak. District Court Judge Charles F. Amidon's conclusion in Townley's bankruptcy case, in which NPL affairs were also investigated. May have been clipped from a Northwestern Service Bureau Editorial Service Sheet (see No. 622).

499. George H. Mallon, Candidate for Lieutenant Governor. Minneapolis: Campaign Committee, [1920]. 1 p. MHS.
   Campaign card. Photograph of Mallon in military uniform with full quotation of his citation for gallantry in WWI on front; Working People's Nonpartisan Political League ballot on reverse. C. Z. Nelson was secretary of Committee.

500. German State Monopoly for Minnesota! What Mr. Townley Fears. St. Paul: Reliance Publicity Service, [1918?]. 7 p. MHS.
   A defense against A. C. Townley's attacks on S. R. Maxwell's pamphlet (see No. 552).

501. Gilbert, A. B. Another Mooney Case Provided by Supreme Court of Minnesota: Frame Up Case of Politicians against Joseph Gilbert and L. W. Martin, Nonpartisan League Workers, Considered Only in Legal Aspects--Astounding Facts in First Trial Ignored. N.p., [Dec. 1918?]. 1 p. MHS.
   Charges that conviction of sedition for speech at Kenyon in Goodhue Co. was miscarriage of justice. May have been clipped from a Northwestern Service Bureau Editorial Service Sheet (see No. 662).

502. Give Us a Fighting Governor for Minnesota: Lindbergh Will Speak Thursday, June 13th. . . . [St. Paul, 1918]. 1 p. MHS.
   Small poster listing five St. Paul locations for appearances of Charles A. Lindbergh, Sr., and other labor candidates in 1918 primary election.

503. Grain Growers and the Nonpartisan League. N.p., [1920]. 3 p. Saskatchewan Archives Board.
   NPL in Canada. Not seen by compilers.

504. Gunn, John W. The Emballoted Farmers: A Story of the Nonpartisan League. People's Pocket Series No. 17, 2d. ed. Girard, Kans.: Appeal to Reason, [1917]. 128 p. State Historical Society of Wisconsin, MHS.
   Includes Abraham Lincoln's "Ideals of Government." MHS has photocopy.

505. Hannah, Margaret A. Your Problem Is Our Problem: Address Delivered by Mrs. Margaret A. Hannah of Big Timber, Montana, at the Co-operators' Congress at Great Falls, Montana, February 26, 1920. N.p.: Women's Nonpartisan Clubs, 1920. 11 p. UND.

506. How Many of These Does Townley Want? N.p., [1918]. 4 p. MHS.
   Reprint of anti-NPL editorial published in Country Gentleman, June 15, 1918. Claims that A. C. Townley purchased 50,000 copies of magazine's earlier pro-NPL edition (probably No. 168) for distribution.

507. How the Farmer Can "Get His." N.p., n.d.
   Anti-NPL. Not located by compilers.

508. Howard, Asher, ed. [Data Regarding Marketing of Grain]. [Minneapolis, 1921?]. 16 p. MHS.
   Reprint of letters and articles from Canada and the U.S. regarding hedging or futures trading in grain and cotton, a practice NPL opposed.

509. _____, comp. The Leaders of the Nonpartisan League: Their Aims, Purposes and Records, Reproduced from Original Letters and Documents. . . . Minneapolis, 1920. 127 p. MHS.
   Collection of documents showing NPL connections with radicals and socialists. Letters of endorsement from Minn. State Senator Ole O. Sageng, former senator J. E. Haycraft, and Captain Frank E. Reed. Illustrated. See also No. 830.

510. The Hundred and Sixteen Nonpartisan League Members of the Sixteenth Legislative Assembly of North Dakota to the Farmers and Other Workers of America. Bismarck, January 8, 1919. 4 p. MHS.
   Reasons for NPL organization and program. List of "splendid measures first enacted" and photographs of the farmers' caucus.

511. If You Are An American Read: Bolshevism Here at Home. N.p., n.d.
   Anti-NPL. Not located by compilers.

512. Independent Voters Association. By-Laws Independent Voters Association, Formerly the Plain Citizens Political Reform Association. N.p.: The Association, n.d. 4 p. SHSND.

513. [_____]. Diagram of Independent State Organization. N.p., n.d. 1 p.
   IVA structure, showing relations of Democrats, Republicans, and Joint Campaign Committee. Not located by compilers.

514. _____. The Facts about the State Owned Mill and Elevator at Grand Forks: What It Is Costing the Taxpayer, the Farmer, the Consumer of Flour and Mill Feed and the Effect It Is Having. . . . N.p: The Association, n.d. 16 p. SHSND.

515. [_____]. If You Want To Help the Townley-McKenzie Combination to Continue to "Work" the People of North Dakota. Grand Forks, n.d. 2 p. SHSND.
   IVA campaign card.

516. [_____]. I'll Vote Friday This Week. N.p., [1921]. MHS.
   Seven IVA post cards mailed election week for Rangvold A. Nestos, M. P. Johnson, and Joseph A. Kitchen. Text and illustrations vary.

517. _____. The Independent Voters Association: Its Plan of Organization and Operation, Its Relation to Republicans and Democrats, Its Stand on Townleyism and Kindred Radicalism. Fargo: The Association, [1921]. 15 p. MHS.
   Information for field workers of IVA; contains IVA bylaws.

518. _____. IVA Plan of Organizing: General Rules and Regulations. Fargo: The Association, [1920]. 4 p. SHSND.
   Contains "Outline of Work and Distribution of Funds," organizational chart, and a plea for strong precinct organizations.

519. _____. IVA Platform. Fargo, [1918]. 2 p. MHS.
   Succinct statement of IVA stance on NPL programs and of IVA proposals, including creation of a Bureau of Markets.

520. _____. IVA Press Bulletin No. 26: Where the Money Has Gone. N.p., [1921]. 2 p. SHSND.
   General news for IVA members. Information on NPL management of state industries and instructions for completing N.Dak. 1921 recall petition drive.

521. _____. Instructions to Petition Circulators. Fargo: The Association, 1919. 24 p. MHS.
   Petition for four initiative measures and seven referenda on laws passed.

522. _____. The Record of North Dakota's State Industries: Their History and Record, Facts and Figures Showing Their Cost to the Taxpayer to Date, Future Cost to be Met. . . . N.p., 1926. 30 p. SHSND.
  Opposes NPL programs still in operation.

523. _____. Townleyism's Future in North Dakota. Fargo: The Association, 1919. 96 p. MHS.
  Manual for anti-NPL forces prepared for 1920 N.Dak. elections. Table of contents, index, and illustrations.

524. Information for League Speakers and Boosters. Bismarck, [1920].
  Compiled from addresses given at Bismarck, Oct. 1920, by state officials, league officers, and league candidates. Not located by compilers.

525. Ingle, J. G. The Story of Farmer J. G. Ingle . . . Explaining in Detail His Experience with A. C. Townley and Other Leaders of the Nonpartisan League When Townley Said: "You farmers are a set of G-- D---- Hogs!" [Dawson, N.Dak.]: North Dakota Farmers Opposed to Socialism Control of the State, 1918. 11 p. NDSU.

526. _____. "You Farmers Are a Set of G-D- Hogs!" Said Townley. Dawson, N.Dak.: Ingle, 1918. 8 p. MHS.
  An anti-Townley, pro-NPL farmer, who had paid $100 for Consumers United Stores Co. Buyer's Certificate, quotes Townley's insulting message to Farmers Union meeting.

527. Invest Your Savings in Bonds of the State of North Dakota. [Bismarck: The Department, 1921?]. 1 p. MHS.
  Encourages sale of bond for state industries by Bank of N.Dak.

528. Joint Campaign Committee. An Enemy of Church and Home. Fargo: The Committee, [1922?]. 15 p. MHS.
  "Documentary proof that the leaders of the Non-partisan League are closely associated with, and heartily approved by[,] deadly enemies of the church and the private home." Page 3 stamped "Paid for and distributed by Independent Voters Ass'n." Illustrated.

529. _____. Facts and Figures. [Fargo]: The Committee, [1920?]. 24 p. MHS.
  Includes tax information by county; loans made by Bank of N.Dak., by county; list of books found by Rep. Olger B. Burtness in Public Library Commission holdings; prominent NPL members; Socialists holding office in N.Dak.; state offices created by NPL and salaries paid.

530. _____. The Independent Program: The Constitutional Amendment. Fargo: The Committee, [1921?]. [4] p. MHS.
  Urges signing of petitions for recall of NPL officials and for initiative measures.

531. _____. Legislative Purposes of the League Leadership and Procedure to Attain It. Fargo: The Committee, [1920?]. 14 p. MHS.
  Argues that NPL had greatly changed its purposes and methods from those first proposed, becoming a new party. Attacks Charles Edward Russell; NPL's socialist connections; NPL plan for state sheriff.

532. _____. The Men in the Recall Election. Fargo: The Committee, 1921. 6 p. MHS.
  IVA biographies of Rangvold A. Nestos, M. P. Johnson, and Joseph A. Kitchen. Contains IVA program and photographs.

533. _____. Our Taxes and the Cost of State Government. [Fargo]: The Committee, [1920?]. 15 p. MHS.
  Detailed criticism of NPL tax laws. Cover stamped "Paid for and distributed by Independent Voters Ass'n."

534. _____. Reasons for the Recall. Fargo: The Committee, [1921?]. [4] p. MHS.
  IVA campaign literature with indictment of Industrial Commission.

535. _____. Reasons Why Good Citizens Cannot Vote for Lynn J. Frazier for United States Senator If They Want to Be Honest with Themselves and Loyal to Their State and Nation. Fargo: The Committee, 1922. 12 p. SHSND.
  Attack on NPL reforms and radicalism with short biography of J. F. T. O'Connor, IVA candidate.

536. _____. Trade Unionism and Townleyism. [Fargo]: The Committee, [1920]. [9] p. MHS.
  Attacks NPL's farmer-labor coalition by connecting it with IWW and Eugene V. Debs. Title page stamped "Paid for and distributed by Independent Voters Ass'n."

537. _____. Grand Forks County. High Spots in the Election Issues (General Election Nov. 7, 1922). N.p., n.d.
  Not located by compilers.

538. Kellogg, Frank B. In Response to Senator La Follette's Address before That Body [U.S. Senate] Bearing upon the Subject of His Speech at the Nonpartisan League Convention in St. Paul on the 20th Day of September, 1917. Washington, D.C., 1917. 8 p. SHSND.
  Attacks Robert M. La Follette's stand on WWI, based on his speech to Producers and Consumers Convention in St. Paul, Sept., 1919.

539. Kerr, J. Edmund. The Psychology of Suspicion as Demonstrated in North Dakota: An Appeal to Reason. St. Paul: Kerr, [1918]. 32 p. SHSND.
  Anti-NPL; discusses NPL relations with IWW.

540. Labor!! Who's Yer Friend?: L. L. Twitchell [sic] and the IVA's Who Voted against All Labor Laws or L. J. Frazier and the Farmer Who Voted and Passed Them, That's the ? What's Your Answer? N.p., [1920]. 14 p. MHS.
  Labor-union support for NPL ticket and program to "elect the men who gave us the workmen's compensation act."

541. Labor's Campaign Committee, St. Paul, Minn. Why Labor Put Up Candidates for Political Offices. St. Paul: The Committee, [1918]. 8 p. MHS.
  Endorsement by State Federation of Labor of D. H. Evans for governor and Thomas Davis for attorney general. Opposes J. A. A. Burnquist and Fred E. Wheaton, Republican and Democratic candidates for governor; lists G. W. Lawson as committee chairman.

542. Labor's Municipal Nonpartisan League. Platform and Candidates Endorsed by Labor's Municipal Nonpartisan League. Minneapolis, [1917]. 4 p. MHS.
  Supports Thomas Van Lear for mayor and other candidates for city and legislative offices. O. E. Nordstrom was secretary of League.

543. Ladd, E[dwin] F. A Revelation of Facts Not Generally Known: Senator E. F. Ladd of North Dakota Makes Timely Reply to Former President Taft's Malicious Attack on the Farmers of the Country. Washington, D.C.: Government Printing Office, 1921. 16 p. North Dakota NPL Collection 1, UND.
  Pro-NPL. Reprinted from Congressional Record, May 2, 1921.

544. Laidley, Frederick W. The Why of the Non-Partisan League. Swift Current, Sask.: League Headquarters, [1916?], 1917. 27, 24 p. Saskatchewan Archives Board.
  Not seen by compilers. There may also be a 1919 edition.

545. Le Sueur, Arthur. An Open Letter to the Governor and Legislature of North Dakota: Take Your Industries Out of Politics. St. Paul, [1920]. 32 p. MHS.
  Pro-NPL. "Friendly Warning" to NPL to depoliticize Bank of N.Dak. and state industries and to be more concerned about their management.

546. _____. Unclogging the Channels of Trade. N.p., [1919]. 2 p. MHS.
  Charges that parasitic businesses clog the farmer's channels of trade; argues that NPL program would solve the problem.

Cover of pro-NPL pamphlet (see No. 540)

547. Light on the League Movement as a Money Mover: Millions of Dollars Have Changed Hands in a Few Years. N.p., [1921]. 4 p. MHS.
  IVA literature objecting to NPL use of members' funds in N.Dak. Pamphlet damaged; missing much text.

548. Lindbergh, Charles A., Sr. Fight for Democracy in Europe, Vote for Democracy in Minnesota: Charles A. Lindbergh for Governor. June 8, 1918. 1 p. MHS.
  Loyalty letter distributed by NPL candidate for governor.

549. _____. The Voter and the Economic Pinch. Little Falls: Lindbergh, [1920?]. 15 p. MHS.
  Author emphasizes independence as a congressional candidate, stating that he fought for NPL's ideals before League's birth.

550. Lundeen, Ernest. *A Farmer-Labor Party for the Nation.* Washington, D.C.: American Commonwealth Federation, [1936?]. 3 p. MHS.
   Credits NPL with helping prepare the public for a Farmer-Labor party. Author was a Minn. congressman (1917-19, 1933-37) and U.S. Senator (1937-40).

551. *March Primary Election, Laws and Constitutional Amendments to be Voted On: Independent Voters' Statement.* N.p., [1924]. 5 p. UND, SHSND.
   IVA explanation of measures in Mar. 18, 1924, primary. Includes references to NPL program.

552. Maxwell, S. R. *The Nonpartisan League.* New York, 1920.
   Not located by compilers.

553. _____. *The Nonpartisan League from the Inside.* St. Paul: Dispatch Printing Co., 1918. 115 p. MHS.
   Author, a former NPL organizer, attacks "autocracy" of NPL and calls upon farmers to assume control. First published as series of articles in *St. Paul Dispatch* in July and Aug. 1918.

554. *Men and Women of North Dakota.* N.p., [1920?]. [2] p. MHS.
   Labels as "indecently suggestive" an unnamed NPL pamphlet by a "has-been pastor" who attacked the moral character of IVA leaders E. W. Everson and Theodore G. Nelson. Includes testimonials from Elizabeth Anderson (president and secretary of N.Dak. WCTU) and J. W. Schannach (president of Fargo Trades and Labor Assembly).

555. Miller, Clarence Benjamin. *The Non-Partisan League and Its Leaders.* Washington, D.C.: Government Printing Office, 1918. 8 p. MHS.
   Speech delivered to U.S. House of Representatives, June 8, 1918, opposing NPL. Quotes extensively from book by Charles A. Lindbergh, Sr. (see No. 62); lists other NPL members convicted in Minn. Author was congressman from Minn. (1909-19).

556. _____. *The Poison Book of Lindbergh, Officially Endorsed by the Townley League Organization: An Expose in Congress by Rep. C. B. Miller.* [St. Paul, 1918?]. 16 p. MHS.
   "Prepared, published and distributed by Tom Parker Junkin." Deals with book by Charles A. Lindbergh, Sr. (see No. 62).

557. Mills, Walter Thomas. *The Articles of Association of the National Nonpartisan League. Together with a Discussion of the Democracy of the League's Purposes. . . .* St. Paul: National Nonpartisan League, [between 1917 and 1919]. 27 p. MHS.
   Points out the essential democracy of the League and its goals.

558. _____. *Your Choice, Government by Plunderers or Producers.* Fargo: North Dakota Nonpartisan League, [192-?]. 16 p. NDSU.
   Not seen by compilers.

559. *Mind Your Own Business.* N.p., [1920]. 4 p. Saskatchewan Archives Board.
   Pamphlet has handwritten notations, possibly by someone connected with the Sask. Grain Growers Assn. Not seen by compilers.

560. Minneapolis League of Women Voters. *What the Candidates Tell You: Election Hand Book, November 4, 1924.* Minneapolis: The League, 1924. 22 p. MHS.
   Short biographies and answers to questions. Many former NPL officials were running as Farmer-Laborites, including Susie Stageberg for secretary of state and Thomas V. Sullivan for attorney general.

561. *The Minnesota Daily Star: A New Daily Newspaper on an Entirely New Plan.* [Minneapolis: Northwest Publishing Co., 1919]. 4 p. MHS.
   Newspaper-like leaflet distributed at Minn. State Fair. Lists daily fair events and announces NPL's soon-to-be-published farmer-worker paper (see No. 722).

562. Minnesota Daily Star. *The Minneapolis Journal Figures Prove Conclusively That the Minnesota Daily Star Is the Third Paper in Minneapolis in City Carrier Circulation.* [Minneapolis: The Star, 1920?]. 1 p. MHS.
   Broadside prepared by advertising manager of *Minnesota Daily Star*; uses *Minneapolis Journal* figures to prove status.

563. Minnesota Economics Society. *Does Minnesota Want "State Insurance": The First Plank in the Socialistic Platform of the Nonpartisan League?: What the Enactment of H.F. 20 and S.F. 176 Would Mean to You, an Employer of Labor.* St. Paul: The Society, 1919. 2 p. MHS.

564. Minnesota Sound Government Association. *. . . Declaration of Principles and By-Laws.* St. Paul: The Association, [1920?]. 8 p. MHS.
   Goals and bylaws of an anti-NPL and anti-radical group.

565. *The Minnesota Train Service Organizations Respond to the Call for Political Action Issued by the Executives of the Sixteen Railroad Labor Organizations.* St. Paul, [1920]. 4 p. MHS.
   Explanation of Working People's Nonpartisan Political League, NPL, and need to support labor candidates; lists candidates.

566. *Mr. Frazier: Please Answer.* N.p., n.d. Anti-NPL. Not located by compilers.

567. *Mr. Townley's Greatest Venture: The Consumers United Stores Company.* Fargo: AASE Publishing Co., [1918]. 30 p. MHS.
   Published to satisfy "demand for as complete and accurate data as it is possible to obtain"; includes articles of incorporation, copy of the agreement circulated by organizers and signed by buyers, A. C. Townley's testimony in his bankruptcy case, and newspaper articles.

568. Montana Loyalty League. *The Great Conspiracy.* Helena, Mont., n.d. MHS.
   Charges A. C. Townley with "conspiracy" in leading farmers who believe in private ownership "step by step, to the ultimate--the world revolution." Includes a curious "working diagram of the Socialists and the Revolutionists" showing relationship with NPL. League's executive secretary was Will A. Campbell. Original not located by compilers; microfilm copy in No. 864.

569. _____. *The New Day in North Dakota: Ten of the Principal Laws Enacted by the Sixteenth Assembly of North Dakota, 1919.* Helena, Mont., 1919. 17 p. North Dakota NPL Collection 1, UND.
   Lists excerpts from and comments critically on NPL legislation.

570. _____. *Who's Who in the Nonpartisan League: Also a Compilation of Quotations from Persons and Publications Friendly to the League.* 2d. ed. Helena, Mont.: The League, 1919. 24 p. MHS.
   Ties NPL to socialists. Describes Mont. Loyalty League as "patriotically opposed to socialism, bolshevism and the 'Revolution in America.'"

571. Morris, Oliver Scott. *The Freedom of the Press: Economic Influences as They Affect the Freedom of the Press: Being the Text of an Address before the Open Forum at the City Hall, St. Paul, on Feb. 29, 1920.* [Minneapolis: Nonpartisan Leader, 1920?]. 18 p. MHS.
   Discussion of influence of advertisers on publications such as the *Saturday Evening Post*. Author was editor of *Nonpartisan Leader*.

572. Morse, J. H. *Red Blood or Yellow?* [Robbinsdale, Minn., 1918]. 3 p. MHS.
   Attacks Charles A. Lindbergh, Sr., for raising questions about Red Cross financing. Compares his view to patriotic editorial by Guy F. Lee (published in *Chicago Tribune*, May 20, 1918).

573. National Civil Liberties Bureau. *War-Time Prosecutions and Mob Violence Involving the Rights of Free Speech, Free Press and Peaceful Assemblage (From April 1, 1917, to May 1, 1918).* New York, 1918. 24 p. MHS.
   Incomplete list of cases from NCLB correspondence and clippings; section one, part three, lists "Political Causes Involving Primarily the Non-partisan League." Edition published in 1918 (*War-Time Prosecutions . . . From April 1, 1917 to May 1, 1918*, 24 p.) not located by compilers.

574. National Nonpartisan League. *1924 Election Blue Book: Facts and Official Figures on Taxes and Other Issues.* Bismarck: Executive Committee of the Nonpartisan League, 1924. 32 p. SHSND.
   Analyzes opposition's administration and presents an NPL-endorsed "Progressive Ticket" for eight statewide offices, including governor, and three congressional seats.

575. _____. *Facts for the Farmer on Conditions Vitally Important to Him as Producer and to the Wage Worker as Consumer.* St. Paul, 1917, 1918. 93, 94 p. MHS.
   Has only chapters 1 ("Grain and Milling Combine"), 6 ("Butter and Egg Market Manipulation"), and 7 ("The Big Packers Methods and Profits"). Paging is not continuous; some pages in both editions are bound upside-down and backwards. For more complete edition see No. 576.

576. _____. *Facts for the Farmer on Conditions Vitally Important to Him as Producer and to the Wage Worker as Consumer (Minnesota Handbook).* St. Paul, 1917, 1919. 136, 135 p. MHS.
   Facts specifically for Minn. Has eight chapters, including the three in No. 575 and others on taxes, corporate land grabs, iron ore, and "Who Rules Minnesota?" Indexed and illustrated. Reprinted in No. 82.

577. _____. *Facts Kept from the Farmer: General Handbook of the National Nonpartisan League.* St. Paul, 1917, 1918, 1919. 79, 82, 74 p. MHS.
   Cites many examples of how corporations "invest" in political campaigns to influence legislation, advertise to influence public opinion, and build "fighting funds" to defeat farmer and labor organizations. Text of all editions virtually the same. Reprinted in No. 82.

578. _____. *The Fighting Program of the National Nonpartisan League. Unanimously Adopted by the National Committee of the National Nonpartisan League in Annual Meeting Assembled at St. Paul, Minnesota, December 3,*

1918. St. Paul: The League, [1918?]. 10 p. MHS.
> NPL's own Fourteen Points, adopted at the end of WWI in response to President Woodrow Wilson's Fourteen Points. They call for such radical ideas as "A United States of the World" and "Public Ownership of Unavoidable Monopolies."

579. _____. Freedom for All Forever: The Spirit That Is Fighting for Democracy at Home and Abroad, the Spirit of 1776. 1918 Souvenir Rally Booklet. Minneapolis: The League, 1918. 40 p. MHS.
> Designed to show NPL support of war effort. Contains fold-out photos of NPL rallies, speech of Charles A. Lindbergh, Sr., songs (some about NPL), etc.

580. _____. How to Finance the Great War. St. Paul: The League, [1918?]. 24 p. MHS.
> Discussion of war profits and conscription of wealth.

581. _____. Memorial to the Congress of the United States Concerning Conditions in Minnesota, 1918. By the National and State Executive Committees of the National Nonpartisan League. St. Paul, 1918. 120 p. MHS.
> Harassment of NPL and denial of its political rights, listing incidents by county. Well done and complete. Same as No. 582.

582. _____. Memorial to the President of the United States Concerning Conditions in Minnesota, 1918. By the National and State Committees of the National Nonpartisan League. St. Paul, 1918. 120 p. MHS.
> Same as No. 581.

583. _____. The National Nonpartisan League: Origin, Purpose and Method of Operation. [St. Paul, 1917]; 32 p.; North Dakota NPL Collection 1, UND, and MHS. N.p., [1918?]; 28 p.; MHS. Minneapolis, 1920; 27 p.; North Dakota NPL Collection 1, UND. Minneapolis: Educational Dept., [1921?]; 16 p.; MHS.
> Pamphlet often sent to correspondents. First edition, adopted June 7, 1917, by National NPL (according to penciled writing on cover of MHS copy; copy at UND of same length not seen by compilers), carries subtitle, War Program and Statement of Principles, and includes statement of principles by Congressman John M. Baer (p. 27-32) and photographs. Edition of [1918?] includes photo of Lynn J. Frazier. Edition of 1920 not seen by compilers. Another edition may have been published in Minneapolis in 1918 (not located by compilers).

584. _____. Non-Partisan Campaign Policy of the Farmers' and Workers' National Non-Partisan League: St. Paul Municipal Auditorium, March 19, 20, 21, 1918. St. Paul, [1918].
> Not located by compilers.

585. _____. The Nonpartisan League, Loyal or Disloyal? N.p., [1918 or 1919]. 1 p. MHS.
> Shows N.Dak. farmers' contributions to Liberty Loan and Red Cross drives.

586. _____. Resolutions Adopted by Farmers' and Workers' National Non-Partisan League Campaign Rally: St. Paul Auditorium, March 19-21, 1918. St. Paul: The League, 1918. 8 p. MHS.
> Concerned with loyalty issue. Mentions Congressman John M. Baer's support for striking employees of Twin City Rapid Transit Co.

587. _____. The Truth about North Dakota Taxes: The Full Facts from the Official Records, Giving the Appropriations of the Legislature, the Cost of the State Industries, the Per Capita Taxes in North Dakota and Other States, together with an Analysis of Typical Tax Statements of Individual Farmers. A Handbook that Will Enable You to Nail the Lies of the Anti-Farmer Press. Minneapolis: The League, 1920. 19 p. MHS.

588. _____. Where the People Rule. North Dakota, a State Where Democracy Is Safe. The Nonpartisan League State. [St. Paul, 1919]; n.p., n.d. 26, 31 p. MHS, State Historical Society of Wisconsin.
> Comprehensive discussion of accomplishments and goals of NPL. Shorter version not seen by compilers.

589. _____. Why Should Farmers Pay Dues? St. Paul: The League, [1918?]. 24 p. MHS.
> Defense of NPL's dues of $8.00 per year. Frequently sent to correspondents of the NPL's general secretary.

590. _____. Winning the War: Nonpartisanship the Test, From the Letters, Messages and Addresses of the President. St. Paul: The League, [1918]. 24 p. MHS.
> Quotes Woodrow Wilson extensively to defend loyalty of NPL ("Democracy . . . [is] worth fighting for in Flanders and it is worth fighting for in America," p. 24). Commentary by NPL.

591. _____. Committee on Resolutions. Resolutions Adopted by the Non-Partisan League Conference Held in St. Paul, Sept. 18-19-20, 1917. St. Paul: The League, 1917. 6 p. MHS.
> Resolutions of Producers and Consumers Conference (here called "Farmer and Worker Conference"), including one on WWI endorsing Pope Benedict XV's peace appeal.

592. _____. Educational Department. The League Correspondence Course: Enrollment Application, Farm Economics, and League Organization

Work, Lessons 1-18. N.p., [1918?]. Varying p. MHS and UND.
   Used to train organizers and to inform them on the issues. MHS has Enrollment Application; Farm Economics, Lessons 3-6, 9-12, and 18; Organization Work, Lessons 7 and 8. UND has Lessons 5-18. Lessons 1 and 2 not located by compilers.

593. _____. Educational Department. What to Read. St. Paul: The Department, [1919]. 4 p. MHS.
   List of NPL publications and other recommended books.

594. _____. Minnesota. Platform and Declaration of Principles Adopted by Delegates to the State Convention of the Minnesota Branch of the National Nonpartisan League, St. Paul, Minnesota, March 19, 1918. St. Paul: The Branch, 1918. 4 p. MHS.
   Lists legislative program with an additional four points of special value to labor; strong statement in support of Russian Revolution.

595. _____. Montana. Questionnaire Prepared by the Conference for Progressive Political Action and Submitted to Legislative Candidates, State and National. Billings, Mont., 1922. 4 p. MHS.
   Eighteen questions NPL asked of Mont. legislative candidates.

596. _____. Nebraska. Progressives Vote Together: Scattered Independent Voters in Nebraska Banded together in an Organized Voting Block, Can Elect Any Candidate for Whom They Conclude to Vote. Lincoln, Nebr.: The League, 1922. 12 p. MHS.
   Candidates endorsed by NPL, Farmers Union, organized labor, and others at Farmer-Labor Convention at Grand Island, Nebr., Aug. 25, 1922.

597. _____. North Dakota. By Laws and Constitution of the North Dakota Nonpartisan League. Stanley, N.Dak.: Sun Print, [between 1916 and 1920]. 16 p. MHS.

598. _____. North Dakota. By Laws National Nonpartisan League, North Dakota Branch. Fargo: Elliott Printing Co., 1921. 15 p. MHS.

599. _____. North Dakota. By Laws of the Nonpartisan League of North Dakota. N.p., [1923]. 8 p. SHSND.
   Adopted at state convention in Bismarck, Mar. 2 and 3, 1923, amended Oct. 10 and 11, 1923.

600. _____. North Dakota. Big Eastern Bond House Buys North Dakota Bonds. Fargo: State Executive Committee, [1921]. 1 p. MHS.
   Published during recall election; attacks IVA.

601. [_____]. North Dakota. Nonpartisan League Candidates: Vote for Each and Every One. Fargo, [1920]. 1 p. MHS.
   Photos of all NPL candidates for N.Dak. state offices.

602. _____. Wisconsin. The New Day: What the Organized Workers and Farmers Have Done for Themselves in North Dakota. Madison, Wis., [1920]. 8 p. MHS.
   Includes NPL platform for Wis. and a statement by Robert M. La Follette in support of League-endorsed candidates.

603. _____. Wisconsin. Principles or Mud Slinging, Which Will You Choose. Madison: Wisconsin Branch of the Nonpartisan League, [1920?]. 4 p. MHS.
   Response to statements made by E. F. Dithmar against ticket backed by NPL and Robert M. La Follett's supporters.

604. Nelson, C. Z. Minnesota's Next Governor, Henrik Shipstead. Minneapolis: [Nelson, 1920]. 6 p. MHS.
   Campaign literature for candidate endorsed by NPL and Working People's Nonpartisan Political League.

605. Nestos, R[angvold] A. The Campaign Issues: Primary Election, 1922, Address Delivered . . . [at] Memorial Park, LaMoure County, June 5. Fargo: Joint Campaign Organization, 1922. 15 p. MHS and UND-A.
   Address by N.Dak. governor defending six months of IVA control.

606. Nestos, R[angvold] A. The Campaign Issues: Primary Election, 1922, Address Delivered . . . [at] Memorial Park, LaMoure County, June 5. Fargo: Joint Campaign Organization, 1922. 15 p. MHS.
   Address by N.Dak. governor defending six months of IVA control.

607. _____. The Spirit of the Northwest: Delivered before the Chamber of Commerce of the State of New York, at Its 155th Annual Banquet, November 15, 1923. Fargo: Knight Printing Co., [1923]. 19 p. SHSND.
   Asserts that Minn. and N.Dak. are not radical havens and that NPL has declined in popularity.

608. _____. What We Promised and What We Have Done: Address Delivered . . . [at] Wilton, North Dakota, September 27, 1922. N.p., [1922?]. 24 p. MHS.
   Nestos's campaign for re-election. Attacks Lynn J. Frazier and William Lemke; touts opening of state mill at Grand Forks.

609. *New Book for Sale: Justice Held for Ransom by Grant S. Youmans, Minot, N.D.* N.p., n.d. 1 p. MHS.
  Cartoons show A. C. Townley as financier, bribe seeker, blackmailer, and corruptionist. In Broadside Collection, Division of Archives and Manuscripts.

610. *The New Day in North Dakota: Synopsis of the Laws Making It.* N.p., 1919. 11 p. MHS.
  "A statement in outline of the character, the contents and changes arising under these new laws." Supports NPL.

611. Nielson, Minnie J. *A Message to Minnesota Womanhood.* [St. Paul: Minnesota Sound Government Assn., 1920?]. 8 p. MHS.
  Anti-NPL pamphlet reprinted from *Minnesota Issues* (see No. 723). Charges that NPL-inspired socialism is corrupting N.Dak. school system.

612. _____. *"Safeguard Your Schools": A Message to Minnesota Womanhood.* St. Paul, 1920. SHSND.
  May be same as No. 611. Not seen by compilers.

613. *Nonpartisan League Meeting.* Sept., [1918]. 1 p. Broadside Collection, Division of Archives and Manuscripts, MHS.
  Announces move of meeting scheduled for Canton, Minn., to Harmony, Minn., where "free speech" is supported. O. M. Thomason and Barlow, speakers.

614. *Nonpartisan League: Methods and Principles.* Waco, Tex., n.d.
  Pro-NPL. Not located by compilers.

615. *Nonpartisans and the Nonpartisan Ballot.* N.p., [1921?]. [2] p. MHS.
  IVA recall election literature calling for party government and party responsibility, not nonpartisanship.

616. *Non Party League Programme.* N.p., n.d. 1 p. Saskatchewan Archives Board.
  NPL in Canada. Not seen by compilers.

617. Norbeck, Peter. *Governor Norbeck Accepts Suggestion of Mr. Bates and Will Accompany Him.* Redfield, S.Dak., 1918. 21 p. MHS.
  Open letter from governor of S.Dak. to Mark P. Bates, his NPL opponent, agreeing to accompany Bates in order to reduce violence at NPL meetings. Dated Oct. 7.

618. _____. *Governor Peter Norbeck Replies.* Pierre, S.Dak., 1918. 4 p. MHS.
  Author responds to NPL charges; addresses pamphlet to Mark P. Bates, his NPL opponent.

619. _____. *Message to the People of South Dakota.* [Redfield, S.Dak., 1918].
  Published as part of author's 1918 re-election campaign. Contrasts his record with that of N.Dak. NPL. Not located by compilers.

620. *North Dakota Bonds Business Politics: A Brief Statement of Facts Relative to State Bonds Now Being Offered for Sale.* Fargo, 1921. 4 p. SHSND.
  "Sponsored by the Republican and Democratic state organizations and the Independent Voters Association." Signed by H. P. Goddard, vice-chairman of Republican State Central Committee; Sveinbjorn Johnson, chairman of Democratic State Central Committee; Theodore G. Nelson, executive secretary of IVA.

621. Northwest Publishing Company. *Soon to Appear: The Minnesota Daily Star, Bringing the Bright Light of Truth, Pointing the Way to Real Progress.* St. Paul: The Company, [1920?]. 4 p.
  Advertises sale of stock in the newspaper. Herbert E. Gaston, president and treasurer; Thomas Van Lear, vice-president; Thomas V. Sullivan, secretary. Not located by compilers.

622. Northwestern Service Bureau. *Editorial Service Sheet.* Nos. 57 and 58. St. Paul: The Bureau, [1917?]. 1 p. MHS.
  Surviving examples of ready-made newspaper copy sent out to newspapers participating in service run by NPL. Sheets include articles on NPL, social conditions, and "fillers." See also Nos. 498, 501, and 675.

623. _____. *The Farmer-owned County Newspaper.* St. Paul: The Bureau, [1918?]. 12 p. MHS.
  Arguments for and advice on establishing farmer-owned newspapers. Publisher (later known as Publishers' National Service Bureau) was NPL auxiliary.

624. O'Connor, J. F. T. *Our Problems and the Senatorship: Address Delivered by Hon. J. F. T. O'Connor, Hankinson, North Dakota, September 15, 1922.* N.p., [1922]. 7 p. SHSND.
  Campaign speech by IVA candidate for U.S. Senate.

625. *O'Connor-Nestos Ticket.* Chicago: Davis Photo Service, [1922]. 2 p. SHSND.
  Seventeen photos of IVA candidates and instructions on voting.

626. O'Hara, Frank. *The Nonpartisan League of North Dakota: A Study and Outlook.* St. Louis, Mo.: Central Bureau of Central Society, 1920. 20 p.

Author, who also wrote an economics textbook, supports NPL. Not located by compilers.

627. Our Socialist Autocracy: Some of the Things They Have Done or Attempted in North Dakota under the Guise of "The Farmers Program." N.p., [1920?]. 4 p. MHS.
   Covers 1919 session.

628. Packard, Frank E. The Farmers' Movement in North Dakota and Taxation: An Address Delivered before the National Tax Association at Atlanta, Georgia, November 15, 1917. N.p., 1918. 8 p. MHS.
   Author was N.Dak. State Tax Commissioner. Discusses tax program; mentions loyalty issue. Pro-NPL.

629. Patterson, Charles. Reds and Radicals in America. N.p., 1920. Rudolph Johnson Collection, Western Historical Collections, University of Colorado at Boulder.
   St. Paulite's address at the Jan. 10, 1920, meeting of the Lawyers Club in N.Y. Attacks NPL government in N.Dak. as socialist. Not seen by compilers.

630. People's Franchise Bureau. Where Will You Be Tuesday? With the Constructionists or Will You Be with the Destructionists? N.p.: The Bureau, [1919]. 1 p. MHS.
   Mailer dealing with vote on franchising Minneapolis street car system. Charges that "All Socialists . . . All I.W.W.'s . . . All Members of the Nonpartisan League . . . All Bolshevists and Communists are Against the Franchise." John H. Ray, Jr., was Bureau's executive secretary.

631. Peterson, Elmer Theodore. American Bolshevism: Address on the Non-Partisan League, by . . . before Groups 7, 8 & 5 of the Kansas Bankers Association, November 11-12-13, 1919. N.p., 1919. 8 p. MHS.
   Cover stamped "Paid for and distributed by Independent Voters Ass'n."

632. Plain Talk by One Who Should Know--Better. Fargo, n.d. 4 p. SHSND.
   Contrasts IVA and NPL farm programs; supports NPL.

633. Political Patrioteers. . . . N.p., [1918?]. 7 p. MHS.
   Statements by George Creel, John Lind, Minnesota Supreme Court, NPL, and others, "which put that charge of disloyalty permanently to rest."

634. Preus, Jacob A. O. A Government Experiment Versus Life Insurance Principles: An Address Delivered at the Fifteenth Annual Meeting of the Association of Life Insurance Presidents at New York, December 9, 1921. N.p., [1921?]. 21 p. MHS.
   Minn. governor's defense of capitalism against NPL attacks in Minn. and N.Dak. Urges "cooperation . . . the opposite of state ownership."

635. Program of the Nonpartisan League as Enacted into Law in North Dakota: Is It Good or Bad? N.p.: Farm Labor State Record, n.d. 4 p.
   Urges votes for Lynn J. Frazier, William Lemke, and John N. Hagan. Published after 1921. Not located by compilers.

636. Progressive Republican Voter's Guide. N.p., n.d. 2 p. SHSND.
   Sample voting card for NPL-endorsed candidates, both statewide and in 27th Legislative District (Burleigh Co.).

637. Proposed Laws Provide for Closing of State Bank and Scrapping of N.D. Program: Rural Credits Act Is Fake Bill That Will Be Blocked If Constitutional Amendment Is Approved--People Would Have Nothing to Say in Nomination of Congressmen in Primary Asked For. Fargo: Elliott Printing Co., [1921]. 4 p. MHS.
   Attacks IVA recall election program of constitutional amendment and initiated measures.

638. Publishers' Circulation Statement (Not Auditor's Report). [Minneapolis: The Star, 1920]. 1 p. MHS.
   Brief statement by Minnesota Daily Star showing distribution of paper, giving figures by mail, carriers, and place.

639. Queering North Dakota: Profit Seekers Use Press of Country to Mislead Public. St. Louis, Mo.: Central Bureau of Central Society, 1921. 4 p. North Dakota NPL Collection 1, UND.
   Supports NPL.

640. Randall, N. S. Should the Farmers of Minnesota Join the Non-Partisan League?: The Text of the Debate Held at Long Prairie, Minn., on Saturday, March 24, 1917, between N. S. Randall, State Organizer for the League and Rudolph Lee, Editor of the Long Prairie Leader. N.p., [1917?]. 46 p. MHS.

641. The Recall: I Have Signed, Have You? Let's Get Rid of Them before They Get Our Goat. [Fargo, 1921]. SHSND.
   IVA pamphlet urging people to sign N.Dak. 1921 recall petition; lists $200 million spent by "Townleyism."

642. Republican Campaign Committee. North Dakota. Facts and Figures of North Dakota Issues. Fargo: Republican Campaign Committee, 1920. 32 p. North Dakota NPL Collection 1, UND.
   Anti-NPL.

643. [Republican Party (Minn.). State Central Committee.] Non-Partisan League Is Only Another Name for "Socialism." N.p., [1918?]. 8 p. MHS.
   Points to real and imagined connections between NPL and socialists. Discusses A. C. Townley and Arthur Le Sueur.

644. Republican State Central Committee. North Dakota. The Truth About the Constitutional Amendments: Every Citizen Should Vote Either "Yes" or "No" on These Important Measures. Fargo, [1918]. 16 p. SHSND.
   Urges passage in Nov. 1918 of the ten amendments that would allow NPL to enact its program.

645. Restiveness in the League. [Grand Forks: Grand Forks Herald, 1918]. 1 p. MHS.
   Reprint from Grand Forks Herald, Aug. 11, 1918; deals with NPL defectors.

646. Richter, Dan E. Independent Campaign Songs. N.p., n.d. [2] p. MHS.
   Songs attacking A. C. Townley and NPL.

647. ____. Weeds: An Exposition of Arthur C. Townley, President of the Non-Partisan League, a Sower of Wind, a Reaper of Weeds. Minneapolis: Loyal Voters Assn., 1919. 8 p. MHS.
   Outline of Townley's career as aspiring "Flax King," socialist organizer, and "Czar of the NPL." Title page of MHS copy stamped "Paid for and distributed by the Independent Voters Ass'n."

648. Russell, Charles Edward. In and Out of the Yoke. A Plain Story of the Farmer and the Nonpartisan League. [St. Paul?, 1921?]. 32 p. MHS.
   Succinct statement of farm problem and origin of NPL; discussion of laws passed and defeated in N.Dak. in 1916. Author, a well-known Socialist, was hired to work on Nonpartisan Leader.

649. Sargent, Noel. I.W.W. Preach Violence. Minneapolis: American Committee of Minneapolis, [1919?]. 8 p. MHS.
   Author was a former University of Minn. economics instructor and a contributing editor of American Economist.

650. ____. Nonpartisan League Leaders Work with I.W.W. St. Paul: Minnesota Sound Government Assn., [1919?]. 8 p. MHS.
   Points to IWW connections including work of David C. Coates, first general manager of NPL, who helped organize IWW.

651. ____. North Dakota Schools under the Nonpartisan League. St. Paul: Minnesota Sound Government Assn., [1920?]. 16 p. MHS.
   Discusses Board of Administration set up by NPL under Senate Bill 134 to control educational, penal, and charitable institutions; describes ousting of Minnie J. Nielson as superintendent of public instruction.

652. ____. The Socialism of 1919. Minneapolis: Sargent, [1919?]. 21 p. MHS.
   Discusses the "dictatorship of socialism."

653. ____. Socialism, the Farmer, the Nonpartisan League. St. Paul: Minnesota Sound Government Assn., [1920?]. 8 p. MHS.
   Points out socialist goals and connections in NPL.

654. Schmahl, Julius A. Address . . . at New Ulm, Minnesota, August 20, 1919, and Kimball, Minnesota, Sept. 27, 1919, on the Occasion of a Home-coming of Soldiers of the World War and of the Fifty-seventh Anniversary of the Repulse of the Sioux Indians. Minneapolis: Syndicate Printing Co., 1919. 22 p. MHS.
   Author, Minn. secretary of state, ties Dakota War and Little Crow to the "embryo I.W.W."; most of speech is directed against NPL, under the heading "Another Evil."

655. Shafer, George F. The Record of North Dakota's State Industries: Their History with Record Facts and Figures Showing Their Cost to the Tax-payer to Date; Future Cost to Be Met, Etc. Fargo: Independent Voters Assn., n.d. 20, 32 p. SHSND.
   IVA analysis of state industries. Longer edition lists no author.

656. Sir Rufus Wallingford Has Thrown Up His Hands!: Truth Is Stranger Than Fiction. N.p., n.d.
   Anti-NPL. Not located by compilers.

657. Six Reasons Why You Should Vote for Mrs. S. V. Haight. N.p.: Thunder Creek Provincial Constituency, [1917]. 1 p. Saskatchewan Archives Board.
   Haight was an NPL-endorsed candidate in 1917 Sask. election. Not seen by compilers.

658. Smelker, R. C. "Putting Up Loyalty": The Patriotism of the People Exploited by Political Profiteers, Documents Furnish Proof. St. Paul: Smelker, [1918]. 8 p. MHS.
   Letters of A. A. D. Rahn planning campaign rally for J. A. A. Burnquist at which Theodore Roosevelt was to question League's loyalty. Issued on behalf of D. H. Evans, Tom Davis, and F. E. Tillquist, NPL-endorsed candidates in Minn.

659. Socialism in North Dakota. Lisbon, N.Dak., and Anoka, Minn.: Standard Publishing Co., [1922]. 8 p. SHSND.
   Anti-NPL review of North Dakota Industrial Commission's annual report.

660. Socialism Is Real Menace in Our State Now. N.p., [1917 or 1918]. 8 p. MHS.
   Includes reprint of a "Dear Comrade" letter signed "George" to William Head of Mitchell, S.Dak. (while he was in prison on a charge of violating the espionage act), saying that NPL is socialism in disguise. Mentions George and L. L. Griffith and George D. Brewer as Socialist organizers.

661. A Socialist Constitution for North Dakota: Do You Want That or the Constitution That Has Stood the Test of 25 Years: A Careful Digest and Comparison, Revised to Latest Amendments of Proposed Constitution. [Grand Forks, 1917?, 1918?]. 20, 24 p. MHS, SHSND.
   Opposes House Bill 44, which proposed enactment of NPL's changes in N.Dak. Constitution. Compares "Present Constitution" with "Proposed Amendments." Longer edition contains more polemical commentary and "Top-Notch Socialist Government" (p. 21-24). Morlan attributed authorship to Jerry Dempster Bacon (see No. 78, p. 102). Title page of MHS 24-p. copy stamped "Paid for and distributed by Independent Voters Ass'n." SHSND also holds a 4th edition, [1920?], and an undated 19 p. edition.

662. Solberg, K. K. Tom Davis for Governor: Vote a Farmer-Labor Ballot. [Minneapolis?, 1918]. 4 p. MHS.
   Davis ran with NPL support as Farmer-Labor candidate in 1918 Minn. general election after defeat of Charles A. Lindbergh, Sr., in primary election. Author was a state senator from Clarkfield, Minn.

663. Soltis, John Gabriel. How Van Lear Works the Workers. Minneapolis: Soltis, 1923. 24 p. MHS.
   Socialist attack on Thomas Van Lear, A. C. Townley, Minnesota Daily Star, and Working People's Nonpartisan Political League.

664. _____. Political Traitors and How They Work: Astounding Revelation of Treason within the Labor Movement. Minneapolis: Soltis, 1924. 29 p. MHS.
   Socialist attack on Working People's Nonpartisan Political League and Thomas Van Lear.

665. _____. The Rise and Fall of the Nonpartisan League.
   "In preparation" notice of this pamphlet printed on back cover of No. 663. Not located by compilers.

666. S.D. Farmers O.K. League Accounts: Special Committee, Representing Members of the State, Finds the Organization Funds Well Managed . . . Nebraska Farmers O.K. League Accounts: "League Funds Safe" Says Committee. N.p., [1918?]. 6 p. MHS.

667. Spalding, Burleigh F., N. C. Young, and Edward Engerud. Analysis of State Bank Law, Comments and Questions. Fargo, 1919. 8 p. MHS.
   Analysis of effect of bank law on county tax funds, addressed "To Municipal and School Officers and Township Treasurers of Cass County, N.D." Authors had served on N.Dak. Supreme Court.

668. Spies, Traitors and the Kept Press!: A Barrage Flung Out by Fear. N.p., [between 1915 and 1921]. 4 p. MHS.
   Compares A. C. Townley's rhetoric with barrage of shells, gas, and smoke bombs on WWI front line.

669. State Mill and Elevator, Grand Forks, North Dakota. N.p., n.d. 32 p. MHS.
   Published after 1922. Includes good photographs of the mill and its operations and recipes calling for "Dakota Maid Flour."

670. Steele, H. H. The Tax Program of the Nonpartisan League and North Dakota. N.p.: National Tax Assn., 1919. 10 p.
   Author was pro-NPL chairman of N.Dak. State Tax Commission. Not located by compilers.

671. [Stewart, A. D.] A Typical Townley Trick. Redwood Falls, Minn., [1918]. 4 p. MHS.
   Concerns quotation of Abraham Lincoln taken out of context and printed in Minnesota Leader. Author was secretary of the State Assn. of Farmers Mutual Insurance Companies.

672. Take This with You to the Polls on October 28: You Will Find It Helpful in Marking Your Ballot. N.p., [1921]. 2 p. MHS.
   Stamped "Sample Copy." IVA ballot for N.Dak. 1921 recall election, showing amendments, initiated measures, and IVA slate for state offices.

673. Talmage, William Henry. Two Nonpartisan League Lectures: "The Mad Captain" and "We'll Stick." Redfield, S.Dak., 1918. 15 p. MHS.
   Includes bylaws of Kans. NPL; argues for a permanent NPL free of Townley's autocratic rule. Author was pastor of St. George's Church in Redfield, S.Dak., and helped organize NPL in Kans.

674. Teigen, Ferdinand A. The Nonpartisan League: Its Origin, Development and Secret Purposes. St. Paul: Economic Research and Publishing Co., 1918. 82 p. MHS.
   Author of first printing listed as "Dr. Mum," supposedly using a pseudonym to protect practice; second printing by Teigen, a de-

fector from NPL during WWI, who said he "had supplied a large part of the material." Texts are identical.

675. Test Townleyism Yourself by Very Simple Method. N.p., n.d. 1 p. MHS.
Anti-NPL articles on a newspaper-like sheet, possibly produced as response to Northwestern Service Bureau's Editorial Service Sheets (see No. 622).

676. To All Anti-League Republicans and Democrats! Bismarck, [1924]. 1 p. SHSND.
Urges support for three anti-NPL election-law reforms.

677. [Townley, Arthur C.] Address of A. C. Townley, President of the National Non-Partisan League, at the Farmers and Workers Conference Held at St. Paul, Sept. 18, 19 and 20, 1917. N.p., 1917. 39 p. MHS.
Excellent example of Townley's speaking style and rhetoric; described in No. 593 as "the best speech Townley ever made and that's going some."

678. Townley and Youmans: The Farmers Want to Know the Truth . . . Dare You Tell Them Mr. Townley? N.p., [1919]. 2 p. MHS.
Prints an excerpt from a letter from Grant S. Youmans to James Manahan and an excerpt from an interview of A. C. Townley; each man charges the other with blackmail. Printed on back of sheet is a letter from farmers asking Townley to debate NPL program with George Murphy, "a farmer and taxpayer, of Berthold."

Arthur C. Townley addressing a meeting from the back of a truck, undated

679. Townley Explains Selection of League Candidates: The Courier-News Says. [Fargo, 1922]. 2 p. SHSND.
Criticism of A. C. Townley extracted from Fargo Courier-News.

680. Townley Made the League. Fargo, 1922. 2 p. SHSND.
Reprints of editorials from Fargo Courier-News discussing Townley's attacks on NPL and "Selling the League."

681. Townleyism. N.p., n.d. 1 p.
IVA broadside. Not located by compilers.

682. Townleyism: A True Story of the Operation of the Non-Partisan League Program in North Dakota, as Told in Official Reports of the Various Departments of the State Government. Fargo: Elliot Printing Co., 1921. 95 p. MHS.
Discusses 1921 recall election in N.Dak.; pro-NPL.

683. Twichell, L. L. Labor Legislation in the Last Session of the North Dakota Legislature: Were the Independents Opposed to Labor Legislation, Did They Oppose or Defeat Any Fair, Necessary, or Reasonable Labor Laws Proposed? N.p., n.d. 6 p. SHSND.
Stamped: "Distributed by IVA." Explanation of IVA labor legislation during N.Dak. legislative session, probably 1921.

684. Uncle John. Frank and Tom Have It Out about the Recall. N.p., [1921?]. 8 p. MHS.
Fictional conversation between two Red River Valley farmers in which former Leaguers decide IVA is right in 1921 N.Dak. recall election.

685. Utah Farm Bureau State Committee. Farmers, Investigate! Shall We Be Governed by a League Affiliated with the I.W.W.? N.p., 1919.
Not located by compilers.

686. Vote for Chas. A. Lindbergh for Governor: The Religious Lie Is Answered Herein. Minneapolis: Lindbergh for Governor Campaign Committee, 1924. 16 p. MHS.
Refers to and answers charges of disloyalty and religious bigotry that were raised in Lindbergh's NPL-backed campaign for governor in 1918.

687. Vote "No" on the Three Constitutional Amendments and the Six Initiating Measures. Fargo, [1921]. 1 p. MHS.
Opposes IVA program, especially law requiring election to be held in the "dead of winter." Includes a cartoon.

688. Voters Information Club, Minneapolis, Minn. Political Committee. Some Things the Local Czars of Socialism Fail to Mention. Min-

neapolis: The Club, [1921?]. 15 p. MHS.
  Attack on Thomas Van Lear and Minneapolis socialist leaders.

689. Warning. N.p., [1922?]. 1 p. SHSND.
  Urges votes for IVA.

690. Weaver, S. Roy. The Nonpartisan League in North Dakota: A Study of a Class War and Its Disastrous Consequences, Together with a Comparison of Bank Services in Canada and Western States. Toronto, Ont.: Canadian Reconstruction Assn., 1921. 96 p. SHSND.
  Compares NPL to possible farmers' movements in Canada. Discusses N.Dak. banking policies.

691. Wehrle, Vincent. The Non-Partisan League: Its Causes and Tendencies. N.p., [1919 or 1920]. 19 p. MHS.
  Author, Roman Catholic bishop of Bismarck, advocates Christian opposition to NPL socialism.

692. ____. The Present Political Situation of the State of North Dakota. [Bismarck]: Wehrle, [1918?]. 36 p. MHS.
  Calls for less government involvment in business affairs.

693. West, Willis Mason. A Statement by . . . Regarding His Suggested Candidacy for Governor, with a Declaration of His Principles and His Views on State Policies. N.p., 1920. 5 p. MHS.
  Declares intent to file if his platform meets the approval of progressive labor and NPL in Minn.

694. What Do You Know about Free Love in North Dakota?: You Might Learn Some Facts from This. N.p., [1920?]. 4 p. MHS.
  Explains that "Free Love Bill" introduced in N.Dak. 1919 legislative session by James A. Harris was not supported by NPL; reprints text of NPL-sponsored Senate Bill 61, which outlawed "prostitution, lewdness and assignation" in order to combat "wide-spread vice and venereal disease" and provided that girls and women convicted under the act report to female probation officers.

695. What Is Your Answer: The Question Is, Shall North Dakota Abolish Its Present Debt and Tax Limit and Change Its Program of Private Ownership of Property to Public Ownership and Go into Limitless Debt? N.p., [1918?]. 2 p. SHSND.

696. What the Cosmopolitan, Everybody's Magazine and Others Say about the Nonpartisan League. Fargo: North Dakota Leader, 1919. 16 p. MHS.
  A supplement to the North Dakota Leader, Apr. 12, 1919, reprinting newspaper and magazine articles.

697. When It Comes to a Show Down, with Whom Will Townley Stick? N.p., [1918?]. 2 p. MHS.
  Attack on "Czar Townley," Arthur Le Sueur, and Joseph Gilbert.

698. When Farmers Stuck Together: The Story of Sixty Thousand North Dakota Farmers Who Are Running Their Own Government and Have Enacted Laws That Will Enable Them to Borrow Money at Fair Rates. . . . St. Paul: Nonpartisan Leader, [1919?]. 27 p. MHS.
  Description of N.Dak. bills that helped the farmer; often sent out by NPL to answer inquiries.

699. Where the Money Went. Fargo, [1921]. 6 p. MHS.
  Figures from official records supporting IVA amendments, initiated laws, and state officials.

700. . . . Will the Ellsworth County Farmers Permit Themselves to be Ruled by a Few Mobbists of Ellsworth City? N.p., [1918]. 1 p. Kansas State Historical Society.
  Broadside showing reproduction of poster produced by county's Council of Defense Action ordering M. L. Amos to leave Ellsworth Co., Kans., before Nov. 29, 1918. Not seen by compilers.

701. Women's Nonpartisan Clubs. Minnesota, the Problems of Her People and Why the Farmers and the Workers Have Organized for Political Action. Minneapolis: National Nonpartisan League, [1921?]. 15 p. MHS.
  Includes information on Women's Nonpartisan Clubs; platforms for Minn. including the Farmer Organization Program and the Labor Organization Program. Mentions matters of particular concern to women.

702. ____. Report of the Fourth Annual Convention, 1925. Minneapolis, 1925.
  Includes a list of names and addresses of earlier secretaries. This report and reports of the first three conventions have not been located by compilers.

703. ____. Women's NPL Clubs: Summary of Audit of July 16, 1921, and Report from July 16, 1921, to April 29, 1922, together with Findings of the Executive Committee of NPL Clubs May 4, 1922. N.p.: Executive Committee of the Women's Nonpartisan Clubs, n.d. 7 p. North Dakota NPL Collection 1, UND.

704. The Workers' Herald Campaign Leaflet. Minneapolis: Committee on Information of the Hennepin County Central Committee for the

Women's Nonpartisan Club No. 18, Renville Co., N.Dak., ca. 1917

Candidates of the Socialist Party, [1918]. 4 p. MHS.
Newspaper-like item supporting Thomas Van Lear for mayor and calling the Lincoln Club "Minneapolis' Tammany Hall." Includes photographs and biographies of Socialist candidates in Hennepin Co.

705. Working People's Nonpartisan Political League. Minnesota Labor Is about to Vote for Itself: Organizing Pamphlet Number 1. Minneapolis: The League, [1919?]. 7 p. MHS.
Call for organizers and members to "help build an organization to overthrow greedy profiteers and their political henchmen." Thomas Van Lear, secretary-treasurer. No other pamphlets in this series have been located by compilers.

706. ____. A New Political Alignment for Minnesota: The Working People's Nonpartisan Political League Is an Organization which Proposes to Place the Government of Minnesota in the Hands of the People. Minneapolis, n.d. 12 p. North Dakota NPL Collection 1, UND.

707. ____. A New Political Movement for Minnesota.
General explanation and membership application. Not located by compilers.

708. ____. Proceedings: Second Annual Convention of the . . . of Minnesota, Held at the Armory, Rochester, Minnesota, Sunday Afternoon and Evening, July 18, 1920. Minneapolis: The League, [1920]. 12 p. MHS.
Reports, constitution, bylaws, and legislative program of Working People's Nonpartisan Political League. Proceedings of first convention have not been located by compilers.

709. ____. Proceedings: Third Annual Convention of the . . . of Minn., Held at Gardner's Hall, Brainerd, Minnesota, Sunday Afternoon and Evening, July 17, 1921. Minneapolis: The League, [1921]. 19 p. MHS.

710. ____. Proceedings: Fourth Annual Convention of the . . . of Minnesota. Minneapolis: The League, [1922]. 20 p. MHS.

711. ____. Voters!!! Which Do You Want? Minneapolis Home Rule or Government by a St. Paul Commission. . . . Minneapolis, [1921]. 4 p. MHS.
Campaign literature for Thomas Van Lear's mayoral race.

712. ____. City Central Committee, Minneapolis. City Platform and Program of the Working People's Nonpartisan League of Minneapolis. Minneapolis: The League, [1921?]. 4 p. MHS.
Supports Thomas Van Lear for mayor; includes platform planks on street railway system, other city monopolies, and various city issues.

713. ____. St. Paul Division, St. Paul, Minn. Platform of the . . . For a Clean Democratic Government for St. Paul. St. Paul: The Division, 1919. 4 p. MHS.
Preamble and seven planks of platform calling for "honest ballot," "municipal ownership" to improve the condition of working people, etc.

714. Young for Congress. Valley City, N.Dak., [1920]. 4 p. MHS.

PAMPHLETS and EPHEMERA

Campaign literature for re-election of IVA-supported Congressman George M. Young.

715. "Yours for the Revolution!": Defiance of the Government. St. Paul: Reliance Publicity Service, [1918]. 1 p. MHS.
  Flyer reprinting two of Arthur Le Sueur's letters and one from William D. Haywood to Le Sueur. Title refers to Le Sueur's closing line in one of the letters and to content of the other.

Periodicals

For more information on the entries in this section, see Introduction.

716. Alberta Non-Partisan (Calgary). Provincial Archives of Alberta.
NPL weekly and biweekly newspaper. Published by William Irvine as Nutcracker, Nov., 1916; changed to Alberta Nonpartisan, Oct. 1917; became Western Independent, 1920.

717. America First (St. Paul). MHS.
Anti-NPL magazine edited and published by Tom Parker Junkin. Published monthly, Apr.-Oct. 1919.

718. Fargo Courier-News. SHSND.
Daily newspaper taken over by NPL, 1916; sold, 1923, and became Fargo Tribune.

719. The Goat (Fargo). SHSND.
Published by Progressive Feature Service Bureau. SHSND has Vol. 1, Nos. 1 (Feb.-Mar. 1920) and 3 (May-June 1920). Not seen by compilers; other copies not located by compilers.

720. Grand Forks American. SHSND.
NPL newspaper. Published daily, Sept. 1918-Mar. 1920.

721. Kansas Leader (Salina). Kansas State Historical Society.
NPL weekly newspaper. Began publication as Ellsworth County Leader (Ellsworth, Kans.), 1919; changed to Kansas Leader (Salina), 1920; became Saline County Independent (Salina), 1926. Ceased publication 1927.

722. Minnesota Daily Star (Minneapolis). MHS.
NPL newspaper. Published daily by NPL, 1920-24; sold and became Minneapolis Star, 1924.

723. Minnesota Issues (St. Paul). MHS.
Anti-NPL magazine, official organ of Minn. Sound Government Assn. Published bi-monthly, Feb. 15, 1920-Mar. 1921.

724. Minnesota Leader (St. Paul). MHS.
NPL newspaper, irregularly published. Began publication Feb. 1918 in St. Paul; moved to Olivia, Minn., Apr. 1920; ceased operation Nov. 1924.

725. Nebraska Leader (Lincoln). Nebraska State Historical Society.
NPL newspaper. Published weekly, 1919-21.

726. Nonpartisan Leader (Fargo, St. Paul, Minneapolis). MHS.
Official NPL national newspaper. Published weekly and semi-weekly in Fargo (1915-18), St. Paul (1918-20), and Minneapolis (1920-23).

727. The Non-Partisan: Official Organ of the Minnesota Non-Partisan League (St. Paul). MHS.
Newspaper published monthly, Aug.-Dec., by Minn. Non-Partisan League, an anti-NPL group sometimes called the "Fake League."

728. Nonpartisan Leader of Western Canada (Swift Current, Sask.). Saskatchewan Archives Board.
NPL newspaper edited by Sidney Godwin. Published weekly, Sept. 1916-Aug. 15, 1917.

729. North Dakota Leader (Fargo). SHSND.
NPL newspaper. Published weekly, 1918-26; publication suspended Oct. 1921-May 1922.

730. Northwest Warriors Magazine (St. Paul). Minneapolis Public Library.
Anti-NPL periodical. Published monthly, Sept. 1919-Mar. 1920.

731. On the Square: A Magazine for Farm and Home (St. Paul). MHS.
Anti-NPL periodical. Published May and June 1918. Copies in MHS library are bound with a clipping from Nonpartisan Leader (St. Paul), June 23, 1918, that prints the publishing contract between "On the Square Publishing Company" and its backers: Russell M. Bennett,

Minneapolis, and Eli S. Warner and Charles Patterson, both St. Paul, "acting as a committee representative of certain interests."

732. Pan-American Anti-Socialist (St. Paul). Anti-NPL magazine. Published 1918. Not located by compilers.

733. The Red Flame (Bismarck). SHSND. IVA magazine. Published monthly, Nov. 1919-Oct. 1920. See No. 92.

734. Rural Independent (Fargo). SHSND. IVA weekly and monthly newspaper. Published as Independent, 1919-21; Independent Review, 1922-ca. 1923; and Rural Independent, ca. 1923-24.

735. South Dakota Leader (Mitchell). MHS. NPL newspaper. Published weekly, 1918-24.

Government Publications

For more information on the entries in this section, see Introduction.

736. Minnesota. Commission of Public Safety. _Preliminary Report to J. A. A. Burnquist, Governor of Minnesota._ N.p., 1918. 53 p. MHS.
   Investigation of NPL activities including Robert M. La Follette's speech in St. Paul in Sept. 1917 and strike against Twin City Rapid Transit Co.

737. _____. Commission of Public Safety. _Report of the Minnesota Commission of Public Safety._ St. Paul, [1918]. 319 p. MHS.
   Wartime hysteria translated into government action. Members of committee included Governor J. A. A. Burnquist, Attorney General Clifford L. Hinton, Special Counsel Ambrose Tighe, and John F. McGee. Special mention of NPL (p. 163-64) is same as No. 736.

738. _____. Commission of Public Safety. Publicity Department. _Wall Street and the War: A Concise Argument Against "Rich Man's War" Propaganda._ St. Paul, n.d. 10 p. MHS.
   Issued to counter contention of NPL and other groups that WWI was waged for profits.

739. _____. Legislature. Senate. Special Investigating Committee. _The Red Menace in Minnesota: An Open Letter to Friends of Constitutional Government in Minnesota together with a Transcript of the Testimony before the Senate Investigating Committee of Harry Curran Wilbur and W. D. Washburn._ [St. Paul, 1923?]. 36 p. MHS.
   "Prepared and circulated" by Harry Curran Wilbur, organizer of Minn. Sound Government Assn., which opposed NPL and Working People's Nonpartisan Political League.

740. North Dakota. Auditor. _North Dakota Directory._ Bismarck, 1917, 1919. 8 p. MHS.
   Lists state officials and their home towns. After 1919, directory was published by Secretary of State (see No. 770).

741. _____. Bank of North Dakota. _The Bank of North Dakota: Purpose, History and Organization, Laws, Regulations, By-Laws, Orders, Rules, Directions, Advice and Information; Series of 1920._ Bismarck, 1920, 1933. 58 p. MHS.
   Author, F. W. Cathro, was director general of Bank of N.Dak. and chairman of General Finance Committee.

742. _____. Bank of North Dakota. _Circulars._ Nos. 5-7, 1919; nos. 1-8, 11, 1920; 1a, 2a, 3, 4, 6, 1921. SHSND.
   On a variety of topics ranging from bond sales to purpose of bank.

743. _____. Bank of North Dakota. _Statement of the Condition of the Bank of North Dakota_ (Bulletins 1-5, series 1919) and _Condensed Statement of the Condition of the Bank of North Dakota_ (Bulletins 1-12, series 1920, Bulletins 1-11, series 1921). SHSND.

744. _____. Board of Administration. _Annual Report._ 1919. 140 p. MHS.
   Includes Charles E. Stangeland's report on Public Library Commission (p. 113-40).

745. _____. Board of Control. _Report on Terminal Grain Elevators Made to the Fourteenth Legislative Assembly by the Board of Control of State Institutions, 1915._ Fargo, 1915. 31 p. SHSND.
   Authorized by 1913 N.Dak. legislature, this study was a response to growing demands for a state-owned grain elevator. Its advice against such an elevator lent support to NPL's organizing efforts.

746. _____. Department of Agriculture and Labor. _Report on the State Experimental Creamery at Werner, North Dakota._ Grand Forks, 1922. [29] p. SHSND.
   Critical of losses at creamery under NPL administration.

747. _____. Department of State. North Dakota Publicity Pamphlet: Constitutional Amendments Initiated and Referred Measures to be Submitted to the Electors at the General Election November 2, 1920. Bismarck, 1920. 13 p. MHS.
   Statements by IVA and NPL regarding issues to be voted upon.

748. _____. Department of State. North Dakota Publicity Pamphlet: Constitutional Measures and Initiated Measures to Be Submitted to the Electors at the Recall Election October 28, 1921. Bismarck, 1921. 39 p. MHS.
   Statements by IVA and NPL on issues in recall election: one constitutional amendment, setting debt limit for state, and six initiated laws, one of which would dissolve of Bank of N.Dak.

749. _____. Department of State. North Dakota Publicity Pamphlet: Measures Enacted by the Sixteenth Legislative Assembly and to be Referred to the Electors at a Special Election June 26, 1919. Bismarck, 1919. 39 p. MHS.
   Arguments for and against seven laws on referendum that IVA opposed and NPL favored.

750. _____. Department of State. North Dakota Publicity Pamphlet: Primary Election, June 28, 1922. Bismarck, 1922. 34 p. MHS.
   Biographies and statements from candidates. Also includes information on constitutional amendment and two initiated measures.

751. _____. Governor. Public Documents of North Dakota, Being the Annual and Biennial Reports of Various Public Officers and Institutions to Governor and Legislative Assembly. 1917-18 (2 vols., 30 reports); 1919-20 (2 vols., 34 reports); 1921-22 (2 vols., 43 reports). UND, SHSND.
   Compilation of reports of various state agencies and commissions, including Board of Administration, Superintendent of Public Instruction, Publication and Printing Commission, Workmen's Compensation Bureau, Minimum Wage Dept., Fire and Tornado Dept., State Banking Board, Commissioner of Immigration, and Hail Commissioner.

752. _____. Home Builders Association. Report of the Home Builders Association by F. E. Diehl, Manager, to the Industrial Commission of North Dakota, December 31, 1922. N.p., 1922. 15 p. SHSND.

753. _____. Immigration Department. North Dakota Invites New Settlers: North Dakota Has Land for the Landless and Homes for the Homeless. Bismarck, [1919], [1921]. 20, 15 p. SHSND.
   Opponents of NPL charged that pamphlets issued by this department were NPL propaganda, which the department was created to disseminate.

754. _____. Immigration Department. North Dakota: Its Resources and Its Opportunities. Vol. 1, nos. 1-8 (Nov. 1919-June 1920) and no. 10 (n.d.). Various pages. SHSND.

755. _____. Immigration Department. North Dakota, the Sunshine State, the Food Basket of the World. Fargo, 1920. 16 p. SHSND.

756. _____. Industrial Commission. Facts and Figures on North Dakota's Rural Credits System.

Lunch at the North Dakota Capitol, ca. 1917: Governor Lynn J. Frazier, seated, left foreground; Superintendent of Public Instruction Minnie J. Nielson, seated, second woman from right; Attorney General William Langer, seated, sixth from right (at end of table). Note newspapers spread to cover table.

[Bismarck]: The Commission, 1922. 31 p. MHS.
Describes actions of Governor Rangvold A. Nestos's administration in management of Bank of N.Dak.'s Farm Loan Department. Reprints report of W. B. DeNoult, director of Farm Loan Department, to Industrial Commission.

757. ____. Industrial Commission. <u>Financial Report of the North Dakota Industrial Program for the Period Ending December 31, 1920</u>. Bismarck: The Commission, 1921. 37 p. MHS.
First report of the Commission. Includes discussion of work on state mill; balance sheets for Bank of N.Dak. and Home Builders Assn.; titles and salaries for employees of these and other NPL programs.

758. ____. Industrial Commission. <u>North Dakota Facts</u>. Minot, N.Dak.: The Commission, [1923]. 4 p. SHSND.
Information on the state's economic standing. May have been used by state government to help sell bonds.

759. ____. Industrial Commission. <u>The North Dakota Industrial Program: A Report on the Organization and Progress of the North Dakota State Industries, and the Administration of Related Laws</u>. . . . Bismarck: The Commission, 1920, 1921. 86, 109 p. MHS.
Report on NPL program, including discussions of Bank of N.Dak., Mill and Elevator Assn., Home Building Assn., Workmen's Compensation Bureau, etc.

760. ____. Industrial Commission. <u>Report . . . for the Year Ending December 31, 1921</u>. Bismarck, [1922]. 68 p. MHS.

761. ____. Industrial Commission. <u>Report . . . for the Year Ending December 31, 1922</u>. Bismarck, [1923]. 41 p. SHSND.

762. ____. Legislative Assembly. 16th Session, 1919. <u>The New Day in North Dakota: Some of the Principal Laws Enacted by the Sixteenth Legislative Assembly 1919</u>. Bismarck: Industrial Commission of North Dakota, [1919]. 156 p. MHS.
Actions of the "farmer legislature," listing progressive measures by House and Senate bills in sections: "State Economics and Industries," "Condition of Labor," "Taxation," and "Miscellaneous." Important document.

763. ____. Legislative Assembly. <u>Supplement to the 1913 Compiled Laws of North Dakota</u>. 1913-25. 1 vol. UND.
Contains statutes enacted by N.Dak. legislature during 1915, 1917, 1919, 1921, 1923, and 1925 regular sessions, and 1918 and 1919 special sessions. Detailed index. Compiler's notes accompany the statutes, along with references to N.Dak and U.S. Supreme Court cases.

764. ____. Legislature. House. <u>Journals</u>. 1917, 1918 (Special Session), 1919, 1919 (Special Session), 1921. 5 vols. UND, SHSND.
House proceedings, including list of members, messages from the governor, records of votes, and other proceedings. Indexed by bill number, subject, and members. Texts of resolutions, special reports, and selected hearings, including hearings on Public Library Commission controversy of 1919 and investigations of state-owned industries.

765. ____. Legislature. House. Audit Committee. <u>Report of House Audit Committee Investigating Bank of North Dakota and Other State Industries, 1921</u>. [St. Paul: Temple, Webb, and Co., 1921]. 76 p. MHS.
After Bishop-Brissman audits of Bank of N.Dak. found no incriminating evidence, N.Dak. House voted to set up its own investigation; no NPL members were appointed to this committee. Report was privately printed in St. Paul because those in control of N.Dak. Publication and Printing Commission tried "to suppress the true condition of the finances of that state as reflected in the reports of the House Audit Committe and the Minority Report of the Senate Audit Committee" (p. 1A). The latter report is included (p. 66-76) in the pamphlet.

766. ____. Legislature. House. Audit Committee. <u>Report on Legislative Investigation of Public Industries</u>. Fargo: Joint Campaign Committee, 1921. 64 p. MHS.
Produced under same circumstances as No. 765.

767. ____. Legislature. House. Committee to Investigate the Public Library Commission. <u>[Hearings, December 10, 1919]</u>. [Bismarck, 1919]. 85 p. MHS.
Supplement to House Journal, Dec. 10, 1919. Hearings to investigate charges by Representative Olger B. Burtness that State Library was corrupting school children by forcing them to read radical literature. Committee, which included IVA members, questioned George A. Totten, chairman of Board of Administration, and unanimously cleared the library of any wrongdoing.

768. ____. Legislature. Senate. <u>Journals</u>. 1917, 1918 (Special Session), 1919, 1919 (Special Session), 1921. 5 vols. UND, SHSND.
Senate proceedings, including list of members, governors' messages, and texts of resolutions and selected hearings. Indexed by bill number, subject, and members. Of special importance are three reports submitted on Mar. 4, 1921, by Bishop Brissman and Co., auditors from St. Paul: "Report of

Special Examination of the State Mill and Elevator of Drake, North Dakota as at December 14, 1920" (p. 1629-50); "Report of Special Examination of the Home Building Association of North Dakota of Bismarck, North Dakota, as at December 3, 1920" (p. 1651-75); "Report of Special Examination and Audit of the Bank of North Dakota, Bismarck, North Dakota, as at December 3, 1920" (p. 1677-2016).

769. _____. Secretary of State. Legislative Manuals. 1913, 1919. Various pages. SHSND.
Also known as Blue Books. Contain biographies and photographs of state officials, voting statistics by county, histories of state agencies and commissions, and other vital information. Volume for 1919 is a particularly important source on NPL legislature.

770. _____. Secretary of State. Official Directory. 1921-22. Various pages. SHSND. Editions for 1919-20 entitled Congressional, State, Judicial, Legislative and County Offices. For previous directories, see No. 740.

771. _____. Workmen's Compensation Bureau. North Dakota Insurance Manual, Rules and Rates . . . No. 4. 1922. 40 p. MHS.
Lists each industry and its taxation rate per $100 payroll.

772. _____. United States Congress. Senate. Committee on Military Affairs. Hearings before the Committee on Military Affairs, United States Senate, Sixty-Fifth Congress, Second Session, on S. 4364. Part 2. Washington, D.C.: Government Printing Office, 1918.
Senate was considering a bill to extend jurisdiction of military tribunals. A. C. Townley testified concerning NPL and its activities.

Court Cases

For more information on the entries in this section, see Introduction.

773. <u>Currie</u> v. <u>Frazier</u>, 186 <u>NW</u> 244 (1921).
N.Dak. Supreme Court voided sale of revenue bonds by Bank of N.Dak., because sale was at less than par. See also No. 793.

774. <u>Gilbert</u> v. <u>Minnesota,</u> 254 <u>US</u> 325 (1920).
Appeal to U.S. Supreme Court of Gilbert's conviction in Minn. District Court of sedition for a speech he made at Kenyon, Minn. Court upheld conviction (see Minn. Supreme Court Case File 21081, Minn. State Archives, MHS), despite dissent by Justice Louis Brandeis. See also No. 791.

775. <u>Green et al.</u> v. <u>Frazier, Governor, et al.</u>, 253 <u>US</u> 233 (1920); <u>Scott et al.</u> v. <u>Frazier, Governor, et al.</u>, 253 <u>US</u> 243 (1920).
These two cases, involving constitutionality of NPL's N.Dak. legislative program of state-owned industries, were heard as one case by U.S. Supreme Court, which affirmed a lower court's ruling that the legislation was constitutional. See also <u>Scott</u> v. <u>Frazier</u>, 258 <u>F</u> 669 (1919), which originated in Federal District Court in N.Dak. (Judge Charles F. Amidon presiding), and <u>Green</u> v. <u>Frazier</u> 1976 <u>NW</u> 11 (1920), which originated in N.Dak. District Court.

776. <u>McCutcheon</u> v. <u>Townley,</u> 266 <u>F</u> 985 (1920).
Suit brought by a N.Dak. creditor against A. C. Townley relating to the bankruptcy of his farm. The creditor, backed by IVA, sought to examine NPL records to make certain that Townley was not diverting funds from NPL for his personal use. Federal District Judge Charles F. Amidon ruled in Townley's favor and took note of political nature of suit.

777. <u>Ray McKaig</u> v. <u>Frank R. Gooding and Statesman Printing Company,</u> Civil Case File No. 7527 (1919), Ada County Third District Records, Idaho Historical Society.
Civil suit brought by McKaig (NPL leader and organizer) against Frank Gooding (Idaho governor and U.S. senator) and a Boise newspaper company (publisher of the <u>Idaho Statesman</u>). Suit charged that defendants libeled McKaig in their accounts of his association with Kate Richards O'Hare during her 1917 sedition trial in Minot, N.Dak. McKaig lost the case.

778. <u>State ex rel. Amerland</u> v. <u>Hagan,</u> 175 <u>NW</u> 372 (1919).
Case challenging NPL-backed law establishing N.Dak. Workmen's Compensation Board (John N. Hagan was Commissioner of Agriculture and Labor). N.Dak. Supreme Court upheld the law's constitutionality.

779. <u>State ex rel. Burtness</u> v. <u>Hall,</u> 163 <u>NW</u> 1055 (1917).
Suit brought by an anti-NPL group over ballot designations for 1917 special congressional election (District 1) in N.Dak. The anti-NPL group had hoped to consolidate its forces behind Olger Burtness, but the N.Dak. Supreme Court ruled that all candidates who had filed had to remain on the ballot. John M. Baer, NPL candidate, won.

780. <u>State ex rel. Kositzky</u> v. <u>Waters,</u> 176 <u>NW</u> 913 (1920).
Suit brought to stop N.Dak. Auditor Carl Kositzky from conducting an audit of the Bank of N.Dak. N.Dak. Supreme Court ruled that examination of the bank was not part of the auditor's duties, thus blocking the audit.

781. <u>State ex rel. Laird</u> v. <u>Hall,</u> 186 <u>NW</u> 284 (1921).
Suit brought by NPL supporters challenging validity of petitions that forced 1921 recall election. N.Dak. Supreme Court ruled that petitions were valid.

782. <u>State ex rel. Langer</u> v. <u>Macdonald,</u> 175 <u>NW</u> 361 (1919) and 170 <u>NW</u> 873 (1919).

Suit brought by N.Dak. Attorney General William Langer against Superintendent of Public Instruction Neil C. Macdonald, who had refused to surrender his office to Minnie J. Nielson (after she won 1918 election), on the grounds that Nielson was unqualified. In first ruling, N.Dak. Supreme Court ordered Macdonald to turn over office to Nielson; in second ruling, N.Dak. District and State Supreme Courts ruled in Nielson's favor.

783. State ex rel. Langer v. Olson, 176 NW 528 (1920).
Case in which N.Dak. Supreme Court ruled that the laws passed at the 1919 special legislative session should take effect on July 1, 1920.

784. State ex rel. Langer v. Totten, 175 NW 563 (1919).
Suit brought before N.Dak. Supreme Court by Attorney General William Langer against State Board of Administration (George A. Totten, chairman) challenging board's authority to take power from State Superintendent of Schools, a post then held by Minnie J. Nielson. The court, over dissent of the chief justice, held that legislature and Board of Administration had acted within their powers.

785. State ex rel. Linde v. Hall, 159 NW 281 (1916).
Case brought before N.Dak. Supreme Court by a group of Bismarck businessmen who were challenging an attempt by a group from New Rockford, N.Dak., to move state capitol from Bismarck to New Rockford. Court ruled that a 1914 state law allowing for popular vote on an issue if "at least 25%" of legal voters signed petitions meant any amount over 25 percent that the legislature decided to set. This ruling meant that NPL would have a difficult time changing state constitution until it controlled both houses of state legislature. See also No. 787.

786. State ex rel. Lofthus v. Langer, 177 NW 408 (1919).
While State Bank Examiner O. E. Lofthus (an NPL supporter) was traveling outside of N.Dak., Deputy State Examiner P. E. Halldorson (under the direction of Attorney General William Langer, an NPL opponent) examined League-owned Scandinavian-American Bank in Fargo and found it insolvent. Halldorson was appointed receiver by a hastily convened State Banking Board meeting. When Lofthus returned to the state, he asked the N.Dak. Supreme Court to place him in charge of the bank. The court ruled in his favor.

787. State ex rel. Twichell v. Hall, 171 NW 213 (1918).
The case grew out of an IVA challenge to NPL's attempt to file petitions asking for N.Dak. voters to approve amendments to state constitution. N.Dak. Supreme Court reversed its own earlier ruling (see No. 785) and allowed vote on amendments to proceed.

788. State ex rel. W. E. Byerley and Theodore G. Nelson v. State Board of Canvassers, 172 NW 80 (1919).
Suit brought by IVA to challenge ruling by N.Dak. Board of Canvassers that all constitutional amendments on 1918 ballot had passed. N.Dak. Supreme Court affirmed board's ruling.

789. State v. A. C. Townley and Another, 168 NW 591 (1918).
Appeal to Minn. Supreme Court of convictions of Townley and Joseph Gilbert of discouraging enlistments by distributing the pamphlet "The Nonpartisan League; Its Origin, Purposes, and Method of Organization" in Martin Co., Minn. Court dismissed the convictions. See also Martin Co. District Court Criminal Case Files 271 and 272 and Minn. Supreme Court Case Files 20926 and 20927, all in Minn. State Archives, MHS.

790. State v. A. C. Townley et al., 182 NW 773 (1920).
Case heard by Minn. Supreme Court appealing convictions in Minn. District Court of Townley and Joseph Gilbert on charges of conspiring to discourage enlistments in Jackson Co., Minn. Convictions were upheld and their request for a new trial was denied (see Jackson Co. District Court Criminal Case Files 627, 628, and 629, and Supreme Court Case File 22086, all in Minn. State Archives, MHS). See also No. 792.

791. State v. Joseph Gilbert, 169 NW 790 (1918).
Appeal to Minn. Supreme Court of Gilbert's conviction in Minn. District Court for sedition in his speech at Kenyon, Minn. (see Goodhue Co. District Court Criminal Case File 894 and Supreme Court Case File 21089, both in Minn. State Archives, MHS). Minn. Supreme Court upheld conviction, which was later also upheld by U.S. Supreme Court (see No. 774).

792. State v. Joseph Gilbert, 171 NW 798 (1919); State v. A. C. Townley, 171 NW 930 (1919).
Minn. Supreme Court rulings that affirmed a lower court's decision to uphold indictments of Gilbert and Townley for conspiracy to discourage enlistments in Jackson Co., Minn. (see Minn. Supreme Court Case Files 21225 and 21226, Minn. State Archives, MHS). Case was sent back to Minn. District Court for trial (see No. 790).

793. Yaeger v. Frazier et al., 186 NW 381 (1921); State ex rel. Lemke v. District Court of Stutsman County, 186 NW 381 (1921).
   State District Court of Stutsman Co. (N.Dak.) had handed down a ruling that severely restricted powers of Bank of N.Dak., especially the selling of revenue bonds. N.Dak. Supreme Court reversed the lower court's ruling. See also No. 773.

Archival and Manuscript Collections

For more information on the entries in this section, see Introduction.

794. Adams, Elmer Ellsworth (1861-1950) and Family. Papers, 1860-1951. 30.5 ft. MHS.
Republican journalist, politician, and businessman from northwestern Minn. who served several terms as state senator and representative. Papers include correspondence and documents relating to struggle of Republican party against NPL, loyalty issue, socialists in NPL, and relationship of Woodrow Wilson's administration to NPL. Parts of collection are restricted.

795. Alexander, Moses (1853-1932). Governor's Records, 1914-18. 20 ft. Idaho State Historical Society.
Idaho governor. Collection includes correspondence regarding NPL.

796. Allen, Henry J. (1868-1950). Papers, 1919-23. 16 ft. Kansas State Historical Society.
Served as Kans. attorney general while NPL was organizing. Papers contain a few items relating to investigations by his office of complaints by and against NPL.

797. America First Association, St. Paul. Minn. Records, 1917-35. 32 items. MHS.
Information on allegations that A. C. Townley and NPL promoted disloyalty.

798. Anderson, William, and Theodore Blegen, comps. Minnesota Political Party Platforms, 1849-1942. 1.5 ft. MHS.
Copies of platforms and resolutions adopted at political conventions in Minn., including material on NPL and Working People's NPL.

799. Ault, Harry E. B. (1883-1961). Papers, 1899-1953. 5 ft. University of Washington Libraries.
Political activist and editor of Seattle Union Record (1918-29). Papers include several letters from Wash. NPL and National NPL.

800. Bacon, Jerry D[empster] (1865-1933). Article, undated. 1 item. MHS.
Carbon copy of 8-page typescript entitled "Resume of the Nonpartisan League, their Officers, Methods, Laws and the Effect on Economic Conditions in North Dakota, Furnished by Farmer Jerry Bacon, of Grand Forks, North Dakota, for Publication in states where requested."

801. _____. Papers, 1933 and 1938. 4 items. NDSU.
Businessman, NPL opponent, and owner and editor of Grand Forks Herald. Biographical sketch and newspaper clippings.

802. Baer, John M. (1886-1970). Papers, ca. 1916-20. 18 items and 22 original cartoon drawings. NDSU.
U.S. congressman from N.Dak. (1917-20) and NPL cartoonist. Correspondence, newspaper clippings, articles, and original cartoon drawings.

803. Bangert, Charles G. (1879-1969). Papers, 1900-66. 2.5 ft. NDSU.
Lawyer, state senator, and NPL member from Enderlin, N.Dak. Extensive correspondence and political and legal papers concerning NPL and one of its papers, Ransom County Farmers Press (Enderlin), which he edited, 1914-25. Some material concerns NPL after 1922.

804. Borah, William E. (1865-1940). Papers, 1905-40. 360 ft. Library of Congress.
NPL-endorsed candidate in Idaho's 1918 U.S. Senate race. Collection includes one folder of correspondence (approximately 80 pages) relating to NPL.

805. Brinton, Job Wells (1883-?). Papers, 1918-20. .5 ft. Nebraska State Historical Society.
Head of Publishers' National Service Bureau.

Active in NPL business endeavors and Consumers United Stores Co. Collection includes correspondence and printed material.

806. Bronson, Harrison A. (1874-1947). Papers, n.d. 5 items. UND.
Chief justice of N.Dak. Supreme Court. Notes for and manuscript of "The Story of the North Dakota State-Owned Mill and Terminal Elevator."

807. Burnquist, Joseph Alfred Arner (1879-1961). Papers, 1884-1961. 15 ft. MHS.
Minn. governor (1915-21). Material on activities of Minn. Commission of Public Safety, including several NPL pamphlets and information on surveillance of NPL meetings.

808. Central Labor Union of Minneapolis and Hennepin County. Records, 1912-62. Approximately 30 ft. MHS.
The Union succeeded Minneapolis Trades and Labor Assembly (1903-25). Two folders of correspondence, circular letters, and publications (1918-23) regarding Working People's NPL. Also included are cartoons by John M. Baer, 1921.

809. Christen, Richard. Papers, 1975. 1 item. SHSND.
Typescript of a Minot State College history paper entitled "Personal Reflections on the Nonpartisan League." Incorporates reminiscences of NPL by Elmer Cart, Jess Joiner, E. P. Christenson, Henry Steinberger, and Lawrence Erickson.

810. Citizens Alliance of Minneapolis. Records, 1903-48. 13.5 ft. MHS.
Business organization established to promote open shop. Papers contain one file on NPL.

811. Colorado State Federation of Labor. Records, 1896-1955. 50 ft. Western Historical Collections, University of Colorado at Boulder.
Resolutions, endorsements, and records of contributions concerning NPL are contained in proceedings of executive board's annual meeting, Jan. 5-6, 1920, and 26th annual convention, Aug. 8-11, 1921.

812. Committee of 48, Minnesota State Central Committee. Records, 1920-24. .5 ft. MHS.
Formed to organize a new national progressive party; later functioned as Liberal party. Correspondence regarding NPL and other topics relating to third parties, mainly between John A. H. Hopkins, chairman of the national executive committee, and Stanley I. Rypins, chairman of the Minn. committee.

813. Consumers United Stores Company. Records, 1921-28. .5 cu. ft. and 2 vols. SHSND.
A cooperative begun with NPL support. Ledgers, financial statements, receipts, and an agreement for various branch stores in N.Dak.

814. Coverdale, John W. (1883-?). Papers, 1922-40. 1 ft. University of Iowa Special Collections.
Secretary of Iowa Farm Bureau Federation (1919) and of American Farm Bureau Federation (1920-24). Manuscript in collection titled "The Early Days of the Farm Bureau in Iowa and the American Farm Bureau Federation" (ca. 1950), by Coverdale and James R. Howard, states Iowa Farm Bureau's view of NPL.

815. Cotton, Donald R. (1883-?). Papers, 1915-19, 1925. 1.25 ft. MHS.
St. Paul businessman prominent in WWI homefront activities. Collection deals with Cotton's civilian work during WWI and his work with Minn. Commission of Public Safety. Also include correspondence with Theodore Roosevelt regarding NPL's influence in N.Dak. and Minn.

816. Dahl, Math (1884-1976). Papers, 1939-56. 33 items. UND.
Early NPL supporter and N.Dak. commissioner of agriculture and labor (1939-64). Speeches, news releases, correspondence, and proceedings of North Central Assn. of Commissioners, Secretaries, and Directors of Agriculture.

817. Dale, Alfred Samuel (1896-1974). Papers, 1921-42. 10 cu. ft. SHSND.
N.Dak. state treasurer (1933-35); member of State Executive Committee of N.Dak. NPL, 1920s-1930s. Papers include records of State Executive Committee, minutes, ledgers, correspondence, platforms, membership records, and rosters of League delegates and precinct committeemen.

818. Davis, David W. (1873-1959). Governor's Records, 1918-22. 24 ft. Idaho State Historical Society.
Idaho governor. Collection includes correspondence regarding NPL.

819. Day, Walter E. (1880-1969). Typewritten transcript of 1967 interview. MHS.
Minn. state representative as member of NPL (1919-33) and Farmer-Labor and DFL (1937-57) parties. Discusses A. C. Townley, NPL, and Minn. politics.

820. Divet, A. Guy (1871-1950). Papers, 1920-48. .25 ft. SHSND.
N.Dak. state representative (1913-21) who opposed NPL. Collection includes some newspaper clippings, speeches, and correspondence regarding his political career and NPL.

821. Dixon, Joseph M. (1867-1934). Papers, 1883-1934. 59.5 ft. University of Montana.
U.S. senator (1907-13) and governor (1921-25) of Mont. Correspondence mentions NPL.

822. Doyle, Stephen J. (1871-1940). Papers, 1890-1960. .2 ft. NDSU.
U.S. marshal, N.Dak. legislator, and Democratic candidate for governor, 1918. Political clippings relating to gubernatorial campaign and correspondence with James A. Farley, Louis Howe, Burton K. Wheeler, James Gronna, G. A. Fraser, C. C. Webber, and others.

823. Duffy, Clyde (1890-1977). Papers, 1918-60. 8 ft. UND.
Attorney and N.Dak. state senator (1949-55). Political correspondence, IVA organization lists and material, and pamphlets concerning NPL.

824. Folwell, William Watts (1833-1929), and family. Papers, 1704-1945. 60 ft. MHS.
Prominent Minn. historian. Includes notes from research on a wide range of historical topics, including NPL.

825. Frazier, Lynn J. (1874-1947). Papers, 1919-20. .3 ft. UND.
NPL-endorsed N.Dak. governor (1917-21) and U.S. senator (1923-40). Papers include correspondence concerning N.Dak. coal strike of 1919.

826. Gilbert, Joseph (1886-1956). Papers, 1886-1954. .4 ft. MHS.
Socialist and NPL organizer. Gilbert and A. C. Townley were convicted of conspiracy to discourage enlistments in Jackson County, Minn. Collection includes a transcript of a 1954 interview in which Gilbert discusses his NPL activities and relations with A. C. Townley and other League leaders.

827. Hagan, John N. (1837-1952). Papers, 1919-38. .25 cu. ft. SHSND.
NPL member and N.Dak. commissioner of agriculture and labor, 1916-22, 1937-38. Autobiography, correspondence, party platforms, financial records, and speeches concerning NPL, politics, and agricultural issues. Correspondents include Lynn J. Frazier and Edwin F. Ladd.

828. Haight, Mrs. S. V. (1875-1963). Papers, 1913-17. .75 ft. Saskatchewan Archives Board.
NPL candidate, Thunder Creek constituency, in 1917 Sask. general election. Collection contains some information on this campaign.

829. Hall, E. George (1865-1938). Papers, 1885-1937. 5 ft. and 7 vols. MHS.
Minn. labor leader, active in several unions and labor organizations. Papers include information on NPL and Working Peoples Nonpartisan Political League.

830. Howard, Asher, comp. Materials Relating to the Nonpartisan League, 1905-20. 1 ft. MHS.
Letters and printed material relating to NPL and other reform organizations. Background material for pamphlet (see No. 509).

831. Johnson, Francis A. Typewritten transcript of 1973 interview. MHS.
Discusses life of Johnson's father, Magnus Johnson (see No. 832) and NPL leaders and campaigns.

832. Johnson, Magnus (1871-1936). Papers, 1923-41. 4.25 ft. MHS.
Early NPL worker, candidate for governor of Minn. (1922), U.S. senator (1923-25), and U.S. congressman (1933-35). Some correspondence with NPL officers and elected officials, although most of collection deals with Farmer-Labor party.

833. Johnson, Rudolph (1883-1971). Papers, 1888-1963. 8 ft. Western Historical Collection, University of Colorado at Boulder.
Secretary of Colo. Grange. Collection contains several items concerning Johnson's opposition to NPL.

834. Kanneberg, Adolph P. (1870-1949). Papers, 1920-22. 10 items. State Historical Society of Wisconsin, Archives.
One file of correspondence concerning NPL and Wis. Progressive Assn.

835. Kansas Attorney General. Records, 1871-1955. 72 ft. Kansas State Historical Society.
Investigation file number 94 includes documents concerning complaints by and against NPL.

836. Ladd, A. J. Papers, 1922. 3 pages. MHS.
Letter concerning Professor A. A. Bruce's printed statements about NPL sympathies of certain Univ. of Minn. professors.

837. Land Finance Company. Papers, 1909-64. 12 ft. UND.
Land company organized in Mexico by NPL leader William Lemke; William Langer was also involved. Correspondence, maps, stocks, canceled checks, board minutes, and advertising.

838. Langer, William (1886-1959). Papers, 1900-59. 837 ft. UND.
N.Dak. attorney general (1917-20) and governo (1933-34, 1937-38), U.S. senator (1941-59), and NPL leader. Collection includes speeches

and clippings, Langer's correspondence as attorney general, and his files as governor.

839. Lemke, William (1878-1950). Papers, 1905-50. 56 ft. UND.
NPL leader and congressman (1933-43, 1943-50) from N.Dak. Correspondence, speeches, court briefs, pamphlets, and photographs. Also includes correspondence (1916-20) of Republican National Headquarters for N.Dak. and of N.Dak. NPL.

840. Le Sueur, Arthur (1870-1950). Papers, ca. 1910-54. 6 ft. MHS.
Legal consultant, educational director (with his wife Marian), and early leader of NPL. Papers include correspondence, subject files, and legal records relating to NPL; extensive information on his work for and eventual break with NPL.

841. Liessman, Charles (1878-1963) and Viola Liessman (1869-1969). Papers, 1909-61. 10 cu. ft. SHSND.
Charles Liessman was an attorney, farmer, organizer for N.Dak. Farmers Union. Papers include material relating to NPL. Access is restricted due to condition of collection.

842. Lindbergh, Charles Augustus, Sr. (1858-1924) and family. Papers, 1808-1960. 7 ft. MHS.
Minn. congressman (1907-17) and NPL candidate for governor, 1918. Collection includes correspondence, political literature, newspaper clippings, and miscellaneous papers concerning campaigns and writings on U.S. involvement in WWI.

843. Losk, Walter (1920-). Papers, 1951. 1 item. UND.
Rough draft of thesis (see No. 964). Author was assistant professor of journalism at UND from 1947 to 1952.

844. Macdonald, Donald C. (1892-1969). Papers, 1896-1969. 15 ft. UND.
Includes correspondence, clippings, and scrapbooks relating to career of his brother, Neil C. Macdonald (see No. 845).

845. Macdonald, Neil C. (1876-1923). Papers, 1890-1923. Ca. 200 items. UND.
N.Dak state superintendent of public instruction during first NPL administration, 1917-19. Collection includes correspondence, speeches, photographs, clippings, memorabilia, and writings on his life and on education in N.Dak.

846. McKaig, Robert Ray (1880-1962). Papers, 1917-49. 6 ft. Idaho State Historical Society.
Important NPL organizer in several states, primarily N.Dak. and Idaho. Collection contains correspondence, subject files, and scrapbooks.

847. McNaughton, Violet Clara (1879-1968). Papers, 1900-64. 44 ft. Saskatchewan Archives Board.
President of Women's Grain Growers Assn. and women's editor, 1925-52, of Western Producer (Saskatoon). Papers include a small amount of correspondence concerning NPL.

848. Mahoney, William (1869-1952). Papers, 1890-1929. .75 ft. MHS.
Minn. Farmer-Labor politician. Letter to editor of St. Paul Daily News (1918?) concerning Charles A. Lindbergh, Sr., and 1918 Minn. election. Includes other material on Minn. Farmer-Labor party.

849. Manahan, James (1866-1932) and family. Papers, 1883-1935. 3.75 ft. MHS.
Lawyer, U.S. congressman (1913-15) from Minn., and NPL supporter. Included are handwritten draft and typed copy of autobiography (see No. 73) and "The Non-Partisan League," a 7-page typed manuscript by his daughter Kathryn Manahan.

850. Martin, William Melville (1876-1970). Papers, 1916-22. 19 ft. Saskatchewan Archives Board.
Premier of Sask. (1916-22). Small amount of NPL material.

851. Martinson, Henry R. (1883-1981). Papers, 1918-76. .5 ft. UND.
NPL organizer, editor of Iconoclast (Minot, N.Dak.), and N.Dak. deputy commissioner of agriculture and labor (1938-62). Papers contain some correspondence, newspaper clippings, prose and poetry, and miscellaneous papers for 1915-22.

852. Masonic Grand Lodge of North Dakota. Historical Collection, 1880s-1960s. 6 ft. NDSU.
Includes newspaper clippings, pamphlets, reprints of articles, and campaign literature relating to NPL. Also contains a 53-page typescript produced by the "Educational Committee, Woman's Non-Partisan League" entitled "The Legal Position of Women and Children in North Dakota, 1922," which reprints laws and asks questions to aid readers in studying them.

853. Meadors, John P. (1872-1954). Papers, ca. 1954. 5 items. NDSU.
Early NPL member. Letters, biographical material, and obituary.

854. Miklethun, John L. (1874-?) and family. Papers, 1909-54. 4 cu. ft. MHS.

N.Dak. state legislator and delegate to NPL conventions. Collection includes convention minutes, delegate lists, printed material, and correspondence relating to NPL.

855. Minnesota Commission of Public Safety. Records, 1917-21. 146.5 ft. MHS.
Minutes, correspondence, and subject files relating to NPL activities.

856. Mostad, Thorwald (1881-1973). Papers, 1916-59. .5 ft. SHSND.
NPL N.Dak. state senator (1916-17). Papers include NPL campaign material, membership cards, and a brief history of League.

857. National Farmers Union Archives. Records, 1902-79. 88 ft. Western Historical Collections, University of Colorado at Boulder.
Collection contains issues of Farmers Union (Salina, which became Kansas Union Farmer, April 27, 1922), weekly newspaper published by Kans. State Farmers Educational and Cooperative Union. Numerous editorials, 1918-21, written by Maurice McAuliffe (editor of paper and president of state union) concerning NPL.

858. Nebraska Constitutional Conventions. Records, 1866-1920. 3 cu. ft. Nebraska State Historical Society.
Correspondence of various groups, including NPL, that worked to change state constitution.

859. Nelson, Knute (1843-1923). Papers, undated and 1861-1924. 82 ft. and 18 items. MHS.
Served Minn. as congressman (1883-89), governor (1892-95), and U.S. senator (1895-1923). Papers include correspondence (1916-20) concerning NPL, IWW, A. C. Townley, Charles A. Lindbergh, Sr., Robert M. La Follette, and anti-German sentiment in Minn. during WWI.

860. Nelson, Theodore G. (1880-1961). Papers, 1906-60. .4 ft. NDSU.
Secretary of IVA, leader of American Society of Equity, realtor, and editor of Rural Independent (see No. 734). Collection contains material concerning American Society of Equity, 1907-10; IVA, 1917-22; Grain Growers Convention, 1907-23; and other subjects relating to grain marketing and inspection.

861. _____. Papers, 1904-24. 1 ft. and 1 roll microfilm. SHSND.
Material on IVA, including minutes, articles of incorporation, correspondence, reports, speeches, petitions, transcripts of investigations and debates, political ephemera, drafts of legislation, news releases, newspaper clippings, publications, and a subscription list of Rural Independent (see No. 734). Subjects covered in IVA records include 1921 recall campaign, William Langer's 1920 gubernatorial campaign, and investigation of Home Building Assn. and other state industries.

862. Nielson Family. Papers, 1875-1952. 5 cu. ft. SHSND.
Papers of Valley City, N.Dak., family, including reports, statements, and other material relating to Minnie J. Nielson and her 1918 campaign for N.Dak. state superintendent of public instruction. Nielson's opponent Neil C. Macdonald is also mentioned.

863. Nonpartisan League. Collection, 1917-64. .3 ft. NDSU.
Correspondence, bylaws, publications, and subject files.

864. _____. Records, 1913-28. 18 rolls microfilm and approximately 88,000 cards on 19 rolls microfilm. MHS.
The most extensive collection of NPL material. Records of national office, located in St. Paul, including correspondence and related files from papers of Henry G. Teigan (see No. 901), membership card files of Minn. NPL chapter, and records of Publishers National Service Bureau, organized in 1917 as Northwestern Service Bureau to acquire newspapers (primarily rural weeklies) and supply NPL news and opinion to affiliated papers. For published guide to collection, see No. 85.

865. _____. Records, 1918-20. 2 items. Nebraska State Historical Society.
Scrapbook, 1918-19, and list of Nebr. NPL committeemen by county.

866. _____. Newspaper clippings, ca. 1920. 2 pages. Kansas State Historical Society.
Opposition to NPL in Kans.

867. Nonpartisan League of North Dakota. Collection 1, ca. 1921-52. 1 ft. UND.
Pamphlets, platforms, minutes, constitution, lists of local precincts, and other material. (NPL collection 2 is dated 1934-72).

868. North Dakota Politics: Trial Transcripts, 1917-35. 1.5 ft. UND.
Includes some from NPL period, such as Scott v. Frazier (see No. 775).

869. North Dakota Socialist Party. Records, 1913-16. 1 vol. SHSND.
Local record book providing names of local members and receipts and disbursements. Many NPL organizers and leaders were drawn from N.Dak. Socialist party.

Nonpartisan League Headquarters, Bismarck, during 1917 N.Dak. legislative session

870. ____, District Two Organizing Department. Records, 1914. 1 vol. SHSND.
Account book listing members and organizers' expenses. Prominent NPL leaders in Organizing Department included A. C. Townley and A. E. Bowen. When Socialist party closed department, many organizers began working for NPL.

871. North Dakota State Archives, State Auditor. Records, 1881-1966. 20 cu. ft. and 27 vols. SHSND.
Records for 1915-22 include audit reports on Bank of N.Dak. and State Mill and Elevator Assn. and records of special examination of Home Building Assn.

872. ____, Bank of North Dakota. Records, 1919-84. 100 cu. ft., 17 vols., and 2 rolls of microfilm. SHSND.
Records for 1915-22 include minutes from Industrial Commission and bank's General Finance and Farm Loan Department committees; general ledgers; records relating to sale of bonds, including ledgers and sample advertisements; case files regarding sale of foreclosed property; loan, deposit, and discount schedule; reports from bank's Farm Loan, Collection, and Land departments; files from the Credit Department; and a card index to closed farm loan files.

873. ____, Council of Defense. Records, 1917-19. 2 cu. ft. SHSND.
Council was established by NPL administration to coordinate state's war preparations. Collection includes minutes of executive committee meetings, reports from film department, and financial records.

874. ____, Department of Immigration. Records, 1919-20. 1 vol. SHSND.
Office of Commissioner of Immigration was created by NPL administration in 1919. Publicity scrapbook of newspaper clippings promoting N.Dak. agriculture.

875. ____, Department of Public Instruction. Records, 1877-1981. 250 cu. ft. and 200 vols. SHSND.
Records for 1915-22 include subject files, reports of county superintendents, minutes of Board of Education meetings, and records relating to teacher certification. Superintendents during this period were Neil C. Macdonald (1916-19) and Minnie J. Nielson (1919-27).

876. ____, Director of Institutions. Records, 1883-1977. 75 cu. ft., 22 vols., and 5 rolls of microfilm. SHSND.
Records for 1915-22 include minutes of meetings of the Boards of Administration and Control. The NPL-dominated legislature abolished Board of Control in 1919 and gave its duties and a wide range of other powers to Board of Administration.

877. ____, Governor. Records, 1884-1984. 1000 cu. ft. and 26 vols. SHSND.
Records for 1915-22 comprise small part of this collection and include incoming letters to Lynn J. Frazier and reports of state agencies and institutions.

878. ____, Industrial Commission. Records, 1923-69. 2 folders. SHSND.
Includes minutes of Commission meetings, 1923-28.

879. ____, Mill and Elevator Association. Records, 1918-79. 45 cu. ft. and 4 vols. SHSND.
A small portion of the collection, including

cash grain records and audit reports, pertains to 1915-22 period.

880. ___, Public Service Commission. Records, 1905-80. 650 cu. ft. and 33 vols. SHSND.
NPL-dominated legislature gave Commission broad regulatory powers in 1919. Records for 1915-22 (a very small portion of the collection) include minutes and case files.

881. ___, Secretary of State. Records, 1885-1981. 300 cu. ft., 100 vols., and 100 rolls of microfilm. SHSND.
Records for 1915-22 constitute a small portion of the collection and include schedules for 1915 state census, recall petitions for 1921 recall election, candidate and initiative petitions, abstracts of election results, and records relating to 1921 investigation of Bank of N.Dak.

882. ___, State Experimental Creamery. Records, 1919-22. 1.5 cu. ft. and 3 vols. SHSND.
State Creamery, started by NPL administration to promote N.Dak.'s dairy industry, operated from June 1, 1920, to Dec. 31, 1921. Collection includes correspondence, payroll records, bank statements, reports, and purchase ledgers (which list names of farmers who sold produce to the Creamery).

883. ___, Supreme Court. Records, 1980-55. 160 cu. ft. SHSND.
Records for 1915-22 include correspondence and case files on NPL lawsuits.

884. North Dakota State Mill and Elevator. Records, ca. 1920-40. 16 items. NDSU.
Pamphlets, newspaper clippings, and NDSU undergraduate papers: Julian Bjornsin, "State Mill and Elevator" (n.d.), and Charles Nyberg, "The Origin of the State Mill and Elevator" (1970).

885. O'Hare, Kate Richards (1877-1948). Papers, 1917 and 1965. .3 ft. UND.
Copy of transcript of O'Hare's 1917 sedition trial in Bismarck along with other documents relating to trial. Also includes unpublished paper "Red Kate: A Case of Midwest Socialism" (n.d.) by James J. Wood. Her connection with the NPL became a campaign issue.

886. Olsness, S. A. (1866-1954). Papers, 1883-1954. 3 ft. NDSU.
Norwegian immigrant and N.Dak. commissioner of insurance. Diaries, newspaper clippings, poetry, and speeches; also correspondence relating to NPL, Socialist party, and other topics.

887. Peterson, Hjalmar Otto (1879-1957). Papers, 1930-54. 1 ft. MHS.
NPL worker in Washington County, Minn., and publisher of Washington County Post (Stillwater), 1920-26. Papers include undated list of NPL members and statement of NPL program. Much of collection deals with Farmer-Labor party after 1922.

888. Pierce, Walter M. Papers, 1888-1969. 88 cu. ft. University of Oregon Library.
State senator (1917-21), governor (1923-27), and U.S. congressman (1933-43). Active in Populist and Democratic politics. Collection includes some NPL material. Not seen by compilers.

889. Pope, James Pinckney (1884-1966). Papers, 1910-31. 15 ft. Idaho State Historical Society.
Lawyer, Democratic politician, and U.S. senator (1933-39) from Idaho. Anti-NPL references in correspondence, case files, and miscellaneous personal material.

890. Preus, Jacob Aall Otteson (1883-1961). Interview, 1960. 114 p. MHS.
Minn. governor (1921-25). Transcript of interview that includes information on Minn. gubernatorial campaigns of J. A. A. Burnquist (1918) and Preus (1920), campaign against NPL by Minn. Commission of Public Safety, and anti-German sentiment in Minn. during WWI. NPL opposed both Preus and Burnquist in their gubernatorial campaigns.

891. ___ and family. Papers, 1853-1946. 15.75 ft. and 5 vols. MHS.
Papers include material on Minn. gubernatorial campaigns of J. A. A. Burnquist (1918) and Preus (1920) and correspondence with N. Dak. IVA leaders. Preus made speeches in N.Dak. for IVA.

892. Proudfoot, Lorne (1880-1977). Papers, 1916-59. .5 ft. Glenbow Archives, Calgary, Alberta.
Alba. politician and member of Farmers Union of Alba. and United Farmers of Alba. Collection includes program of Nonpartisan Political League and two newspaper clippings on NPL.

893. Quigley, Walter Eli. "Out Where the West Begins." Unpublished manuscript, 1932. 106 p. MHS.
Reminiscences of NPL development through 1932 convention of Farmer-Labor party in Minn.

894. Research Papers in North Dakota History, 1950-65. 1.5 ft. UND.
Collection of undergraduate papers with approximately 20 on topics related to NPL, 1915-22, including works on Magnus Johnson, Edwin F. Ladd, Clyde Duffy, William Langer, William Lemke, and Lynn J. Frazier; NPL sup-

port for woman suffrage in 1917 and 1919 N.Dak. legislative session; sedition trial of Kate O'Hare; 1921 recall election; N.Dak. disloyalty trials; German-Russian participation in NPL; and 1917 N.Dak. legislative session. Also includes papers by Hiram Drache ("North Dakota and the Farm Bloc, 1921-1923," 1958) and by Charles Haug ("Pie in the Sky: A History of the IWW in North Dakota," 1968) on N.Dak. activities of the IWW, its affiliate the Agricultural Workers Industrial Union, and the NPL.

895. Robinson, James E. (?-1933). Papers, 1916-21. .25 ft. UND.
Associate justice of N.Dak. Supreme Court (1917-22). Papers consist of letters that were published in Bismarck Tribune as "The Saturday Evening Letter" column. They dealt with court proceedings and contained Robinson's opinions on N.Dak. politics and justice during much of NPL period.

896. Roylance, William. Papers, 1921. 23 items. SHSND.
Director of statistics and publicity, Bank of N.Dak. Papers consist of reports concerning organization of state agencies by NPL.

897. Saskatchewan Grain Growers Association. Records, 1902-26. 3 ft. Saskatchewan Archives Board.
Minutes contain references to NPL.

898. Seattle Port Commission. Records, 1911-60. 6 ft. University of Washington Libraries.
Contains three letters (1916-19) from NPL to Robert Bridges, president of the Port Commission, including invitation to speak to 1917 Producers and Consumers Convention in St. Paul.

899. Sorenson, Christian Abraham (1890-1959). Papers, 1907-59. 60 ft. Nebraska State Historical Society.
Lawyer, Nebr. state attorney general (1929-33), and early NPL supporter. Collection includes correspondence for 1917-20, the period of NPL activity in Nebr.

900. Strout, Irwin Charles (1893-1954). Papers, 1922-39. 12.5 ft. MHS.
Clipping in collection identifies Strout as a former NPL organizer in N.Dak.; later a Farmer-Labor organizer in Minn. Papers are primarily concerned with Farmer-Labor party of 1922 and later.

901. Teigan, Henry George (1881-1941). Papers, 1916-41. 51 ft. MHS.
NPL secretary (1916-23); also active in N.Dak. Socialist party and Minn. Farmer-Labor party. Papers include correspondence (1916-23) from files of National NPL office. These files were filmed as part of MHS microfilm edition of National Nonpartisan League Papers (see No. 864).

902. Thomason, Otto Monroe (1874-1960) and family. Papers, 1916-62. 15 items. MHS.
NPL leader (known as O. M. or Oliver Thomason) and editor of Nonpartisan Leader. Collection includes manuscript by Thomason describing his early activities in organizing NPL in N.Dak. and his association with A. C. Townley and A. E. Bowen. Papers also include poem by Thomason for NPL.

903. Thompson, Martin O. (1882-1948). Papers, 1906-48. 3 ft. NDSU.
Ransom County, N.Dak., judge (1923-48) and NPL member. Collection includes correspondence relating to NPL with William Langer, Gerald P. Nye, Henry Helgeson, John M. Baer, Asle F. Gronna, Robert M. La Follette, and others.

904. Townley, Arthur C. (1880-1959). Papers, 1917-59. .3 ft. UND.
Founder of NPL. Copies of Townley's speeches and of newspaper and journal articles concerning Townley and NPL. Material collected by Alice Poehls for her master's thesis (see No. 983).

905. _____. Papers, 1919-21. 1 ft. UND.
Photocopies of briefs, transcripts, and other material from 1919 trial in Jackson, Minn., on charges of conspiracy to discourage enlistments. Also includes clippings and articles relating to Townley, NPL, and Townley's debates with William Langer in 1921.

906. _____. Speech, 1917. 39 pages. State Historical Society of Wisconsin, Library.
Delivered to Producers and Consumers Convention (here called Farmers and Workers Conference) at St. Paul, Sept. 18-20, 1917.

907. Washington State Federation of Labor. Records, 1906-57. 50 ft. University of Washington Libraries.
Includes five letters (1922) from National NPL.

908. Wefald, Knud (1869-1936). Papers, 1817-1936. 18.5 ft. MHS.
Minn. state representative (1912-16) and congressman (1916-22). Papers include material relating to Wefald's bid for NPL endorsement of his 1922 congressional campaign; Henrik Shipstead's 1922 campaign for U.S. Senate (on Farmer-Labor ticket); decline of NPL and rise of Minn. Farmer-Labor party; Joseph Gilbert's conviction for sedition for his speech at Kenyon in Goodhue Co.; and NPL leaders William Lemke, Lynn J. Frazier, and A. C. Townley.

909. Wehrle, Bishop Vincent (1885-1941) and the NPL, 1916-21. 1 roll microfilm. SHSND.
Newspaper and magazine clippings, pamphlets, and other items pertaining to attacks on NPL by the bishop of Roman Catholic Diocese of Bismarck. Originals in Assumption Abbey Archives, Richardton, N.Dak.

910. Wisconsin Nonpartisan League. Records, 1920-24. .5 ft. State Historical Society of Wisconsin, Archives.
Primarily correspondence devoted to organizational work of Wis. chapter of NPL.

911. Wisconsin State Historical Society Library. Papers, 1907-49. 39 items. UND.
Photocopies of library's collection of correspondence and speeches of major N.Dak. political figures, including William Lemke, A. C. Townley, R. A. Nestos, Edwin F. Ladd, Lynn J. Frazier, and other NPL leaders.

912. Wold, Eva Emerson (1880-1961). Typewritten manuscript, 1953. 43 pages. MHS.
"A Short Biography of the Honorable Carl A. Wold and Autobiography of Mrs. Eva Emerson Wold," written by the superintendent of schools in Douglas County, Minn. (1919-27). The Wolds were active in NPL and other political movements; Carl was editor of Park Region Echo (Alexandria, Minn.).

913. Wooster, Charles (1843-1922). Papers, 1861-1920. 9.5 cu. ft. Nebraska State Historical Society.
Newspaper editor, populist, and NPL supporter. Collection contains correspondence concerning NPL and Nebr. Council of Defense.

914. Zimmerman, Phil (1879-1965). Papers, 1900-65. 2 rolls microfilm. Kansas State Historical Society.
Prominent Kans. Republican and state hotel commissioner (1925-29). Correspondence and newspaper clippings concerning Zimmerman's work against NPL and IWW in Kans.

Unpublished Papers

915. Anderson, F. W. "Some Political Aspects of the Grain Growers' Movement (1915-1935) with Particular Reference to Saskatchewan." Master's thesis, University of Saskatchewan (Saskatoon), 1949. 203 p.
   Succinct history of NPL in Canada (Sask., Alba., and Man.), including an analysis of reasons for NPL's rise and discussion of its relationship with existing Canadian political groups, Canadian platform, and influence on Canadian politics of 1920s and 1930s. Puts NPL's Canadian history into larger political and social context of agrarian reform.

916. Anderson, Raymond V. "Adoption and Operation of Initiative and Referendum in North Dakota." Ph.D. diss., University of Minnesota, 1962. 607 p.
   Includes analysis of NPL's use of and legislation pertaining to initiative and referendum. Gives details on mechanics and political tactics that surrounded drives. Deals mostly with post-1922 period.

917. Baglien, David B. "The McKenzie Era, A Political History of North Dakota from 1880-1920." Master's thesis, NDSU, 1951. 159 p.
   Political biography of Alexander McKenzie. Mainly covers N.Dak. politics before NPL, but includes discussion of 1916 election and interesting analysis of relationship between A. C. Townley and McKenzie.

918. Bahmer, Robert Henry. "The Economic and Political Background of the Nonpartisan League." Ph.D. diss., University of Minnesota, 1941. 518 p.
   Thorough treatment of Upper Midwest farm economy, 1870-1920. Includes discussion of Populism and American Society of Equity.

919. Bakken, Larry A. "The Bank of North Dakota, 1922-1941." Master's thesis, NDSU, 1969. 91 p.
   Economic conditions leading to formation of NPL and establishment of Bank of N.Dak. Based in part on interviews with former bank employees.

920. Bandza, Alfred. "An Analysis of the Electoral Response to the Initiative and Referendum in North Dakota, 1918-1960." Master's thesis, UND, 1963. 207 p.

921. Bates, James L. "Senator Walsh of Montana, 1918-1924: Liberal under Pressure." Ph.D. diss., University of North Carolina (Chapel Hill), 1952. 247 p.
   NPL in 1920 Mont. campaign. Thomas J. Walsh supported NPL's candidate for governor, Burton K. Wheeler.

922. Beyer, Carlyle. "The People's Lawyer: A Study of the Life of James Manahan and His Part in the Progressive Movement of the Middle West." Undergraduate paper, Hamline University, 1937. MHS. 39 p.
   Biography of League attorney with brief discussion of NPL.

923. Blackorby, Edward C. "Political Strife in North Dakota from 1920 to 1932." Master's thesis, UND, 1938. 116 p.
   Includes a short history of NPL, 1916-20; a longer analysis of events leading to recall election of 1921; and some statistical analyses of N.Dak. elections, 1920-30.

924. _____. "Prairie Rebel: The Public Career of William Lemke." Ph.D. diss., UND, 1958. 339 p.
   Emphasizes Lemke's role in NPL, 1915-22, and in Union party, 1936. Describes inner workings of NPL based on interviews of politicians of 1915-22 period. Basis for later book (see No. 5).

925. Bloom, Howard E. "Violence against the Nonpartisan League in Minnesota during the World War." Undergraduate paper, Macalester College, [1930?]. 58 p. MHS.

Relates problems NPL faced because of loyalty issue.

926. Brackett, Edmund C. "Anti-Conservatism in North Dakota from 1920-1932." Master's thesis, UND, 1972. 129 p.
Examination of political protest, including analysis of 1920 state and national elections in N.Dak. Briefly discusses NPL before 1920.

927. Brake, Robert J. "A Rhetorical Criticism of Selected World War One Speeches of Arthur C. Townley." Master's thesis, State University of South Dakota, 1961. 132 p.
History of NPL with emphasis on Townley's role. Includes texts and analyses of some Townley speeches.

928. Brennan, James William. "A Political History of Saskatchewan, 1905-1929." Ph.D. diss., University of Alberta, 1976. 827 p.
A sound work that places NPL in context of Sask. political history, exploring economic and ethnocultural influences on political events. Attributes NPL's lack of success to divisions within farmers' movement.

929. Brewer, Philip Edwin. "The Nonpartisan League in North Dakota." Master's thesis, University of Wisconsin, 1933. 85 p.
Straightforward history of NPL including discussion of economic background and reasons for decline.

930. Brudvig, Glenn Lowell. "Public Libraries in North Dakota, the Formative Years, 1880-1920." Master's thesis, University of Minnesota, 1962. 129 p.
Includes brief discussion of N.Dak. Public Library Commission controversy of 1919.

931. Cooke, Gilbert William. "The North Dakota Industrial Program." Ph.D. diss., University of Wisconsin, 1936. 132 p.
Comprehensive history of state-owned industries program, 1919-34. Discusses operation and history of Hail Insurance Commission, Home Building Assn., Mill and Elevator Assn., and Bank of N.Dak. programs; gives numerous statistics on production and operation of industries.

932. Cravens, Hamilton. "A History of Washington Farmer-Labor Party, 1918-1924." Master's thesis, University of Washington, 1962. 270 p.
Populist and Progressive background of Farmer-Labor party. NPL is briefly mentioned in connection with anti-war activity in Wash. Good discussion of interaction among NPL, Socialist party, organized labor, and other farm groups.

933. Crews, Cecil R. "Farmer-Labor Parties in the U.S., 1918-1925." Master's thesis, University of Wisconsin, 1935. 160 p.
Not seen by compilers.

934. Deforth, Shirley Jean. "The Montana Press and Governor Joseph M. Dixon, 1920-1922." Master's thesis, Montana State University (Missoula), 1959. 229 p.
Deals with 1920 campaign in Mont., in which NPL endorsed Burton K. Wheeler for governor. Includes an analysis of press reaction.

935. Dovre, Paul John. "A Study of Nonpartisan League Persuasion, 1915-1920." Ph.D. diss., Northwestern University, 1963. 329 p.
A study of rhetorical style of NPL leaders and organizers. Discusses NPL's audience,

NPL meeting in Carver Co., Minn., 1918

organizing methods, and program; analyzes selected League speeches; and offers reasons for NPL's decline.

936. Ellsworth, Scott A. "Origins of the Nonpartisan League." Ph.D. diss., Duke University, 1982. 313 p.
Analysis of influence on NPL of earlier agrarian groups, including Populists, American Society of Equity, and N.Dak. Socialist party. Discusses NPL history through 1916 N.Dak. elections. Appendix examines controversy surrounding birth of NPL.

937. Enerson, Rozanne L. "The Bank of North Dakota: Implications for State-Ownership in a Modern Capitalist Economy." Ph.D. diss., University of Oregon, 1981. 392 p.
Thorough discussion of origins and operation of state bank from its beginnings to late 1970s. Analyzes political and economic history of bank within theoretical context of economic democracy movement and left-populist tradition. Gives an account of NPL history as it relates to bank, and includes appendices of statistics relating to bank's farm loans.

938. Fligelman, Henrietta. "Nonpartisan League in North Dakota." Master's thesis, Columbia University, 1926.
Not seen by compilers.

939. Fossum, Paul R. "The Agrarian Movement in North Dakota." Ph.D. diss., Johns Hopkins University, 1924. 175 p.
Includes chapter on NPL, concentrating on legislative program, especially state-owned industries.

940. Fritz, Nancy R. "The Montana Council of Defense." Master's thesis, University of Montana, 1966. 150 p.
Contains information on suppression of NPL during WWI, including arrest of NPL organizer A. J. (Mickey) McGlynn.

941. Goldberg, Ray. "The Nonpartisan League in North Dakota: A Case Study of Political Action in America." Undergraduate paper, Harvard University, 1948. 95 p. UND, NDSU.
History of NPL, 1915-48, based in part on 51 interviews conducted in 1947. Includes discussion of NPL political tactics.

942. Gracie, Bruce Alan. "The Agarian Response in Prairie Canada to Industrialization and Urbanization: 1900-1935." Ph.D. diss., McMaster University, 1976. 311 p.
Argues (p. 172-78) that example set by NPL strengthened Canadian grain growers' associations by increasing their group awareness, training their leaders, and encouraging political action; maintains that League's political tactics were not effective within Canada's parliamentary system.

943. Hagen, E. Bruce. "The North Dakota State Mill and Elevator Association: History, Organization, Administration, and Operation." Master's thesis, UND, 1955. 388 p.
Comprehensive analysis of economic background (ca. 1880s-1917) and history of mill and elevator (1918-55). Administrative history of Bank of N.Dak. and an account of the politics surrounding its establishment.

944. Harris, Lyle E. "Dr. E. B. Craighead's New Northwest: 1915-1920." Master's thesis, University of Montana, 1967. 141 p.
Study of newspaper published in Missoula, Mont., and its coverage of NPL and Mont. Council of Defense. Includes details of NPL activities in Mont.

945. Hart, John Edward. "William Irvine and Radical Politics in Canada." Ph.D. diss., University of Guelph, 1972. 337 p.
Biography of the "chief organizer and propagandist for the League" in Canada, with analysis of his actions. Argues that NPL offered a vehicle for political involvement to Irvine, who (as an urban minister and editor) was ineligible to join United Farmers of Alba. Extensive discussion of relations between United Farmers and NPL, showing that League's activism forced United Farmers to become more political. Mentions attacks on NPL in Canada during WWI.

946. Hennessey, Leo D. "History of the Valley City State College, 1890-1970." Master's thesis, UND, 1971. 236 p.
Concentrates on 1946-70 period, but includes account of NPL's attempt in 1918 to dismiss George A. McFarland from his post as president of Valley City State College. Briefly discusses two NPL legislative programs--establishment of Board of Administration, to consolidate administration of state schools, and expansion of Valley City from two-year normal school to four-year teachers' college.

947. Hofland, Carl J. "The Nonpartisan League in South Dakota." Master's thesis, University of South Dakota, 1940. 86 p.
History of NPL in S.Dak., with analysis of its decline and inability to capture state's government.

948. Hornbacher, Perry Joel. "The Forgotten Heritage: The North Dakota Socialist Party." Master's thesis, NDSU, 1982. 155 p.
Covers N.Dak. Socialist party to 1916-17, relying heavily on the socialist newspaper, Iconoclast (Minot, N.Dak.), and on the words of Henry Martinson. Attributes decline of party in part to NPL strengh; discusses con-

troversy in Organizing Department (headed by A. C. Townley) brought about by its emphasis on farmers over laborers and its increasing domination of the party. Speculates that Townley's inability to gain official recognition for his department led to birth of NPL.

949. Hudson, Edwin E. "A Comparison of the Farmers' Alliance and the Nonpartisan League in Minnesota." Undergraduate paper, University of Minnesota, 1924. 36 p. MHS.
    Brief discussion of both groups' origins, methods of organization, and activities.

950. Jenson, Carol Elizabeth. "Agrarian Pioneer in Civil Liberties: The Nonpartisan League in Minnesota During World War I." Ph.D. diss., University of Minnesota, 1968. 361 p.
    Thorough examination of NPL's legal struggle for free speech with focus on Minn. 1918 campaign. Deals with Minn. Commission of Public Safety (as well as similar local committees) and legislation and legal cases that affected NPL.

951. Johansen, Sigurd A. "Trends in Farmers' Movements in Minnesota and Adjacent States." Master's thesis, University of Minnesota, 1934. 127 p.
    Agrarian politics in the Upper Midwest, ca. 1860-1935. Briefly compares NPL to other agrarian political organizations from Grange to Farm Holiday Movement. Analyzes economic statistics, membership figures, voting returns, and contents of farm publications.

952. Johnson, Alice Jane. "The Public Career of J. F. T. O'Connor." Master's thesis, UND, 1956. 132 p.
    Includes account of O'Connor's relationship with NPL.

953. Johnson, Gordon W. "William Langer's Resurgence to Political Power in 1932." Master's thesis, UND, 1970. 90 p.
    Primarily concerned with Langer's activities, 1928-32, but discusses his early life and his support of and eventual break with NPL, ca. 1915-22.

954. Johnson, Kenneth C. "The Bank of North Dakota: An Analysis of its Value." Master's thesis, UND, 1957. 97 p.
    Origins of NPL and state bank. Primarily an analysis of reasons for bank's founding and evolution of its functions to 1956.

955. Kane, Ralph James. "Edwin Fremont Ladd, North Dakota's Pure-Food Crusader." Master's thesis, UND, 1960. 234 p.
    Discusses Ladd's career to ca. 1909.

956. Kingsley, Robert. "Recent Variations from the Two-Party System as Evidenced by the Nonpartisan League and the Agricultural Bloc." Master's thesis, University of Minnesota, 1923. 47 p.
    Traces evolution of NPL's political tactics in Minn. and N.Dak. Includes discussion of 1917, 1919, and 1921 legislative sessions and details of campaign tactics.

957. Kloske, Ralph L. "Nonpartisan Leaguers in Minnesota: A Consideration of Organizers, Members, and Voters." Master's thesis, University of Wisconsin (Madison), 1976. 247 p.
    Analyzes economic and ethnic backgrounds of NPL members, careers of NPL organizers, and NPL elections in Minn. Uses NPL membership files (see No. 864) and other statistical sources.

958. Koessler, Mary Lou Collins. "The 1920 Gubernatorial Election in Montana." Master's thesis, University of Montana, 1971. 169 p.
    Study of election in which Burton K. Wheeler ran with NPL endorsement against Joseph M. Dixon.

959. Lamb, Charles R. "Up from the Wheatfields: The Nonpartisan League's Expansion into Minnesota." Unpublished paper, 1978. 86 p. MHS.
    Analysis of ethnic and economic background of Minn. NPL, based on tax records, a 1918 farm census, and NPL membership files (see No. 864). Similar to No. 238.

960. Larsen, Lawrence Harold. "William Langer, Senator from North Dakota." Master's thesis, University of Wisconsin, 1955. 111 p.
    Short account of Langer's tenure as Morton Co. (N.Dak.) state's attorney and N.Dak. attorney general and his break with NPL in 1919.

961. Larson, Bruce Llewellyn. "Charles A. Lindbergh, Senior, of Minnesota: A Political Biography." Ph.D. diss., University of Kansas, 1971. 431 p.
    Basis for book (see No. 59).

962. Larson, Henrietta M. "The Social Significance of the Nonpartisan League." Master's thesis, Columbia University, 1920. 48 p.
    NPL's effect on various social issues. Claims that NPL made farmers more receptive to new ideas, but farmers needed to use techniques of scientific farming to improve their economic status.

963. Laycock, David H. "The Political Thought of William Irvine." Master's thesis, University of Toronto, 1977.
    Not seen by compilers.

964. Losk, Walter S. "The Nonpartisan League, the Farmer's Union, and the Press of North Dakota." Master's thesis, University of Minnesota, 1951. 119 p.
    History of NPL, ca. 1915-22, and Farmer's Union, ca. 1912-50. Contrasts methods of organizing and use of the press.

965. McDonald, Annabelle. "A History of the Nonpartisan League in Colorado." Master's thesis, Colorado State Teachers College, 1930. 173 p.
    History of NPL in Colo., ca. 1917-25. Fairly detailed narrative, focusing on rise of NPL, 1920 elections, and NPL's relationship to Colo. farm and labor groups. Uses newspaper articles, interviews, and manuscript material; includes seven appendices of reports, resolutions, and other manuscript material relating to NPL.

966. Mader, Joseph H. "The Political Influence of the Nonpartisan League on the Press of North Dakota." Master's thesis, University of Minnesota, 1937. 170 p.
    Detailed account of NPL's newspaper laws in N.Dak. and operation of Northwestern Service Bureau (later Publishers National Service Bureau). Includes sample copies of articles of incorporation for Bureau newspapers. See also No. 267.

967. Melby, Alfred C. "A Chemist in the Senate: Edwin Fremont Ladd, 1921-1925." Master's thesis, UND, 1967. 124 p.
    Contains account of NPL's endorsement of Ladd for U.S. Senate in 1920 and ensuing campaign.

968. Merritt, Howard A. "The Farmer-Labor Party of Minnesota." Master's thesis, University of Wisconsin, 1937. 93 p.
    Summarizes NPL activities in Minn. and N.Dak. as background to development of Farmer-Labor party in Minn., with details of the transition.

969. Miller, Clark. "Unlucky Lindy: The NPL and the Origins of the Farmer-Labor Coalition in Minnesota." Paper presented at 3rd Annual Meeting of Social Science History Association, Columbus, Ohio, Nov. 3-5, 1978. 71 p. MHS.
    Quantitative study of NPL and Farmer-Labor elections, concentrating on 1918 Minn. elections. Argues that German-American voters remained in Democratic party rather than supporting Charles A. Lindbergh, Sr. (p. 51-53).

970. Morlan, Robert L. "The Political History of the Nonpartisan League." Ph.D. diss., University of Minnesota, 1950. 2 vols., 861 p.
    Possibly the most complete narrative history of NPL in 1915-22 period. Similar to, but longer than, author's book (see No. 78).

971. Morrison, Paul W. "The Position of Senators from North Dakota on Isolation, 1889-1920." Ph.D. diss., University of Colorado, 1954. 384 p.
    Brief section on NPL concentrates on 1916 elections. Discusses political strife of NPL years as background to activities of U.S. Senators Asle J. Gronna and Porter McCumber.

972. Naftalin, Arthur. "A History of the Farmer-Labor Party in Minnesota." Ph.D. diss., University of Minnesota, 1948. 382 p.
    Detailed analysis of NPL in Minn., ca. 1918-23, as prelude to Farmer-Labor party.

973. Nelson, Harold L. "A History of the Minnesota Daily Star." Master's thesis, University of Minnesota, 1950. 186 p.
    Includes brief discussion of NPL's relationship with organized labor and efforts to establish newspapers in N.Dak. and Minn. Minnesota Daily Star was jointly operated by NPL and organized labor.

974. Nodtvedt, Magnus. "The Nonpartisan League and the Cities of North Dakota." Master's thesis, Columbia University, 1920. 48 p.
    Addresses conflict between urban and agricultural interests; gives NPL legislative history.

975. Nord, David P. "Socialism in One City: A Political Study of Minneapolis in the Progressive Era." Master's thesis, University of Minnesota, 1972. 221 p.
    Socialist activity in Minneapolis, ca. 1900-20s, emphasizing career of Socialist Mayor Thomas Van Lear (1917-18). Includes analysis of labor coalition (which included Working People's Nonpartisan Political League) that was a major force in Minneapolis politics during this period.

976. Olson, Richard O. "The Public Career of Peter Norbeck, 1908-1921." Master's thesis, University of South Dakota, 1941. 78 p.
    Addresses relationship of S.Dak. Republican Governor (1917-21) and U.S. Senator (1920-36) Norbeck to NPL, especially during 1918 campaign.

977. Olson, Ronald V. "William Langer's Rise to Political Prominence in North Dakota." Master's thesis, UND, 1967. 96 p.
    Biography of Langer through his election as N.Dak. attorney general in 1916.

978. Omdahl, Lloyd B. "The Switch of the Nonpartisan League to the Democratic Column." Master's thesis, UND, 1962. 314 p.
    First chapter is an account of NPL, 1915-22. Primarily a discussion of merger of NPL with Democratic party, 1947-ca. 1960.

979. Panting, G. E. "A Study of United Farmers of Manitoba to 1928." Master's thesis, University of Manitoba, 1954. 281 p.
   Very brief mention of NPL and its relationship to established Canadian political parties and farm groups.

980. Phillips, Elmo Bryant. "The Non-Partisan League in Nebraska." Master's thesis, University of Nebraska, 1951. 127 p.
   Excellent account of NPL activities of State Council of Defense, Business Men's Protective Assn. (Omaha), and other anti-NPL organizations; League's involvement in 1919 constitutional convention and 1920 campaign; Oliver S. Evans's efforts as NPL organizer; formation of Nebraska Workers Nonpartisan League; and R. A. Moore's account of spying on and disrupting League meetings.

981. Phillips, William W. "The Growth of a Progressive: Asle J. Gronna." Master's thesis, UND, 1952. 204 p.
   Short discussion of Gronna's relationship to NPL.

982. ____. "The Life of Asle J. Gronna: A Self-Made Man of the Prairie." Ph.D. diss., University of Missouri, 1958. 738 p.
   Includes a brief history of NPL and a discussion of Gronna's attitude toward it.

983. Poehls, Alice C. "An Analysis of Selected Speeches of A. C. Townley, 1915-1921." Master's thesis, UND, 1978. 115 p.
   Includes full text of several speeches and a biography of Townley. See also No. 904.

984. Prochazka, Frank John. "Autobiography and Family History." Unpublished paper, 1925, 1932. 2 vols., 60, 69 p. SHSND.
   Author ran an NPL newspaper in Walsh County, N.Dak. Gives short account of activities and thoughts on NPL.

985. Putnam, Jackson K. "The Socialist Party of North Dakota, 1902-1918." Master's thesis, UND, 1956. 215 p.
   Contains chapter on relationship between NPL and Socialist Party of N.Dak.

986. Raff, Willis H. "Civil Liberties in Minnesota, World War One Period." Master's thesis, University of Minnesota, 1950. 203 p.
   Treats NPL as case history, concentrating on 1918 Minn. election campaign. Expanded in No. 987.

987. ____. "Coercion and Freedom in a War Situation." Ph.D. diss., University of Minnesota, 1957. 298 p.
   Civil liberties during WWI in Minn. Briefly analyzes NPL's role in 1918 campaign; discusses Minn. Commission of Public Safety at length. An expansion of No. 986.

988. Rice, Stuart A. "Farmers and Workers in American Politics." Ph.D. diss., Columbia University, 1924. 217 p.
   Same as No. 357.

989. Ruetten, Richard T. "Burton K. Wheeler, 1905-1925: An Independent Liberal under Fire." Master's thesis, University of Oregon, 1957. 209 p.
   Includes discussion of NPL in Mont. and its 1920 endorsement of Wheeler.

990. Saloutos, Theodore. "Farmer Movements since 1902." Ph.D. diss., University of Wisconsin, 1940. 432 p.
   NPL's relationship with organized labor, in context of early 20th-century farm organizations (ca. 1900-30), including American Society of Equity and Farm Bureau.

991. Schaffer, Ronald. "Jeanette Rankin, Progressive Isolationist." Ph.D. diss., Princeton University, 1959. 277 p.
   Biography of Mont. congresswoman who ran, with NPL backing, for U.S. Senate from Mont. in 1918.

992. Selke, Albert G. "A History of the Initiative in North Dakota." Master's thesis, UND, 1940. 132 p.
   Adoption and use (by both NPL and IVA) of initiative in N.Dak., ca. 1914-39.

993. Shankweiler, Paul W. "The Nonpartisan League and the Local Community." Master's thesis, Columbia University, 1921. 66 p.
   Account of popular reaction to NPL. Author spent summer of 1920 in Ward Co., N.Dak.

994. Sherman, William C. "Assimilation in a North Dakota German-Russian Community." Master's thesis, UND, 1965. 160 p.
   Case study of Pierce Co.; includes brief examination of community's loyalty to NPL.

995. Sim, John C. "The History of the North Dakota Press Association." Master's thesis, University of Minnesota, 1940. 189 p.
   Includes discussion of NPL newspaper legislation and Peoples Press Assn.. (later Progressive Press Assn.), a group of editors who split from N.Dak. Press Assn. and supported NPL.

996. Smemo, Irwin K. "Progressive Judge: The Public Career of Charles Fremont Amidon." Ph.D. diss., University of Minnesota, 1967. 392 p.
   Biography of N.Dak. federal court judge who heard some of court cases involving NPL programs and activities. Includes discussion of

Amidon's views on sedition charges brought against NPL. Bibliography includes list of cases heard by Amidon.

997. Stolee, Leif G. "The Parliamentary Career of William Irvine." Master's thesis, University of Toronto, 1977.
Not seen by compilers.

998. Swenson, Karl R. "A Study of Early Banking and Bank Failures in North Dakota." Master's thesis, NDSU, 1965. 90 p.
Deals in part with bank failures of 1920s in N.Dak. Concludes that Bank of N.Dak. had "very little effect on the private banks."

999. Talbot, Ross B. "The Politics of Farm Organizations in North Dakota." Ph.D. diss., University of Chicago, 1953. 323 p.
Gives a short account of NPL in context of other N.Dak. farm organizations, including Grange, Farmers Union, American Society of Equity, and Farm Bureau. Draws general conclusions about structure and operation of N.Dak. farm organizations. Evidence primarily from 1930-50 period.

1000. Thompson, Robert. "The History of the South Dakota Farmers Union, 1914-1952." Master's thesis, University of South Dakota, 1953. 122 p.
Briefly contrasts Farmers Union with NPL.

1001. Torian, James W. "The Origin and Development of the Bank of North Dakota, 1919 to 1970." Ph.D. diss., University of Arkansas, 1975. 173 p.
Economic and political conditions that led to bank's creation. Analyzes effect of change to IVA state government, including influence of Governor Rangvold A. Nestos.

1002. Tostlebe, Alvin S. "The Bank of North Dakota: An Experiment in Agrarian Banking." Ph.D. diss., Columbia University, 1924. 205 p.
Discussion of political and economic background of NPL. Includes details of NPL's legislative program. Uses studies of NPL by Charles E. Russell and Herbert E. Gaston.

1003. Vadnais, Irene. "The North Dakota Nonpartisan League and the State Newspapers; Recent Activity of the League as Reflected by Representative Papers." Master's thesis, University of Montana, 1933. 111 p.
Primarily concerned with NPL in the 1930s, but includes NPL history from its origins. Makes heavy use of N.Dak. newspapers.

1004. Wasson, Stanley P. "The Nonpartisan League in Minnesota: 1916-1924." Ph.D. diss., University of Pennsylvania, 1955. 669 p.
Discusses loyalty issue and reasons behind decline of NPL. Strongest on NPL's relations with organized labor, latter days of NPL in Minn., and emergence of Farmer-Labor party.

1005. Weber, Elaine J. "William Langer: The Progressive Attorney General (1917-1920)." Master's thesis, UND, 1967. 131 p.
Langer's activities as attorney general, including enforcement of prohibition, Public Library Commission controversy, and break with NPL. Also discusses Langer's 1920 gubernatorial candidacy.

1006. Wentz, Leonard. "The Nonpartisan League: A Quest for Community." Master's thesis, UND, 1968. 80 p.
Author theorizes that N.Dak. farmers lacked a sense of community due to rural isolation, mix of ethnic groups, and the results of uprooting families to N.Dak.; uses newspaper editorials to argue that NPL provided a "pseudo-community" that supported its rapid rise to power.

1007. Wilcox, Benton H. "A Reconsideration of the Character and Economic Basis of Northeastern Radicalism." Ph.D. diss., University of Wisconsin, 1933. 252 p.
Comprehensive study of agrarian protest groups and their economic background, ca. 1870-1920. Includes analysis of NPL in Minn., N.Dak., S.Dak., Nebr., Wis., Iowa, and Kans. and includes interesting discussion of reasons behind decline of NPL.

1008. Wilkins, Robert P. "North Dakota and the European War, 1914-1917: A Study in Public Opinion." Ph.D. diss., West Virginia University, 1954. 340 p.
Important study of foreign policy questions during NPL period. Suggests that North Dakotans opposed U.S. entry into WWI because of ideological distrust of financial and industrial capitalist classes, not because of ethnic considerations.

1009. Youngdale, James M. "Populism in New Perspective: An Analysis of Political Radicalism in the Upper Midwest." Ph.D. diss., University of Minnesota, 1972. 339 p.
Psychohistory of midwestern farm and labor radicals. Includes brief account of NPL in a discussion of origins of Farmer-Labor party in Minn.

1010. Zimmerman, Carle C. "Farmers' Marketing Attitudes." Ph.D. diss., University of Minnesota, 1925. 54 p.
See Nos. 130 and 131.

Political button

Index

ACORN, 1
Aberdeen (S.Dak.) Daily American, 434
Adams, Elmer Ellsworth and family, papers, 794
Adamson, Madeleine, author, 1
Advertising, influence, 571, 577; depicted, p. 6
Agrarian movements, as context for NPL, 4, 56, 141, 335, 936; history, 61, 102, 123, 427, 951, 1007
Agricultural Workers Industrial Union, 894
Airplanes, campaigning depicted, p. 29
Alberta, NPL history and activities, 74, 79, 103, 108, 915; agrarian movements, 127. See also Canada
Alberta Non-Partisan (Calgary, Alba.), 716
Alexander, Moses, Idaho governor, 795
Allen, Henry J., papers, 796
Ambrose, Rev. F. Halsey, author, 435
America First (St. Paul), 717
America First Assn., St. Paul, founded, 436; records, 797
America First League, 179
American Bar Assn., criticism of NPL, 140; Committee to Oppose Judicial Recall, 457
American Committee of Minneapolis, 437, 438; publications, 472, 649
American Economist, 649
American Farm Bureau Federation, 814
American Federation of Labor, 132
American Red Cross, financing, 572, 585
American Society of Equity, 73, 860, 865, 918; role in NPL, 176, 275, 330, 335, 345, 454, 936, 990, 999. See also Equity Cooperative Exchange
Amerland v. Hagen, lawsuit, 778
Amidon, Charles F., judge, 498, 776, 996
Amos, M. L., political activist, 700
Anaconda Copper Mining Co., 52, 72, 120
Anderson, D., author, 133
Anderson, Ed, labor activist, 474
Anderson, Elizabeth, temperance activist, 554
Anderson, F. W., author, 915

Anderson, Raymond V., author, 916
Anderson, William, author, 798
Andre, Pearl, editor, 2
Appel, Livia, author, 43
Arnold, Ronald C., candidate, 120
Asher, Robert, author, 135
Association of Community Organizers for Reform Now, see ACORN
Association of Life Insurance Presidents, convention, 338, 634
Assumption Abbey Archives, Richardton, N.Dak., 909
Astoria, Oreg., convention, 423
Ault, Harry E. B., papers, 799

BABCOCK, C. D., author, 137
Bacon, Jerry Dempster, 115, 330; author, 82, 440-46, 661; papers, 800, 801
Baer, John M., 223, 290, 344, 375, 403, 586, 779; cartoons, 133, 344, 802, 808; author, 583; papers, 802; correspondence, 903; cartoon depicted, p. 26
Baglien, David B., author, 917
Bahmer, Robert Henry, author, 918
Baker, Berta E., NPL member, 2
Bakken, Douglas, author, 138
Bakken, Larry A., author, 919
Balance of power, tactic, 217
Bandza, Alfred, author, 920
Bangert, Charles G., papers, 803
Bank of North Dakota, farm diversification programs, 40; history and operations, 114, 139, 213, 306, 399, 407, 741, 759, 919, 937, 943, 954, 998, 1001, Loan Department, 159, 756, 937; controversies, 162, 228, 359, 545, 637; bond sales, 236, 285, 307, 310, 313, 317, 399, 527, 742, 773, 793; criticisms, 314, 479; economic condition, 376, 743, 757; legislative history, 389, 452; loans, 529; proposed dissolution, 748; investigation, 765, 768, 881; audit reports, 765, 780, 871; court decision, 773, 793; records, 871, 872
Banks and banking, 114, 125, 159, 228, 274, 279, 306, 307, 310, 334, 359, 389, 447, 452, 479; credit, 114, 485; foreclosure moratorium, 195; bank failures, 303, 404, 998; in Canada, 463, 690; loans in N.Dak., 529; N.Dak. bank law, 667; court cases, 786, 793. See also individual banks
Barlow, ___, 613
Barnes, C. W., author, 448, 449
Barr, W. H., speech, 273
Bates, James L., author, 921
Bates, Mark P., candidate, 93, 617, 618
Baum, Dale, author, 141
Beach Publicity Assn., publications, 497
Beecher, John, author, 3
Behling, Robert, compiler, 50
Benedict XV, Pope, peace appeal, 591
Bennett, Russell M., businessman, 731
Berger, Victor, author, 451
Beyer, Carlyle, author, 922
Billings County (N.Dak.) Pioneer, 17
Bishop Brissman and Co., auditors, 768
Bismarck Tribune, 895
Bizzell, W. B., author, 4
Bjornsin, Julian, author, 884
Black, John D., author, 131
Blackorby, Edward C., author, 5, 923, 924
Blaine, John J., candidate, 93
Blakely, Herbert, editor, 259
Bland, Salem, NPL organizer, 126
Blegen, Theodore C., compiler, 798
Bloom, Howard E., author, 925
Blue Books, 769
Boise, Idaho, harassment of NPL, 260
Bonds, revenue, see Revenue bonds
Borah, William E., Idaho senator, 51, 69, 229; papers, 804
Borgos, Seth, author, 1
Borner, Florence, author, 6, 453
Bouck, William, Grange master, 19
Bowen, A. E., Socialist organizer, 870, 902
Boyle, James E., author, 142, 143
Brackett, Edmund C., author, 926
Brake, Robert J., author, 927
Brandeis, Louis, Supreme Court justice, 774
Brennan, James William, author, 928
Brewer, George D., Socialist organizer, 660

[77]

Brewer, Philip Edwin, author, 929
Bridges, Robert, candidate, 93, 898
Briley, Ronald, author, 144
Brinton, Job Wells, 477; author, 7, 454, 455; criticism of, 497; papers, 805
Brommel, Bernard J., author, 145
Bronson, Harrison A., papers, 806
Brookhart, Smith W., Iowa senator, 167, 360
Brown, Robert L., author, 456
Brown, Rome G., author, 146, 457, 458; quoted, 435
Bruce, Andrew Alexander, author, 8, 836
Brudvig, Glenn Lowell, author, 930
Bryan, Charles W., politician, 93, 360
Buell, C. J., author, 147
Bullard, F. L., author, 148
Burbank, Garin, author, 149
Burdick, Usher L., author, 9, 10
Burgess, Eugene Willard, author, 11
Burke, H. T., author, 150
Burke, John, N.Dak. governor, 46, 454
Burleigh Co., N.Dak., 89
Burnquist, Joseph Alfred Arner, Minn. governor, 42, 448, 449, 460, 541; author, 459-61; loyalty issue, 482, 658; campaign, 658, 890, 891; papers, 807
Burtness, Olger B., politician, 529, 767, 779
Burtness v. Hall, lawsuit, 779
Business Men's Protective Assn., Omaha, 87, 980
Buttree, J. Edmund, author, 12, 462
Byerley and Nelson v. State Board of Canvassers, lawsuit, 788

CAIN, MYRTLE, politician, 107
Campaigns, NPL platforms and strategies, 86, 217; airplane depicted, p. 29. See also Elections, Primaries
   1916, Minn., 16; N.Dak., 319, 403
   1918, Minn., 16, 59, 62, 77, 91, 97, 281, 448, 950, 986, 987; Idaho, 71; Mont., 246; N.Dak., 352; cartoon depicted, p. 26
   1920, 52; N.Dak., 44, 395; Minn., 97; Mont., 921, 934
   1922, Texas, 36; Mont., 72, 113; Minn., 97
   1924, Minn., 118
   1980, N.Dak., 352
Canada, history, 28; NPL history and activities, 79, 286, 503, 616, 915, 979; history of agrarian movement, 124, 127, 164, 915, 942. See also Alberta, Manitoba, Saskatchewan
Canadian Reconstruction Assn., 463; publications, 690
Carroll, D. H., author, 152
Cart, Elmer, reminiscences, 809
Cartoons, 1, 133, 223, 299, 310, 323, 344, 409, 687, 802, 808; anti-NPL, 609; depicted, p. 11, p. 26
Carver Co., Minn., meeting depicted, p. 71

Cathro, F. W., author, 464, 741
Central Labor Union of Minneapolis and Hennepin County, records, 808. See also Minneapolis Trades and Labor Assembly
Chafee, Zechariah, Jr., author, 13
Chamberlain, F. A., political activist, 438
Cheney, Charles B., reporter, 14
Chicago, conference, 81
Children, 356, 767
Chipman, George, political activist, 79
Chrislock, Carl H., author, 15, 16, 153
Christen, Richard, papers, 809
Christenson, E. P., reminiscences, 809
Citizens Alliance of Minneapolis, records, 810
Clackamas Co., Oreg., NPL candidates, 243
Clancy, James M., 494; author, 468
Coates, David C., 198, 650
Coates, W. C., author, 471
Cole, Wayne S., author, 17
Colegrove, Kenneth, author, 156
Collins, Peter W., author, 472, 473
Colorado, NPL history and activities, 190, 263, 282, 965; NPL election strategy, 217; 1920 elections, 227, 249; 1918 elections, 242
Colorado State Federation of Labor, proceedings, 474, 475; records, 811
Committee of 48, Minnesota State Central Committee, records, 812
The Commonwealth (Seattle, Wash.) 19
Communist party, 23; role in Farmer-Labor party, 412
Conrad, Charles, author, 18
Conrad, Joyce, author, 18
Conscription, see Draft, Enlistment
Conspiracy, trial in Jackson, Minn., 73, 91, 170, 224, 232, 234, 264, 294, 302, 303, 411, 481, 790, 792, 905
Constitutional amendments, N.Dak., 244, 410, 637, 644, 661, 687, 747-50, 787, 788; Nebraska, 858
Consumers United Stores Co., organization and financing, 151, 272, 330, 350, 477, 567, 805; records, 287, 813; buyer's certificate, 526; articles of incorporation, 567
Cook, Gilbert W., author, 159, 160, 931
Cooper, Charles, candidate, 120
Cooperative Commonwealth Federation, Canada, 65, 126, 149
Cooperative movement, 84, 111; membership study, 130; relationship to NPL, 282, 330; marketing, 338, 364. See also individual associations
Co-operators' Congress, Great Falls, Mont., 505
Cottage Grove (Oreg.) Sentinel, 431
Cotton, Donald R., papers, 815
Cotton, futures trading, 508
Council of Defense Action, Kans., 700
Country Gentleman, 163, 168, 330, 506

Courville, L. D., author, 114
Coverdale, John W., papers, 814
Craig, Minnie D., politician, 2
Craighead, E. B., newspaper editor, 38, 944
Cravens, Hamilton, author, 165, 932
Crawford, Harriet Ann, author, 19
Crawford, Lewis F., author, 20
Creameries, state-owned, 381, 746, 882
Credit, see Banks and banking
Creel, George, support of NPL, 80, 261; author, 166, 167, 219; loyalty issue, 203, 633
Crews, Cecil R., author, 933
Currie, Barton W., author, 168
Currie v. Frazier, lawsuit, 773

DAHL, MATH, papers, 816
Daily Republican (Mitchell, S.Dak.), 25
"Dakota Maid Flour," recipes, 669
Dakota State Journal (Minot, N.Dak.), 476
Dale, Alfred Samuel, author, 478; papers, 817
Davenport, Frederick M., author, 169, 170
Davies, W. P., author, 171
Davis, David W., Idaho governor, 818
Davis, Thomas, candidate, 541, 658, 662
Day, Walter E., politician, 819
Dean, Ezra C., author, 481
Debs, Eugene V., Socialist, 536
Deering, N.Dak., origin of NPL, 346
Deforth, Shirley Jean, author, 934
Democratic party, relationship to NPL, 89, 170, 217; NPL merger, 396, 978
Dennis, Bruce, newspaper editor, 393
DeNoult, W. B., banker, 756
Devine, Edward T., author, 172
Diehl, F. E., bureaucrat, 752
Disloyalty, see Loyalty issue
Dithmar, E. F., 603
Divet, A. Guy, papers, 820
Dixon, Fred, NPL organizer, 126
Dixon, Joseph M., Mont. governor, 52, 934, 958; papers, 821
Doan, Edward N., author, 21
Dockage law, 452
"Dr. Mum," author, 674
Douthit, Davis, author, 22
Dovre, Paul John, author, 173, 935
Doyle, Stephen J., papers, 822
Drache, Hiram, author, 894
Draft, NPL opposition, 126, 145, 224, 232. See also Enlistment, Loyalty issue
Drake, N.Dak., state mill and elevator, 768
DuBois, Fred T., political activist, 424
Dues, see Nonpartisan League, dues
Duffy, Clyde, 894; papers, 823
Duncan, L. J., NPL leader, 25
Dunne, William F., labor leader, 72
Durham, ___, labor leader, 474
Durocher, Leon, author, 483
Dyson, Lowell K., author, 23, 174

EARLY, DELBERT, speech, 437
Education, N.Dak., 32, 265, 274, 275, 466, 611, 612, 651, 767; teaching of German, 358
Election law, reforms, 52, 676
Elections, NPL strategies, 217, 266; NPL-endorsed legislators, 401, 402. See also Campaigns, Primaries
 1916, Minn., 16, 280; N.Dak., 169, 171, 280, 319, 366, 430, 917, 971; Idaho, 280, 424; Iowa, 280; Kans., 280; Mont., 280; Nebr., 280; S.Dak., 280; Wash., 280
 1917, N.Dak., 290; Sask., 657, 828
 1918, Idaho, 75, 218, 242; Minn., 216, 242, 848, 969; Colo., 242; Mont., 242; Nebr., 242; N.Dak., 242, 410; S.Dak., 242
 1920, Minn., 97, 158, 227, 249; Wis., 227; Colo., 227, 249; Mont., 227, 249, 958; NPL votes, 227, 384; N.Dak., 227, 249, 299, 395, 442, 523, 926; Nebr., 249
 1922, Minn., 97, 360, 400; N.Dak., 298, 489, 495, 537; Iowa, 360; Nebr., 360; Wis., 360
 1921, N.Dak. recall, 150, 152, 284, 317, 320, 322, 520, 637, 641, 682, 684, 748, 894, 923
 1921, Minneapolis, 154
 1924, Oreg., 243
 1948-56, N.Dak., 396
Elevators, see Grain elevators
Ellison, James H., 438
Ellsworth, Scott A., author, 121, 176, 936
Ellsworth Co., Kans., 700
Ellsworth County Leader (Ellsworth, Kans.), 240, 721
Emme, Julius, politician, 494
Enerson, Rozanne L., author, 937
Engerud, Edward, author, 667
Enlistments, NPL opposition, 126, 145, 224, 232, 789, 790, 792, 826. See also Draft; Gilbert, Joseph; Loyalty issue; Townley, Arthur C.
Equity Cooperative Exchange, 10, 372, 487. See also American Society of Equity
Erickson, Lawrence, reminiscences, 809
Evans, D. H., candidate, 541, 658
Evans, Oliver S., NPL organizer, 87, 980
Everson, E. W., IVA leader, 554

FARGO COURIER-NEWS, 419, 452, 488, 674, 680, 718
Fargo Trades and Labor Assembly, 554
Fargo Tribune, 718
Farley, James A., correspondence, 822
Farm Bureau, Iowa, 87; relationship to NPL, 53, 54, 100, 990, 999; membership study, 130
Farm Bureau Federation, 9
Farm Holiday, relationship to NPL, 335, 951
Farmer and labor parties, history, 24, 105, 357, 933; organizing methods, 362. See also Farmer-Labor party

Farmer-Labor Federation of Minnesota, publications, 490, 491
Farmer-Labor party, Minn., 33, 42, 278, 392, 832, 848, 969, 972, 1009; transition from NPL, 59, 67, 207, 288, 491, 550, 893, 968, 972, 1004; activities and history, 118, 174, 231, 412, 421, 596, 887, 900; political power, 360. See also Farmer and labor parties
Farmers' Alliance, Minn., 949
Farmers and Workers Conference, see Producers and Consumers Convention
Farmers Educational and Cooperative Union, see Farmers Union
Farmers' International, see Red Peasant International
Farmers' Publicity Assn., 497
Farmers Sentinal, 488
Farmers Union (Farmers Educational and Cooperative Union, National Farmers Union), 9, 964; N.Dak., 18, 55, 348, 350, 841; relationship to NPL, 100, 296, 335, 348, 350, 857, 999, 1000; role in NPL, 275, 330, 345; meetings, 526; records, 857
Farmers Union (Salina, Kans.), 857
Farmers Union of Alberta, 892
Farmers' Union Progressive Alliance, formation, 417
Farms and farmers, economic problems, 40, 177, 250, 363, 648, 918; marketing, 81, 130, 131, 546; methods, 81; image, 235; role of women, 269, 388; depicted, p. 15. See also Nonpartisan League, origins and early history
Fine, Nathan, author, 24
Fite, Gilbert C., author, 25, 91, 180-82
Fligelman, Henrietta, author, 938
"The Flivver Campaign," poem, 6
Folwell, William Watts, author, 26; papers, 824
For Home and Country League, St. Paul, 494
Fossum, Paul R., author, 27, 939
"Fourteen points," 578
Fraser, G. A., correspondence, 822
Frazier, Lynn J., N.Dak. governor, 144, 167, 355, 377, 540, 583, 635, 894, 908, 911; author, 81, 197; 1921 recall, 150, 496; criticism of, 467, 535, 566, 608; papers, 825, 877; correspondence, 827; depicted, p. 55
Frederick, John T., author, 183
"Free love," 120, 694; cartoon depicted, p. 11
Free Trade League, Canada, 79
Freeman, J. L., NPL organizer, 19
Friesen, Gerald, author, 28
Fritz, Nancy R., author, 940
Frost, James, author, 497
Fryburg (N.Dak.) Pioneer, 17
Fussell, E. B., author, 498
Futures trading, 508

GASTON, HERBERT E., newspaper editor, 414, 621; author, 29, 184, 1002
Geelan, Agnes Kjorlie, author, 30, 31

Geiger, Louis G., author, 32, 185
German Americans, political allegiance, 153
German language, taught in schools, 358
German Russians, immigrants, 96
Gieske, Millard L., author, 33
Gilbert, A. B., author, 34, 186-91, 501
Gilbert, Joseph, NPL organizer, 129, 697; trials at Jackson, Minn., 13, 22, 73, 91, 224, 234, 411, 481, 790, 792; Martin Co. trial, 22, 789; Goodhue Co. trial, 501, 774, 791, 908; indictment, 302; speeches, 491; papers, 826
Gilbert v. Minnesota, lawsuit, 774
Gillette, John M., author, 192, 193
Glaab, Charles N., author, 46, 194
The Goat (Fargo), 719
Goddard, H. P., political activist, 620
Godwin, Sidney, 728; author, 196
Goldberg, Ray, author, 35, 941
Goodhue Co., Minn., trial, 501, 774, 791, 908
Gooding, Frank R., Idaho governor, 51; sued for libel, 252, 777
Gordon, F. C. R., author, 198
Gould, James F., political activist, 438
Gracie, Bruce Alan, author, 942
Grain, grading, 142; attempts to reform trade, 364, 365, 369; trading, 364, 508, 860; inspection, 860. See also Wheat
Grain elevators, 142; state-owned and -operated, 160, 514, 669, 745, 768, 806, 884, 943. See also Mills, North Dakota Mill and Elevator Assn.
Grain Growers Convention, 860
Grain Growers' Grain Co., 103
Grand Forks, N.Dak., mill and elevator, 514, 608, 669
Grand Forks American, 488, 720
Grand Forks Herald, 171, 330, 440, 455, 645, 801
Grange, in Wash., 19; relationship with NPL, 87, 275, 300, 423, 833, 951, 999; history, 102; in Oreg., 296, 300, 423
Great Bend, Kans., harassment of NPL, 239, 380
Great Britain, NPL visa problems, 309
Green, James R., author, 36, 199
Green v. Frazier, lawsuit, 775
Gregg, William C., author, 200, 201
Griffith, L. L., NPL organizer, 272, 660
Griggs County Sentinel-Courier (Cooperstown, N.Dak.), 17
Gronna, Asle J., candidate, 395, 971, 981, 982; correspondence, 903
Gronna, James, correspondence, 822
Groves, Donald B., author, 37
Gunn, John W., author, 504
Gutfeld, Arnon, author, 38

HAGAN, JOHN N., 496, 635, 778; papers, 827
Hagen, E. Bruce, author, 943
Hagen, Rhea, NPL member, 2

Haight, S. E., NPL organizer, 74, 124
Haight, Mrs. S. V., candidate, 657; papers, 828
Haines, Austin P., author, 202, 203
Haines, Dora B., author, 39
Haines, Lynn, author, 39
Hall, Covington, NPL organizer, 36
Hall, E. George, labor leader, 829
Halland, J. G., author, 467, 485, 486
Halldorson, P. E., bank examiner, 786
Hannah, Margaret A., author, 505
Hanson, John, film maker, 50, 269
Harding, William, Iowa governor, 37
Harger, C. M., author, 204, 205
Hargreaves, Mary Wilma M., author, 40
Harmony, Minn., NPL meeting, 613
Harris, James A., politician, 694
Harris, Lyle E., author, 944
Hart, John Edward, author, 945
Haug, Charles J., author, 206, 894
Hawkins, Oscar F., letters, 110
Hawley, Edward W., candidate, 456
Haycraft, J. E., politician, 509
Haynes, Frederick Emory, author, 41, 207
Haynes, John Earle, author, 42
Haywood, William D., letters, 715
Head, William, political activist, 660
Healy, Paul F., author, 120
Hedges, M. H., author, 207
Helgeson, Henry, correspondence, 903
Henke, Warren A., author, 209
Hennepin Co., Minn., election, 704
Hennessey, Leo D., author, 946
Hicks, John D., author, 100, 210
Hildreth, Melvin D., author, 211
Hilton, Clifford L., politician, 470
Hilton, O. A., author, 212
Hodgson, Larry, St. Paul mayor, 494
Hofland, Carl J., author, 947
Hofstadter, Richard, historian, 141
Holbrook, Franklin F., author, 43
Holl, Jack M., author, 88
Holtan, Orley I., author, 214
Holzworth, John Michael, author, 44
Hopkins, John A. H., correspondence, 812
Hornbacher, Perry Joel, author, 948
Horwill, A. K., author, 215, 216
Howard, Asher, editor, 508, 509, 830
Howard, James R., author, 814
Howard, Joseph Kinsey, author, 45
Howard, Thomas W., editor, 46
Howe, Frederic Clemson, author, 47
Howe, Louis, correspondence, 822
Howell, R. B., politician, 93, 360
Hudson, Edwin E., author, 949
Hunter, W. H., author, 405
Huntington, Samuel P., author, 217

IVA, see Independent Voters Assn.
IWW, see Industrial Workers of the World
Iconoclast (Minot, N.Dak.), 109, 851, 948
Idaho, NPL history and activities, 51, 190, 229, 252-56, 263, 280, 302, 304, 424; 1918 elections, 71, 75, 218, 242, 424; elections, 217, 280; harassment of NPL, 254, 256, 260; Farmer-Labor party, 288
Idaho Federation of Agriculture, 71
Idaho Statesman, libel suit, 252, 777
Immigration and emigration, 103, 209, 751, 753-55; impact of German Russians, 96
Independent (Fargo), see Rural Independent
Independent Voters Assn., 44, 46, 84, 228, 435, 442, 485, 1001; campaigns, 30, 515, 516; publications, 472, 479, 513-23, 528, 533, 536, 547, 551, 631, 647, 655, 661, 681, 683, 733, 734; sample ballots, 484, 489, 495, 672; recall election literature, 496, 615, 520, 641, 748; bylaws, 512, 517; organizational structure, 513, 517, 518; platform, 519; campaign literature, 534, 605; criticism of, 600; support of, 606, 689, 699; farm programs, 632; analysis of state industries, 655; labor legislation, 683; lawsuit, 788; endorsed candidates, 624, 625, 714; records, 861. See also Plain Citizens Political Reform Assn.
Indians, reform legislation, 144
Industrial Workers of the World (IWW), 76, 206, 330, 394, 426, 439, 480, 536, 649, 654, 859, 894; relationship to NPL, 539, 605, 650
Ingle, J. G., author, 525, 526
Initiative, 521, 530, 637, 687, 747, 748, 750, 916, 920, 992
Insurance, state, 563, 751, 931; N.Dak. manual, 771
Insurance Federation of Oregon, 137
Iowa, NPL history and activities, 146, 190, 202, 280, 330, 360, 1007; elections, 280, 360
Iowa Farm Bureau Federation, 37, 814
Iowa State Bar Assn., address, 458
Iron ore, in Minn., 576
Irvin, Louis S., candidate, 120
Irvine, William, author, 48; NPL organizer, 74, 79, 126, 716, 945, 963, 997

JACKSON, MINN., trial, 73, 91, 170, 224, 232, 234, 264, 294, 302, 303, 411, 481, 790, 792, 905
Janes, George Milton, author, 49
Jelliff, Theodore B., author, 116
Jenkinson, Clay, author, 50
Jenson, Carol Elizabeth, author, 221, 950
Joachim, L. H., author, 222
Johansen, Sigurd A., author, 951
Johnson, Alice Jane, author, 952
Johnson, C. R., author, 224-28; criticism, 359
Johnson, Claudius O., author, 51
Johnson, Francis A., interview, 831
Johnson, Gordon W., author, 953
Johnson, H. W., political activist, 79
Johnson, Harry, NPL organizer, 74
Johnson, Kenneth C., author, 954
Johnson, Magnus P., candidate, 93, 532, 831, 894; campaign, 516; recall, 532; papers, 832
Johnson, Roger T., author, 230
Johnson, Rudolph, papers, 833
Johnson, Sveinbjorn, party official, 620
Joiner, Jess, reminiscences, 809
Joint Campaign Committee, N.Dak., publications, 528-37; recall petition drive, 530
Joint Campaign Organization, N.Dak., publications, 606
Junkin, Tom Parker, magazine editor, 556, 717

KANE, RALPH JAMES, author, 955
Kane, Thomas, college president, 32
Kanneberg, Adolph P., papers, 834
Kansas, NPL history and activities, 100, 239, 240, 280, 330, 360, 373, 409, 834, 866, 1007; elections, 217, 280; harassment of NPL, 239, 380; NPL bylaws, 673
Kansas Bankers Assn., meeting, 631
Kansas Leader (Salina), 721
Kansas State Farmers Educational and Cooperative Union, 857
Kansas Union Farmer (Salina), 857
Karlin, Jules A., author, 52
Kellogg, Frank B., author, 538
Kempfer, Hannah, politician, 107
Kennedy, John C., author, 231
Kenyon, Minn., speech, 501, 774, 791, 908
Kerr, J. Edmund, author, 539
Kile, Orville Merton, author, 53, 54
King, Judson, author, 232-34
Kingsley, Robert, 956
Kitchen, Joseph A., candidate, 516, 532; recall, 532
Kloske, Ralph L., author, 957
Knight, Harold V., author, 55
Knutson, Alfred, NPL organizer, 174
Koessler, Mary Lou Collins, author, 958
Korth, Philip A., author, 235
Kositsky, Carl, auditor, 780
Kositsky v. Waters, lawsuit, 780
Kramer, Dale, author, 56
Kreuter, Gretchen, editor, 107
Kvale, Ole J., NPL supporter, 123, 129

LABOR, 762; strikes, 73, 236, 303, 468, 586, 736, 825; N.Dak. groups, 76, 115; relationship to NPL, 76, 115, 198, 204, 275, 308, 330, 332, 373, 392, 397, 400, 420, 973, 990, 1004; relationship with farmers, 132, 184, 419; role in WWI, 153, 305; newspaper unions, 161; newspapers, 237; and Socialist party, 305, 948; thirdparty movement, 392; involvement in Farmer-Labor party, 412. See also individual labor organizations
Labor Representative League, Alba., 74
Labor's Campaign Committee, Minn., 541
Labor's Municipal Nonpartisan League, 542. See also Municipal Nonpartisan League, Working People's Nonpartisan Political League

Ladd, A. J., papers, 836
Ladd, Edwin Fremont, N.Dak. senator, 129, 167, 168, 185, 395, 894, 911, 967; support of NPL, 325; wheat-grading methods, 330; author, 543; correspondence, 827
La Follette, Bell C., author, 57
La Follette, Foca, author, 57
La Follette, Robert M., Wis. senator, 21, 57, 360, 859; 1917 speech, 21, 57, 326, 538, 736; 1924 presidential bid, 68; support of NPL, 602, 603; correspondence, 903
La Grande (Oreg.) Observer, 393
Laidley, Frederick W., author, 544
Laird v. Hall, lawsuit, 781
Lamb, Charles R., author, 238, 959
Land Finance Co., papers, 837
Langer, Lydia Cady, NPL member, 2
Langer, William, N.Dak. attorney general, 30, 44, 46, 121, 195, 351, 782, 784, 837, 894, 953, 960, 977, 1005; author, 58; 1917 Minot raid, 270; papers, 838; gubernatorial campaign, 861, 1005; correspondence, 903; 1921 debates, 905; depicted, p. 55
Langer v. MacDonald, lawsuit, 782
Langer v. Olson, lawsuit, 783
Langer v. Totten, lawsuit, 784
Larsen, Lawrence Harold, author, 230, 960
Larson, Bruce L., author, 58, 239, 240, 961
Larson, Henrietta M., author, 962
Laws and legislation, affecting NPL, 80, 93, 136, 168; affecting banking, 114; NPL programs, 148, 172, 192, 193, 215, 274, 276, 311, 318, 321, 328, 373, 376, 487, 510, 594, 610, 635, 644, 939, 1002; affecting newspapers, 267, 336, 337, 374, 966, 995; N.Dak. tax policy, 391; labor, 683
Lawson, G. W., 541
Lawyer's Club, N.Y., speech, 629
Laycock, David H., author, 963
Leach, George E., candidate, 154
League of Nations, NPL position, 353
Lee, Guy F., author, 572
Lee, Rudolph, newspaper editor, 640
Lemke, William, 5, 121, 467, 635, 837, 894, 908, 911, 924; recall, 496; criticism of, 608; papers, 839
Lemke v. District Court of Stutsman Co., lawsuit, 793
Le Sueur, Arthur, biography, 60, 373, 460, 643; cricitism of NPL, 100; author, 245, 545, 546, 715; picnic speech, 437; criticism of, 480, 697; papers, 840
Le Sueur, Marian, political activist, 60, 129, 840
Le Sueur, Meridel, author, 60
Levine, Louis, author, 246
Lewis, Robert W., author, 50
Liberal party, 812
Liberty Loan, fundraising, 585
Library scandal, 1919, 172, 349, 529, 764, 767. See also North Dakota Public Library Commission
Liessman, Charles, papers, 841
Liessman, Viola, NPL member, 2; papers, 841

Liggett, Walter W., author, 247, 488
Limvere, Karl, author, 61
Lincoln, Abraham, quoted, 504, 671
Lincoln Club, Minneapolis, 704
Lind, John, loyalty issue, 633
Lindbergh, Charles A., Sr., 16, 39, 59, 106, 129, 848, 859, 961; campaign, 39, 59, 63, 91, 448, 502, 662, 686, 969; author, 62, 63, 548, 549, 556; defense, 449, 686; speeches, 491, 579; quoted, 555; criticism of, 572; loyalty issue, 686; papers, 842; advertisement depicted, p. 6
Linde v. Hall, lawsuit, 785
Lindstrom, David E., author, 64
Lipset, Seymour M., author, 65, 149, 164
Loans, see Banks and banking
Locke, Walter, author, 249
Lofthus, O. E., bank examiner, 786
Lofthus v. Langer, lawsuit, 786
Loftus, George Sperry, Equity official, 10, 73, 121
Lombard, Norman, businessman, 250
Long, Andrew, author, 251
Long Prairie, Minn., debate, 640
Losk, Walter S., papers, 843; author, 964
Lovin, Hugh, author, 252-56
Loyalty issue, in WWI, 15, 16, 36, 51, 91, 153, 179, 202, 203, 212, 216, 221, 229, 241, 261, 330, 331, 332, 355, 393, 397, 422, 446, 482, 548, 586, 590, 628, 633, 658, 686, 794, 894, 925, 1004. See also World War I, civil liberties
Lundberg, George A., author, 257
Lundeen, Ernest, speeches, 67; author, 550

McAULIFFE, MAURICE, author, 857
McConnell, Grant, author, 66
McCumber, Porter, politician, 971
McCurry, Dan C., editor, 67
McCutcheon v. Townley, lawsuit, 776
McDonald, Annabelle, author, 965
Macdonald, Donald C., papers, 844
Macdonald, Neil C., 32, 265, 844, 862, 875; court case, 782; papers, 845
MacDonald, William, author, 258
McFarland, George, college president, 265, 946
McGlynn, A. J. (Mickey), NPL organizer, 52, 113, 940
McGuire, Patrick, author, 259
McKaig, Ray, NPL organizer, 51, 71, 255, 256, 423; libel suit, 252, 777; author, 260-64; papers, 846
McKaig v. Gooding and Statesman Printing Co., lawsuit, 777
MacKay, Kenneth Campbell, author, 68
McKenzie, Alexander, politician, 46, 917
McKenzie, Roderick, political activist, 79
McKenna, Marian C., author, 69
McKinney, Louise, political activist, 79
McMillan, James, author, 265
McMinnville, Oreg., Grange, 300
McNally, Winnifred, author, 265

McNaughton, Violet Clara, papers, 847
MacPherson, C. B., author, 70
MacPherson, O. L., political activist, 79
McVey, Frank, college president, 32
Mader, Joseph H., author, 267, 966
Magazines, anti-NPL, 717, 723, 730-32
Mahoney, William, politician, 42, 118, 128, 129, 490, 491, 494; papers, 848
Mallon, George H., politician, 499
Malone, Michael P., author, 71, 72
Manahan, James M., 129, 678, 922; author, 73, 849; streetcar strike, 468; papers, 849
Manahan, Kathryn, author, 849
Manitoba, NPL history and activities, 79, 142, 196, 915, 979. See also Canada
Manitoba Grain Growers' Assn., 79
Manley, Robert N., author, 268
Mardiros, Anthony, author, 74
Markusen, Ann, author, 50, 269
Martin, Boyd A., author, 75
Martin, L. W., NPL organizer, 501
Martin, Michael J., author, 270
Martin, William Melville, papers, 850
Martin Co., Minn., trial, 22, 789
Martinson, Henry R., 128, 948; author, 76, 271, 272; papers, 851
Masonic Grand Lodge of N.Dak., historical collection, 852
Maxwell, S. R., author, 500, 552, 553
Mayer, George H., author, 77
Meadors, John P., NPL member, 853
Meitzen, E. R., NPL organizer, 36
Melby, Alfred C., author, 967
Merritt, Howard A., author, 968
Merz, Charles, author, 274, 275
Mexican-American relations, NPL position, 353
Meyer, Mrs. E. A., handicraft depicted, p. 21
Midland Cooperator, 22
Miklethun, John L., papers, 854
Mikolasak, V. F., author, 276
Miles City, Mont., beating of NPL organizer, 113. See also McGlynn, A. J.
Mills, state-owned and -operated, 160, 514, 608, 669, 745, 757, 768, 806, 884, 943. See also Grain elevators, North Dakota Mill and Elevator Assn.
Miller, Clarence Benjamin, author, 555, 556
Miller, Clark, author, 969
Mills, Walter Thomas, Farmer-Labor organizer, 291; author, 557, 558
Minneapolis, city council, 456; streetcars, 630, 712; elections, 711, 712
Minneapolis Grain Exchange, 365
Minneapolis Journal, circulation, 562
Minneapolis League of Women Voters, voters guide, 560
Minneapolis Star, 277, 289, 722
Minneapolis Trades and Labor Assembly, 437. See also Central Labor Union of Minneapolis and Hennepin County

Minneapolis Tribune, 14
Minnesota, NPL history and activities, 16, 100, 137, 146, 147, 186, 190, 202, 221, 226, 263, 280, 302, 332, 360, 373, 412, 421, 576, 640, 815, 819, 949, 956, 957, 959, 968, 972, 986, 1004, 1007; loyalty issue, 16, 330, 925; 1916 elections, 16, 280; 1918 elections, 16, 77, 97, 216, 225, 242, 281, 502, 662, 848, 950, 969, 986, 987; history, 26; 1918 gubernatorial campaign, 59, 62, 91, 448; 1920 elections, 97, 158, 208, 227, 249; 1922 elections, 97, 360, 400; 1924 Farmer-Labor campaign, 118; WWI politics, 153, 950; NPL election strategy, 217; 1919 special legislative session, 226; NPL membership, 238, 864; harassment of NPL, 241, 581, 582; analysis of 1916-22 elections, 257; governor's addresses, 461; agrarian movements, 951
Minnesota Commission of Public Safety, 16, 26, 43, 80, 91, 166, 358, 406, 448, 449, 807, 815, 950, 987; campaign against NPL, 212, 219, 890; publications, 736-38; records, 855
Minnesota Daily Star (Minneapolis), 29, 184, 237, 289, 378, 387, 414, 419, 456, 561, 562, 663, 772, 973; circulation, 562, 638; stock offering, 621
Minnesota Economics Society, publications, 563
Minnesota Issues (St. Paul), 611, 723
Minnesota Leader (St. Paul), 671, 724
Minnesota Non-Partisan League, "fake League," 727
Minnesota Safety Commission Act, 406
Minnesota Sound Government Assn., 564, 739; publications, 650, 651, 653, 723
Minnesota State Fair, 561
Minnesota State Federation of Labor, 135, 541
Minnesota Supreme Court, loyalty issue, 633; rulings, 774, 789-92
Minors, working conditions, 356
Minot, N.Dak., raid, 270
"A Modern Hiawatha," poem, 6, 453
Montana, NPL history and activities, 38, 100, 120, 263, 280, 282, 371, 373, 415, 944, 989; history, 45, 72; 1922 elections, 72, 113, 595; NPL election strategy, 217; 1920 elections, 227, 249, 921, 934, 958; 1918 elections, 242, 246; 1916 elections, 280; Socialist party, 415
Montana Council of Defense, 38, 940, 944
Montana Development Assn., 120
Montana Labor League, 52
Montana Loyalty League, 568-70
Moore, R. A., political activist, 980
Moorhead, F. G., author, 280
Morlan, Robert L., author, 78, 92, 281, 970; reviewed, 324
Morris, Oliver Scott, author, 282-85, 571

Morrison, Paul W., author, 971
Morse, J. H., author, 572
Mortgages, see Banks and banking
Morton, W. L., author, 79, 286
Mostad, Thorwald, politician, 856
Moum, Kathleen, author, 287
Municipal Nonpartisan League, 305. See also Labor's Municipal Nonpartisan League, Working People's Nonpartisan Political League
Murphy, Paul L., author, 80

NAFTALIN, ARTHUR, author, 972
National Civil Liberties Bureau, publications, 573
National Conference on Marketing and Farm Credits, Chicago, 81
National Farmers Union, see Farmers Union
National Founder's Assn., 273
National Nonpartisan League, see Nonpartisan League
National Producers' Alliance, 18, 491
National Tax Assn., 628; publications, 670
Nebraska, NPL history and activities, 100, 138, 190, 202, 263, 268, 277, 280, 282, 296, 330, 360, 899, 980, 1007; NPL election strategy, 217; 1918 elections, 242; 1920 elections, 249, 980; 1916 elections, 280; 1922 elections, 360, 596; constitutional conventions, 858, 980; NPL committee members, 865
Nebraska Farmers Union, 296
Nebraska Leader (Lincoln), 725
Nebraska State Council of Defense, 268, 913, 980
Nebraska Workers Nonpartisan League, 980
Nelson, Bruce Opie, author, 83
Nelson, C. Z., 499; author, 604
Nelson, Harold L., author, 289, 973
Nelson, Knute, politician, 859
Nelson, Theodore Gilbert, author, 84, 605; IVA leader, 554, 620, 788; papers, 860, 861
Nestos, Rangvold A., N.Dak. governor, 150, 489, 495, 532, 756, 911, 1001; campaign, 516, 608, 625; recall, 532; author, 606-8
Neubeck, Deborah Kahn, author, 85
The New Day in North Dakota, 762
New Deal, 63
New Northwest (Missoula, Mont.), 38, 944
New York, NPL chapter, 175, 408
New York World, criticism of NPL, 155
Newspapers, 17, 25, 29, 38, 74, 109, 123, 171, 184, 240, 414, 419, 561, 562, 621, 973, 1003; NPL, 17, 19, 22, 98, 161, 263, 277, 289, 378, 716, 718, 720-22, 724-26, 728, 729, 735, 984; laws and legislation, 136, 267, 292, 293, 316, 336, 337, 374, 966, 995; cooperative, 161; labor, 161, 237; news services, 251, 622; anti-NPL, 333, 727; reactions to NPL, 347; farmer-owned, 471, 623; circulation, 562, 638. See also

Publishers and publishing, individual news services, individual papers
Nicholas, E. H., author, 294
Nielson, Minnie J., 875; dispute with NPL, 172, 265, 274; firing, 466, 651; author, 611, 612; court cases, 782, 784; campaign, 862; depicted, p. 55
Nielson family, papers, 862
Nodtvedt, Magnus, author, 974
The Non-Partisan: Official Organ of the Minnesota Non-Partisan League (St. Paul), 727
Nonpartisan Leader, 22, 34, 98, 109, 235, 419, 571, 648, 698, 726, 902; cartoon depicted, p. 26
Nonpartisan Leader of Western Canada (Swift Current, Sask.), 124, 728
Nonpartisan League, criticisms of, 3, 7, 8, 92, 94, 111, 117, 120, 140, 146, 155, 197, 198, 201, 245, 273, 295, 297, 314, 361, 395, 425, 444, 465, 480, 497, 506, 511, 539, 547, 553, 555, 566, 568, 611, 631, 642, 646, 654, 656, 675, 739, 800, 909; origins and early history, 4, 50, 58, 78, 259, 275, 287, 346, 368, 403, 504, 544, 583, 648, 674, 893, 926,936, 948, 954, 964, 970; conventions, 21, 81, 459, 460, 538, 591; legislative program, 34, 148, 172, 192, 193, 215, 274, 276, 311, 318, 321, 328, 361, 373, 376, 466, 487, 510, 594, 610, 632, 635, 644, 661, 939, 1002; in N.Dak., history, 35, 46, 79, 92, 94, 100, 101, 133, 137, 142, 146, 156, 171, 186, 190, 197, 202, 211, 258, 263, 280, 282, 298, 302, 323, 360, 370, 373, 412, 421, 434, 463, 588, 626, 682, 690, 815, 867, 894, 902, 923, 929, 938, 941, 956, 959, 999, 1003, 1007; legislative history, 41, 114, 974; tax program, 47, 95, 172, 328, 533, 628, 670; endorsed candidates, 52, 106, 401, 402, 604, 636, 657, 658, 989; voting reform drives, 52, 676; membership, 61, 130, 238, 280, 287, 341, 401, 529, 887, 957, 959; leaders and organizers, 64, 79, 111, 123, 168, 272, 362, 444, 461, 509, 570, 592, 935, 957; records and collected papers, 85, 817, 863-67, 901; campaign platforms, 86, 452, 748, 798; municipal policy, 187; dues, 191, 589; factors in decline, 191, 265, 278, 288, 388, 908, 929, 935, 1004, 1007; factors in rise, 192, 193, 364, 379, 323, 362, 404, 510, 579, 613; election strategy, 217, 266, 396; suppression and harassment, 239, 248, 380, 807, 980; publications, 267, 574-603; organization, 272, 510, 935; organizing methods, 330, 362; foreign policy, 353, 429; economic background, 366, 401, 403, 666; merger with Democratic party, 396, 978; articles of association, 557; bylaws and constitution, 597-99; meetings depicted, p. 1, p. 71; organizer depicted, p. 20; headquarters depicted,

[82]

INDEX

p. 66. See also North Dakota, state history
Norbeck, Peter, S.Dak. governor, 91, 182, 976; campaign, 25, 619; author, 617-19
Nord, David P., author, 975
Nordstrom, O. E., political activist, 542
North Central Assn. of Commissioners, Secretaries, and Directors of Agriculture, 816
North Dakota, history of agrarian movement, 9, 27, 329, 939; state history, 20, 94, 122, 894; 1920 elections, 44, 208, 227, 233, 249, 299, 395, 442, 450, 469, 523, 601, 926; laws and legislation, 93, 648, 683, 757, 763; 1919 legislative session, 93, 136, 292, 293, 476, 488, 493, 510, 627, 757, 769, 783; 1921 recall election, 150, 152, 284, 317, 320, 322, 520, 637, 641, 672, 682, 684, 861, 894, 923; 1916 elections, 169, 171, 280, 319, 366, 403, 430, 917, 971; 1917 legislative session, 183, 275, 894; anti-business attitude, 230, 692; coal strike, 236, 303, 825; 1918 elections, 242, 352, 410; constitutional amendments, 244, 410, 637, 644, 661, 687, 747-50, 787, 788; analysis of 1916-22 elections, 257; 1917 elections, 290; 1922 elections, 298, 315, 484, 489, 495, 537, 750; financial crisis, 310, 313; economic conditions, 311, 376, 443, 758; 1919 referendum election, 316, 318, 749; 1980 election, 352; 1948-56 elections, 396; taxes, 529, 587, 628, 667, 670, 695; NPL-created offices and salaries, 529, 531, 757; 1924 primary, 551; directory, 740, 770; House and Senate publications, 762-69; court transcripts, 868. See also Nonpartisan League, in N.Dak. history; State industries
North Dakota Agricultural College, support of NPL, 325
North Dakota Board of Administration, 651, 751, 767, 876
North Dakota Board of Canvassers, lawsuit, 788
North Dakota Board of Control, 876
North Dakota Council of Defense, 152, 195; records, 873
North Dakota Democratic-NPL Women, 2
North Dakota Department of Public Instruction, records, 875
North Dakota Farm Bureau, 100
North Dakota Farmers Opposed to Socialism Control of the State, 525
North Dakota Farmers Union, 18, 55, 348, 350, 841
North Dakota Fire and Tornado Department, reports, 751
North Dakota Hail Commissioner, reports, 751, 931
North Dakota Home Builders Assn., 752, 757
North Dakota Home Building Assn., 759, 931; investigation, 768, 861, 871
North Dakota Immigration Department, 753-55; records, 874. See also Immigration and emigration
North Dakota Industrial Commission, 114, 119, 534, 659, 872; publications, 756-62; records, 878. See also State industries, individual industries
North Dakota Leader (Fargo), 452, 488, 696, 729
North Dakota Mill and Elevator Assn., 759, 871, 931, 943; records, 879, 884. See also Grain elevators, Mills
North Dakota Minimum Wage Department, reports, 751
North Dakota Press Assn., 337, 374, 995; publications, 136, 292, 293
North Dakota Public Library Commission, 1919 controversy, 172, 349, 529, 744, 764, 767, 930, 1005. See also Library scandal
North Dakota Public Service Commission, records, 880
North Dakota Publication and Printing Commission, 751, 765
North Dakota State Banking Board, reports, 751. See also Bank of North Dakota
North Dakota State Board of Health, 354
North Dakota State Creamery, records, 882
North Dakota State Federation of Labor, 76, 115
North Dakota State Tax Commission, 328, 391, 628, 670. See also Taxation
North Dakota Superintendent of Public Instruction, controversy, 172, 265, 651; reports, 751, 875; court cases, 782, 784
North Dakota Supreme Court, cases, 136, 292, 293, 773, 775, 778-88, 793; records, 883
North Dakota v. Gilbert, lawsuit, 791, 792
North Dakota v. Townley, lawsuit, 789, 790, 792
North Dakota Workmen's Compensation Bureau, 31, 356, 751, 759, 771; constitutionality, 778
Northern Lights, film, 50, 269
Northwest Loyalty Meetings, St. Paul, 436
Northwest Publishing Co., 29, 414, 621
Northwest Warriors Magazine (St. Paul), 730
Northwestern Service Bureau, Editorial Service Sheet, 498, 501, 622, 623, 675; records, 864; operations, 966. See also Publishers' National Service Bureau
Norwegians, in WWI, 15
Nutcracker (Calgary, Alba.), 716
Nyberg, Charles, author, 884
Nye, Gerald P., politician, 17, 121; correspondence, 903
Nye, Russell B., author, 87, 324

O'CONNOR, J. F. T., candidate, 333, 467, 489, 535, 952; campaign, 624, 625
O'Donoghue, Martin, Catholic priest, 469
O'Hara, Frank, author, 326, 626
O'Hare, Kate Richards, author, 88; trial, 145, 777, 885, 894; papers, 885
Oklahoma, NPL history and activities, 36, 181; agrarian socialism, 149; NPL election strategy, 217
Oliver, E. L., NPL organizer, 422
Olsness, S. A., politician, 886
Olson, Floyd B., Minn. governor, 77
Olson, Richard O., author, 976
Olson, Ronald V., author, 977
Omdahl, Lloyd B., author, 89, 978
On the Square: A Magazine for Farm and Home, 731
Oregon, 251, 291; NPL lack of success, 218, 244, 302, 431, 433; 1924 election, 243; NPL history and activities, 296, 327, 382, 383, 423
Oregon Agricultural College, support of NPL, 325
Oregon Agricultural Economic Conference, 413
Oregon Farmers Union, endorsement of NPL, 296
Oregon State Grange, relationship to NPL, 296, 300, 423
Organizers, see Nonpartisan League, leaders and organizers; individual organizers
Organizing Department, see Socialist party

PACKARD, FRANK E., author, 328, 628
Pan-American Anti-Socialist (St. Paul), 732
Panting, G. E., author, 979
Park Region Echo (Alexandria, Minn.), 912
Parker, Arthur D., fictionalized Townley character, 109
Patrons of Husbandry, see Grange
Patterson, Charles, 731; author, 629
Patterson, Robert George, author, 329
Penniman, Howard R., author, 90
People's Franchise Bureau, Minneapolis, 630
People's Press Assn., N.Dak., 374, 995
Peterson, Elmer Theodore, author, 631
Peterson, Hjalmar Otto, papers, 887
Peterson, Horace C., author, 91
Phillips, Elmo Bryant, author, 980
Phillips, William W., author, 981, 982
Pickett, John E., author, 330
Picnics, 437
Pierce, Walter M., Oreg. governor, 300; relationship to NPL, 331; papers, 888
Pierce Co., N.Dak., 112, 994
Plachy, Frank, Jr., author, 332
Plain Citizens Political Reform Assn., 512. See also Independent Voters Assn.
Plentywood, Mont., Socialist party, 415
Plowing Up a Storm, television special, 102
Poehls, Alice C., 904; author, 983
Poetry, pro-NPL, 6, 453, 902

[83]

INDEX

Pomona Grange, Oreg., 300
Pope, James Pinckney, papers, 889
Populism, 128, 141, 918, 1009; relationship to NPL, 222, 330, 936
Pratt, William C., author, 335
Preus, Jacob Aall Otteson, Minn. governor, 338, 634; interview, 890; papers, 891
Primaries, direct, 69, 266; Mont. law, 120. See also Campaigns, Elections
   1920, Minn., 208; N.Dak., 208, 233, 395, 450, 469
   1918, Minn., 225, 502; N.Dak., 225
   1922, N.Dak., 315, 750
   1924, N.Dak., 551
"Printing Bill," 316
Prochazka, Frank John, author, 984
Producers and Consumers Convention, St. Paul, 301, 326, 397, 538, 591, 898, 906
Progressive Feature Service Bureau, 719
Progressive News (Wadena, Minn.), 471
Progressive party, 73; Canada, 79, 164; N.Dak., 194
Progressive Press Assn., 374, 995
Prohibition, 1005
Proudfoot, Lorne, politician, 892
Public utilities, 119
Publishers and publishing, N.Dak., 316; anti-NPL, 333; supporting NPL, 374; associations, 337, 374. See also Newspapers, North Dakota Publication and Printing Commission
Publishers' National Service Bureau, 17, 623, 805, 966; records, 864. See also Northwestern Service Bureau
Putnam, Jackson K., author, 340, 985

QUIGLEY, HAROLD S., author, 341
Quigley, Walter Eli, 63; reminiscences, 893

RAFF, WILLIS H., author, 986, 987
Rahn, A. A. D., political activist, 658
Railroads, unions, 565
Ramsey, Alexander, Minn. governor, 482
Randall, N. S., author, 640
Rankin, Jeannette, politician, 52, 113, 246, 991
Ransom County Farmers Press (Enderlin, N.Dak.), 803
Ratcliff, Beulah Amidon, author, 342
Recall, 1921 N.Dak., 150, 152, 284, 317, 320, 322, 496, 520, 530, 637, 641, 682, 684, 748, 781, 861, 894, 923; IVA position, 615, 637, 684
Red Cross, see American Red Cross
The Red Flame (Bismarck), 92, 733; cartoons, 206; cartoon depicted, p. 11
Red Peasant International, 174
Reed, Frank E., endorsement of NPL, 509

Referendum, 316, 318, 395, 521, 747, 749, 916, 920
Reid, Bill G., author, 343, 344
Reliance Publicity Service, publications, 500, 715
Remele, Larry, author, 46, 78, 102, 121, 345-53
Republican party, relationship to NPL, 170, 182, 217, 416, 794; publication, 642; correspondence, 839
Revenue bonds, for state industries and bank, 236, 285, 307, 310, 313, 317, 399, 527, 600, 620; direct sale, 312; lawsuits, 773, 793
Rice, Hazel F., author, 356
Rice, Stuart Arthur, author, 93, 357, 988
Richter, Dan E., author, 646, 647
Rippley, La Vern J., author, 358
Roberts, Lillian Lindbergh, author, 62
Robinson, Elwyn B., author, 94
Robinson, James Eugene, 168; author, 95; papers, 895
Rockwell, James E., 384; author, 359
Rodgers, Fred S., candidate, 36
Rodvik, Sigvard, publicist, 15
Roeder, Richard B., author, 72
Rogin, Michael Paul, author, 96
Roman Catholic Diocese of Bismarck, 909
Roosevelt, Theodore, loyalty issue, 658; correspondence, 815
Rorvik, Peter, politician, 52
Ross, Alex, NPL organizer, 74
Ross, C. Ben, biography, 71
Ross, Martin, author, 97
Rowell, Chester H., author, 360
Roylance, William G., author, 361; papers, 896
Royster, W. W., political activist, 658
Rude, Leslie G., author, 362
Ruetten, Richard T., author, 989
Ruhl, Arthur, author, 363
Rural Credits Act, 637
Rural credits system, 756. See also Banks and banking; Bank of North Dakota, Farm Loan Department
Rural Independent (Fargo), 734, 860, 861
Russell, Charles Edward, author, 98, 99, 364-69, 648, 1002; criticism of, 531
Russian Revolution, 353, 398, 594
Rypins, Stanley I., correspondence, 812

SABY, RASMUS S., author, 370
Sageng, Ole O., politician, 509
St. George's Church, Redfield, S.Dak., 673
St. Paul, Minn., 1917 Producers and Consumers Convention, 301, 326, 397, 538, 591, 898, 906; 1918 NPL convention, 459, 460
St. Paul Assn., streetcar strike, 468
St. Paul Dispatch, 553
Saline County Independent (Salina, Kans.), 721
Saloutos, Theodore, author, 100, 371-73, 990

Sargent, Noel, author, 649-53
Saskatchewan, NPL history and activities, 79, 103, 124, 142, 164, 915, 928; agrarian movements, 127, 149; 1917 election, 657, 828. See also Canada
Saskatchewan Grain Growers' Assn., 103, 124, 559; records, 897
"The Saturday Evening Letter," column, 895
Saturday Evening Post, 571
Scandinavian-American Bank, 334, 404; investigation, 274, 279, 479, 786; failure, 303
Schaffer, Ronald, author, 991
Schannach, J. W., labor official, 554
Schmahl, Julius A., author, 654
Schmidt, Paul C., author, 374
Schneider, Richard, author, 101
Schrader, Frederick, author, 375
Schutz, Mary Neal, author, 102
Scott, Frank R., author, 376
Scott v. Frazier, lawsuit, 775, 868
Seattle Port Commission, records, 898
Seattle Union Record, 799
Sedition, Goodhue Co. trial, 501, 774, 791, 908. See also Conspiracy
Schafer, George F., author, 655
Shamer, Daniel, criticism of NPL, 424
Shankweiler, Paul W., author, 993
Sharp, Paul F., author, 103
Sherman, William C., author, 994
Shimmons, Earl W., author, 378
Shipstead, Henrik, candidate, 93, 97, 106, 167, 360, 400; campaign, 604, 908
Sim, John C., author, 995
Simons, A. M., author, 379
Simpson, John A., farm leader, 180
Slosson, Edwin E., author, 380
Smelker, R. C., author, 658
Smemo, Irwin K., author, 996
Smith, A. E., politician, 494
Smith, Glenn H., author, 46, 270, 381
Smith, Robert E., author, 382
Socialist party, relationship to NPL, 36, 100, 137, 156, 186, 259, 271, 335, 340, 373, 415, 435, 451, 531, 570, 643, 653, 660, 794, 932, 936, 948; 1920 campaign, 104; opposition to WWI, 305; in N.Dak., 259, 340, 529, 869, 870, 886, 948, 985; 1918 Minn. campaign, 439, 704; Organizing Department, 870, 948
Society of Equity, see American Society of Equity
Solberg, K. K., author, 662
Soltis, John Gabriel, author, 663-65
Songs, 579, 646
Sorenson, Christian Abraham, papers, 899
South Dakota, NPL history and activities, 25, 100, 182, 190, 263, 280, 282, 373, 947, 1007; elections, 242, 280; Farmer-Labor party, 288
South Dakota Leader (Mitchell, S.Dak.), 25, 735
Spafford, D. S., author, 385
Spalding, Burleigh F., author, 667

Stageberg, Susie, NPL supporter, 129, 491, 560
Stallard, H. H., defense of NPL, 386
Stangeland, Charles E., author, 744
Starr, Karen, author, 388
State Assn. of Farmers Mutual Insurance Companies, 671
State industries, 58, 142, 143, 160, 162, 201, 205, 220, 244, 247, 285, 317, 341, 381, 390, 402, 410, 413, 432, 478, 514, 520, 527, 545, 587, 608, 655, 669, 745, 746, 759, 762, 764-66, 768, 775, 861, 882, 884, 931, 939, 943; Supreme Court decision, 390, 410, 432, 775; criticism, 245, 545, 695; cost, 587, 655; investigation, 764-66, 768, 861. See also North Dakota Industrial Commission, individual industries
State sheriff, controversy, 531
Statesman Printing Co., libel suit, 777
Steele, H. H., author, 391, 670
Steinberger, Henry, reminiscences, 809
Stenehjen, Emma, NPL member, 2
Stedman, Murray Salisbury, Jr., author, 105
Stedman, Susan W., author, 105
Stewart, A. D., author, 671
Stolberg, Benjamin, author, 392
Stolee, Leif G., author, 997
Stolin, O. A., NPL organizer, 87
Streetcars, Minneapolis, 630, 712
Strikes, see Labor, strikes
Strout, Irwin Charles, papers, 900
Stuhler, Barbara, author, 106, 107
Sullivan, Thomas V., politician, 470, 560, 621
Swenson, Karl R., author, 998
Swigart, A. W., NPL organizer, 19
Sykes, D. J., political activist, 79

TAFT, PHILIP, author, 394
Taft, William Howard, author, 395; opposition to NPL, 416, 543
Talbot, Ross B., author, 396, 999
Talmage, William Henry, author, 673
Taxation, NPL policies, 47, 95, 172, 328, 533, 574, 670; N.Dak., 391, 464, 529, 587, 628, 667, 670, 762, 771; Minn., 576. See also North Dakota State Tax Commission
Taylor, Eleanor, author, 397
Teigan, Henry George, author, 399-403; speech, 491; papers, 864, 901
Teigen, Ferdinand A., author, 674
Texas, NPL history and activities, 36, 199; 1922 campaign, 36
Thatcher, Kenneth, author, 37
Third-party movements, 210, 217, 385, 392
This Mighty Dream, exhibit, 1
Thomas, L. G., author, 108
Thomason, Otto Monroe (O. M., Oliver), 123, 613; author, 109, 902; papers, 902
Thompson, J., author, 405
Thompson, Martin O., judge, 903
Thompson, Robert, author, 1000
Thunder Creek Provincial Constituency (Sask.), publications, 657
Tideman, Philip L., editor, 110

Tighe, Ambrose, author, 406
Tillquist, F. E., candidate, 658
Tittemore, James N., author, 111
Tofsrud, Ole T., author, 112
Toole, K. Ross, author, 113
Torian, James W., author, 1001
Tostlebe, Alvin Samuel, author, 114, 407
Totten, George A., bureaucrat, 767, 784
Townley, Arthur C., NPL leader, 6, 18, 50, 77, 83, 109, 112, 121, 129, 132, 134, 141, 148, 156, 192, 214, 262, 322, 343, 351, 363, 483, 500, 643, 819, 826, 859, 870, 902, 908, 911, 917, 983; trials and appeals, 91, 170, 224, 232, 234, 264, 294, 302, 303, 411, 481, 789, 790, 792, 905; break with Langer, 30, 905; testimony, 62, 772; bankruptcy, 279, 498, 567, 776; criticism of, 297, 339, 440, 441, 455, 467, 480, 483, 497, 525, 526, 646, 647, 663, 668, 671, 673, 678-80, 697; retirement, 298; re-election, 327; role in NPL, 335, 927; speeches, 491, 677, 906, 983; cartoons, 609; papers, 904-6; work for Socialists, 948; depicted, p. 48
"Townleyism," 146, 439, 441, 445, 446, 458
Tselos, George, author, 412
Tweton, D. Jerome, author, 46, 115, 116
Twichell, L. L., 540; author, 683
Twichell v. Hall, law suit, 787
Twin City Rapid Transit Co., 73; strike, 468, 586, 736

UNION PARTY, 924
United Brotherhood of Carpenters and Joiners, 115
United Farmers Education League, 174
United Farmers of Alberta, 48, 70, 74, 79, 103, 892; relationship to NPL, 286, 945
United Farmers of Manitoba, 979
United States Committee on Public Information, 166
United States Congress, committee hearing, 774
United States Supreme Court, rulings, 390, 410, 432, 774
University of Minnesota, NPL sympathies, 836
University of North Dakota, history, 32; Bureau of Governmental Affairs, 86
Utah Farm Bureau State Committee, publication, 685

VADNAIS, IRENE, author, 1003
Valley City State College (N.Dak.), 265, 946
Van Lear, Thomas, Minneapolis mayor, 128, 154, 305, 414, 542, 621, 704, 705, 975; criticism of, 663, 664, 688; campaign, 711, 712
Veblen, Thorstein, author, 117
Villard, Oswald Garrison, author, 414

Vindex, Charles, author, 415
Vissers, A. A., author, 111
Vivian, James F., author, 416
Voters Information Club, Minneapolis, publications, 688
Voting, registration form, 439; statistics, 769

WALKER, R. H., NPL organizer, 272
Wallace, Henry, author, 417
Wallace, James F., politician, 456
Wallingford, Sir Rufus, 656
Walsh, Thomas J., politician, 921
Wannamaker, Olin D., author, 418
Ward Co., N.Dak., criminal elements, 270
Warner, Arthur, author, 419-21
Warner, Eli S., businessman, 731
Washington, NPL history and activities 165, 280, 282, 302; elections, 217, 280; Farmer-Labor party, 288, 932; anti-war activity, 932
Washington County Post (Stillwater, Minn.), 887
Washington State Federation of Labor, records, 907
Wasson, Stanley P., author, 1004
Waters, J. R., author, 455
Weaver, S. Roy, author, 463, 690
Webber, C. C., correspondence, 822
Weber, Elaine J., author, 1005
Wefald, Knud, NPL supporter, 129; papers, 908
Wehrle, Vincent, author, 691, 692; attacks on NPL, 909
Weinsten, James, author, 118
Weir, James, political activist, 79
Weist, Edward, author, 119
Wells, Merle T., author, 424
Wentz, Leonard, author, 1006
Wenzel, H. C., politician, 494
West, Willis Mason, author, 693
Western Farm Credit Co., 250
Western Independent (Calgary, Alba.), 716
Western Producer (Saskatoon, Sask.), 847
Wheat, grading, 168, 330; prices, 440; grading depicted, p. 15. See also Grain
Wheaton, Fred E., candidate, 541
Wheeler, Burton K., candidate, 52, 167, 246, 989; campaigns, 72, 113, 120, 921, 934, 958; autobiography, 120; correspondence, 822
"Where the League Begins," poem, 6
Whitaker, Reginald, author, 48
Whitman, Alden, author, 121
Wilbur, Harry Curran, political activist, 739
Wilcox, Benton H., author, 427, 1007
Wilkins, Robert P., author, 46, 122, 428-30, 1008
Wilkins, Wynona H., author, 122
Willis, Hugh E., author, 432
Wilson, Woodrow, relationship to NPL, 80, 261, 794; loyalty issue, 203, 590; fourteen points, 578; quoted, 590
Wisconsin, NPL history and activities, 100, 282, 360, 373, 910, 911, 1007; elections, 217, 227, 360; NPL platform, 602
Wisconsin Progressive Assn., 834

Wisconsin State Historical Society Library, papers, 911
Witham, James W., author, 123
Wold, Carl A., political activist, 912
Wold, Eva Emerson, political activist, 912
Women, in politics, 2, 52, 88, 107, 113, 991; role in NPL, 50, 269, 388; suffrage, 62, 388, 420, 450, 894; working conditions, 356; handicraft depicted, p. 21; group depicted, p. 50
Women's Christian Temperance Union, N.Dak., 554
Women's Grain Growers Assn., 847
Women's Nonpartisan Clubs, 2, 505; publications, 701-3; conventions, 702; group depicted, p. 50
Wood, H. W., NPL organizer, 79
Wood, James J., author, 885
Wood, Louis Aubrey, author, 124
Woodsworth, J. S., NPL organizer, 79, 126
Wooster, Charles, papers, 913
Worker's compensation, in Minn., 135, 540. See also North Dakota Workmen's Compensation Bureau
Workers' Herald, campaign leaflet, 704
Working People's Nonpartisan Political League, 42, 59, 77, 118, 128, 154, 305, 400, 490, 491, 494, 565, 663, 664, 808, 829, 975; endorsed candidates, 106, 604; publications, 705-13; constitution and bylaws, 708; conventions, 708-10; legislative program, 708, 892; criticism of, 739; platforms, 711, 712, 798. See also Labor's Municipal Nonpartisan League, Municipal Nonpartisan League
World War I, civil liberties, 13, 80, 166, 986, 987; Norwegian-American experience, 15; Texas, 36; NPL position, 43, 94, 147, 166, 168, 178, 202, 203, 353, 579; anti-war treatise, 62; suppression of NPL, 91, 254, 256, 940, 945; Minn., 153, 815; N.Dak., 166, 1009; Socialist opposition, 305; 1916 election, 430; war profits, 580, 738; peace appeal, 591; anti-German sentiment, 859, 890

YAKIMA, WASH., convention, 19
Yamhill Co., Oreg., 243, 300
Yeager v. Frazier, lawsuit, 793
Youmans, Grant S., 609; author, 125, 678
Young, E. A., depicted, p. 20
Young, George M., campaign, 715
Young, N. C., author, 667
Young, Walter D., author, 126, 127
Youngdale, James M., author, 128, 129, 1009

ZIMMERMAN, CARLE C., author, 130, 131, 1010
Zimmerman, Phil, papers, 914
Zumach, W. C., political activist, 100